CANADIAN SUMMITS

SELECTIONS
FROM
THE
CANADIAN ALPINE JOURNAL

1907-1994

R. W. SANDFORD
GEOFF POWTER

EDITORS

THE ALPINE CLUB OF CANADA

This publication of the Alpine Club of Canada was made possible by generous donations to the Mountain Guides' Ball held at Chateau Lake Louise in October, 1993. Donors were Abbot Pass Trading Company, Altitude Publishing, the Association of Canadian Mountain Guides, Banff Designs, the Banff Festival of Mountain Films, Best Western Wayside Inn in Revelstoke, Glen Boles, Canadian Helicopters, Canadian Mountain Holidays, Canmore Helicopters, Canmore Printcraft, Ken Curley, *Explore* Magazine, Hans Gmoser, Sue Gottsleig, Marjory Hind, Integral Designs Inc., Lake O'Hara Lodge, Mona LeDuc and Canadian Pacific Hotels and Resorts, Purcell Lodge, Virginia Hemingson, Donna Jo Massie, Monod Sports Ltd., Pat Morrow, Mount Assiniboine Lodge, Mountain Avens Gallery, Harry Nowell, Wendy Oliver, Powder Designs, William L. Putnam, R.K. Heli-Ski Panorama Inc., Rocky Mountain Ski Lodge, Rosehill Auction Services Ltd., Alice Saltiel-Marshall, Selkirk Tangiers Helicopter Skiing Ltd., Storm Quest, Skiing Louise, Spoke 'n Edge, The Timberline Lodge, The Treasure Chest, Elizabeth Wiltzen, Yak Alpine Enterprises, Yamnuska Inc., and the Whyte Museum of the Canadian Rockies.

For Vi and Shelly

CANADIAN CATALOGUING IN PUBLICATION DATA

Main entry under title:

   Canadian Summits : selections from the Canadian
Alpine Journal, 1907–1994

ISBN 0-920330-30-4

   1. Mountaineering — Canada. I. Sandford, Robert. W.
II. Powter, Geoffrey S., 1957–. III. Alpine Club of Canada.

GV199.44.C2C36 1994   796.5´22´0971   C94-900757-9

DESIGN/LAYOUT
Digital Banff
James Swanson
Geoff Powter

EDITORIAL ASSISTANT
Abbie Swanson

OCR TECHNICIAN
Bev Bendell

IMAGE SUPERVISION
Zac Bolan
qnb creative inc., Calgary

PRE-PRESS
Guideline Graphics, Calgary

PRINTING
Kromar Printing, Winnipeg

Front cover. Descending King's Trench, Mount Logan. Photo by Pat Morrow
Back cover: Malachite and Horseman Spires, Purcell Mountains. Photo by Roger Laurilla
Title page: The Bugaboos from Septet Lake. Photo by Roger Laurilla

THIS BOOK IS A TRAVELOGUE: a journey through the years of the *Journal*;
a voyage through our land, moving through the lives of our fellow climbers, from the past into the future.
It is not meant to be the "Best of the *Canadian Alpine Journal*," nor is it meant to be
completely representative of the 77 volumes. Scientific articles, though an important component
of the *Journal* over the years, are not represented, nor are basic route descriptions.
Articles have been edited for clarity and consistency.

Mount Robson, North and Emperor Faces. Photo: Greg Horne

Photographs donated to the project include historical material from
the Whyte Museum of the Canadian Rockies, and work from several
contemporary Canadian artists. Readers interested in obtaining
prints of the photos should turn to page 189 for contact addresses.

CONTENTS

Contents

A BRIEF HISTORY OF THE ALPINE CLUB OF CANADA

R.W. SANDFORD, VICE-PRESIDENT, PUBLICATIONS, ALPINE CLUB OF CANADA

The completion of the Canadian Pacific Railway in 1885 did more for Canada than simply tie the country together with a ribbon of steel. Suddenly a great and still largely unmapped west was opened up for exploration and settlement. While most saw only an opportunity for free land and exploitable natural resources, there were a few who saw access to the west in a vastly different light. Among these were mountaineers. When they looked at the almost limitless expanses of broken peaks and crumbling glaciers that composed Canada's western cordillera, they saw a different and far more romantic history waiting to be made.

At first most Canadians were too busy with the practical insistences of building a nation to think seriously about their own mountains. It took nearly two decades for visiting mountaineers to convince the locals of the value of what they had. By the turn of the twentieth century, however, the railway had installed Swiss guides at many of its mountain hotels and had begun to promote the country's alpine potential.

One of the first Canadians to be exposed to the burgeoning alpine aesthetic established by the early Swiss guides was a young surveyor named Arthur Oliver Wheeler. At the turn of the twentieth century, Wheeler conducted a survey of the railway belt through the Selkirk Range of British Columbia. Through this work he became a competent climber and was exposed to the mountaineering culture brought to Glacier House by the first Swiss guides. He went on to meet or encourage every mountaineer of note who visited the Rockies or the Selkirks for the next thirty years. A tireless champion of a uniquely Canadian sense of the alpine, Wheeler also lobbied hard for the creation of an Alpine Club in Canada.

Despite the fact that Canada was a world centre for mountaineering by the turn of the twentieth century, Wheeler found it very difficult to create an alpine association in this country. Though many clubs all over the world had been formed in the tradition of the Alpine Club created in England in 1857, Canadians didn't seem interested in forming an organization of their own. After several failed attempts at creating a Canadian organization, Wheeler was ready to accept the American Alpine Club's offer to establish a wing of that organization in Canada.

Ultimately, it was a letter Wheeler wrote to the Winnipeg Free Press that hit the nationalistic nerve that brought the notion of a Canadian Alpine Club to life. That letter prompted an article in the paper by a staff writer named Elizabeth Parker, who claimed that it was downright un-Canadian to subject local mountaineers to the dictates of a foreign alpine institution. The article went on to give Canadians a tongue-lashing for their lack of patriotism and willingness to give into American imperialistic zeal. Parker joined forces with Wheeler and helped organize the club's founding meeting in Winnipeg in March of 1906. Wheeler became the Alpine Club's first President and Parker became the organization's first secretary. The rest, as they say, is history.

In the nearly nine decades since the formation of the Club, climbing in Canada has changed as dramatically as the country. Even the remotest parts of Canada have become known and accessible. Gradually most of the country's major peaks fell to the rope and the ice-axe. By 1950, the passion for first ascents necessarily evolved into a fascination with more difficult routes. This led in the 1960s and 1970s to a great interest in big walls and, finally, to the contemporary interest in ice and sport climbing.

Despite continuous evolution in the technique and aesthetic of climbing, the Alpine Club of Canada continues to grow in size and influence. One of the enduring attractions of membership in ACC is the access it gives to the living its reputation as the central repository for the history and literature of Canadian mountaineering. For decades, the club's *Canadian Alpine Journal* was the sole domestic vehicle by which climbers could share reports of the events that shaped their lives on Canadian peaks. Only the war years prevented its annual publication. Over time this journal became a thread that continues to connect generations of climbers and alpine enthusiasts with mountains and memories of mountains in this land. *Canadian Summits* is as much a history of the Canadian mountaineering aesthetic as it is a history of the events that shaped the way we think about mountains.

A SHORT HISTORY OF THE CANADIAN ALPINE JOURNAL

GEOFF POWTER, EDITOR, THE CANADIAN ALPINE JOURNAL

One of the greatest joys in becoming editor of the *Canadian Alpine Journal* is the inheritance of a dog-eared editor's collection of the *CAJ*. Receiving my set felt like discovering a secret path into a previously undiscovered wilderness, complete with towers of rock, virgin snow and companions enough to last a lifetime. The first days with these back editions meant a locked door, a phone off the hook, and a deep dive into the rich history of exploration, exultation, tragedy, faith and friendship that fills the 77 volumes of the *CAJ*. I found the history of our hearts, told in the actual voices of the heroes and the pathfinders — from Kain, MacCarthy, and the Mundays, through Beckey, Croft, and Clarke. I found photographs bringing back warm memories of my own adventures, and images of adventures which can never again be: places now swarming with people; glaciers that have receded or disappeared; legends long ago lost. The only sadness in me was the recognition that few readers of the *Journal* would ever have access to the entire set, and would miss the pleasure of the span of the *Journal* — hence the book in your hands.

The *Journal* has undergone tremendous change from 1907 to 1994, as have we as a nation, as has climbing as a sport, as has the environment we travel through. The *CAJ* began life as 196-page book, printed on rag paper, with stunning photographic reproductions even then. The cost of the first edition was 75 cents. Virtually all the reports in the volume were of first ascents of Canadian peaks.

The early tales from the *Journal* are full of the self-certainty of the times, with writers awed by the majesty of their mountains, but resolute in their ability to conquer. Their exploration had many faces: they were pioneers establishing very new ground; they were scientists dissecting the world; they were Canadians claiming what was "theirs;" but most of all, they were incredibly hard.

The initial volumes of the *Journal* had an emphasis on the practice of science in the mountains, reflecting a need for better understanding of the mountain world, but also the academic background of many of the writers — several notable contributions to the fields of gelogy and glaciology can be found in the *Journal*. Then, from the mid-1960s on, the writing took on a more humanistic tone, with a far greater degree of self-effacement, and much less seriousness about the sport of climbing.

Through the years, the voices in the *Journal* have softened in some cases, gained a cynical edge in others, lost some of their initial bravado and innocence, but remain true in their love of the mountains and the mountain people. Even though some of the problems of travel have been lessened over the years, the development of techniques and technology have done little to tenderize the mountain spirit.

This collection charts a course much like Canada's own: brave beginings, carving a path through a hard wilderness in small teams; strong connections to the motherland, with great influence by the European immigrants; world-class skills quietly developed as Canadians came into their own right; slow growth of a Canadian mountain voice — a modest, self-deprecating, humour-filled and respectful voice, with a clear appreciation of the beauty and the privilege this country has to offer, and an open invitation to others to come along and enjoy it as well.

A note of thanks needs to be given to the one group whose efforts run somewhat invisibly through the course of this book. The editors of the *CAJ* through its history have taken on a thankless task, working on a project that is clearly a labour of love. The editors have been:

Arthur O. Wheeler 1907–1930	Pat. A. Boswell 1969
AA. McCoubrey 1931–1940	Andrew Gruft 1970–1973
M.D. Fleming 1941–1952	Moira Irvine 1974–1984
Phyllis Munday 1953–1968	David Harris 1985–1992
	Geoff Powter 1993–

Seracs on Asulkan, circa 1903. Photo: Vaux family. Whyte Museum of the Canadian Rockies

1907 : THE ALPINE CLUB OF CANADA

ELIZABETH PARKER

The objects of the Club are: (1) the promotion of scientific study and the exploration of Canadian alpine and glacial regions; (2) the cultivation of Art in relation to mountain scenery; (3) the education of Canadians to an appreciation of their mountain heritage; (4) the encouragement of the mountain craft and the opening of new regions as a national playground; (5) the preservation of the natural beauties of the mountain places and of the fauna and flora in their habitat; and (6) the interchange of ideas with other Alpine organizations. When the Club was organized in March, 1906, it was a red-letter day to some who had long felt the reproach of Canadian apathy to Canadian mountains. For, while English and American mountaineers had, year by year, seized the summers following the advent of the railway, and had explored and climbed, an increasing few of our own people had also been climbing for love of it. Thus learning of the immensities of the alpine regions of their own land, they became jealous for their compatriots' sake. Why should not mountaineering become one of our national sports?

Not until November, 1905, did any positive movement towards organization begin. The response from all parts of the Dominion was a surprise, and ought to have been a rebuke to us who had loudly lamented Canadian indifference to a sport for which Nature had provided so vast a playground on our own immediate territory. We had awakened out of sleep, and would redeem the past by a vigorous mountaineering organization. But whatever the Alpine Club of Canada achieves of climbing, of discovery, of purely scientific work; whatever the Club may eventually become, it must never forget how great and splendid service, and affectionate withal, has been rendered to our mountains and Canadian mountaineering by the members of the Appalachian Mountain Club, the American Alpine Club, and the Alpine Club of London. They have done the work, and published the tidings in a series of publications that already make a considerable library of Rocky Mountain literature. When the Canadian Alpine Club was organized, it counted itself honored to confer honorary membership upon some representatives of these Clubs, and happy to receive others as active members. The first life-member on our list is Professor Herschel C. Parker of Columbia University, one of the boldest pioneers of them all.

What does the Alpine Club of Canada propose to do? Does it take itself too seriously? There may be learned cosmopolitan alpinists whose many years' experience of hardy holidays among the glaciers and upper snows of the mountain ranges of the world, would incline them to look with patronage, if not incipient scorn, upon an organized effort to popularize the exclusive sport. They might say that to popularize was to vulgarize. Not so. Mountaineering is too toilsome, too hard a sport, and demands qualities of mind and character quite other than vulgar. Many pastimes and sports, many vocations and avocations may become vulgarized. But it must be obvious to any who know ever so

Winnipeg Free Press *journalist Elizabeth Parker was one of the stellar lights of the early ACC. Although her health prevented active mountaineering, her spirit was possessed by the alpine; and although she disguised her gender in pseudonyms as a writer in the popular press, she openly championed women's roles in the Club, setting an enduring precendent.*
– GP

little about the glaciers and névés and precipices — the unimaginable visions from the upper heights; it must be obvious that, from the very nature of the sport, to popularize mountaineering is not to vulgarize nor degrade it. The mountains themselves hold the high effort and achievement in fee. The vulgar reach the mountain summits by a way against which the Alpine Club of Canada will set a face of flint. We know what way that is: the way of the monster, Mammon. By virtue of its constitution, the Alpine Club is a national trust for the defence of our mountain solitudes against the intrusion of steam and electricity and all the vandalisms of this luxurious, utilitarian age; for the keeping free from the grind of commerce, the wooded passes and valleys and alplands of the wilderness. It is the people's right to have primitive access to the remote places of safest retreat from the fever and the fret of the market place and the beaten tracts of life.

It is the Club's business to support the picturesque and wholly enjoyable transit to the mountain-places by pack-horse and saddle, and to promote the too much neglected exercise of walking. Your true lover of Nature is also a man of the unfamiliar roads and forest trails. It would be a great thing for young Canadians if all the automobiles vanished into space and walking for pleasure became the fashion. As soon as prudence will warrant, huts will be built in remote strategic situations for the convenience of the members, and persons put in charge for the season; bivouacs will be established on the long trails at distances of a day's journey; and the Club will cooperate, where possible, with the Railway and the Government, in making new trails, giving comfortable access to all the places already known or yet to be discovered. And it is the Club's business to support all measures towards preservation for all time of the fauna and flora in their wild habitat. All members are expected to be alert to this end. First named among the reasons for the Club's existence is the claim of science: "the promotion of scientific study and the exploration of Canadian alpine and glacial regions." This clause makes its appeal to the exclusive class already referred to, whose work is of the schools, a thing apart from, though it may and ought to include, mountaineering as an ennobling, ethical and æsthetic pastime. This section has a distinct work to do, and will, we hope, include a considerable number of men of science. And though much snow may fall upon the mountains and much water run in torrents from the glaciers ere it achieves its predestined high place in alpine and glacial science, its progress towards that consummation is in safe guidance. The President

will look to that. He is keen for progress, and has withal an appalling capacity for dogged hard work — and for making other people work.

Concerning the cultivation of Art, prizes are to be given for the best photographs, and as soon as circumstances will permit, a competition in oils and water colors will be opened for active members. A reliable guide-book, too, which will include instruction on the details of mountaineering, will be published for the benefit of any who come to climb in the Canadian Alps.

There is nothing quixotic about the Alpine Club of Canada; it is a sane, sober institution, organized by sane, sober men. As indicated, its mission is manifold. The education of Canadians to an appreciation of their alpine heritage is of itself a *raison d'être*. The Canadian Rocky Mountain system, with its unnumbered and unknown natural sanctuaries for generations yet unborn, is a national asset. In time we ought to become a nation of mountaineers, loving our mountains with the patriot's passion. Among other correctives, none is more effective than this of the exercise of the mountain-craft. No sport is so likely to cure a fool of his foolishness as the steady pull, with a peril or two of another sort attending, of a season's mountain climbing in one of those "thrilling regions of thick-ribbed ice" in the wild alpine playground of Canada. The ethical value of mountaineering is a subject upon which our statesmen would do well to ponder; and there is a considerable Canadian Alpine literature from which they may gather data.

Any young man of latent intellectual and moral force, who comes to close grips with the waiting, challenging mountains, and puts one summit after another beneath the soles of his feet, has gained immensely in the Spartan virtues. Moreover, he has, by climbing to these skiey stations and standing face to face with Infinitude, learned some things he may not tell, because they are unspeakable. It is given to very few, to utter such experiences. But there comes to the mountaineer of pure mind and willing spirit the sense of which Wordsworth tells, of the presence interfused in Nature; the presence that dwells among the sheer peaks and in the living air and the blue sky and in the mind of man; the motion and the spirit that rolls through all things. Browning sums it in his swift way: "which fools call Nature and I call God." To this climber is given a key to many an utterance of the Masters, which else remained for him unlocked. It is quite true that every climber has not, nor may not, acquire the philosophic mind that is curious regarding the divine interpretation of Nature; but traversing the sources of the great ice-rivers and breathing the virgin air above their mute snows is conducive to that philosophic mind. And whether or no, if that high exercise and that environment fail to arouse a sense of Nature malignant and Nature benignant, his case is hopeless as one who stands among men at the making of the nation. One word more: the standard for membership may not be lowered. That it will be raised is almost certain; just as, with the progress of education, the standards for matriculation in a new university are raised.

Packtrain ascending to Jonas Pass in snow, Columbia Icefield trip, 1924. Photo: Byron Harmon. Whyte Museum of the Canadian Rockies

Moraine Lake, 1899. Photo: Walter Wilcox. Whyte Museum of the Canadian Rockies

1907 : THE CANADIAN ROCKIES, A FIELD FOR AN ALPINE CLUB

ARTHUR O. WHEELER

The first question is: What constitutes a field for an Alpine Club? The second question, and one of primary importance, is: Do the Rocky Mountains of Canada fill the required conditions?

With reference to the former, it is necessary to trace the origin of the word *alpine*. We have the Latin word *alpes*, meaning a high mountain, and said to be of Celtic origin. The Irish *ailp* and its Gaelic equivalent *alp* have the same meaning as the Latin. The word *alp* is identical with the word *alb*, which would seem to be synonymous with the word *albus*, meaning white. We have, therefore, by a process of deduction, a meaning for the word *alps*, of high white mountains, or mountains clad with snow, holding stored in their recesses more or less extensive bodies of the same material. An Alpine Club is one that has for its field of operations a tract of country fulfilling the above conditions. And herein lies the difference between an Alpine and a Mountain club: while any mountain tract will supply the requirements of the latter, those of the former can only be satisfied by a region where there is a permanent snow line, above which snow and ice may be found throughout the year.

Do the Rocky mountains of Canada fulfil the required conditions? To ascertain this fact, it is only necessary to apply to the Department of the Interior at Ottawa for a topographical map of the Rocky or Selkirk mountain ranges, or to look up the maps and text in *Baedeker's Guide to Canada*. Better still, pay a visit to the region. It will not be necessary to leave the train to obtain a view of vast snow-fields and glaciers. If you can spend a few days by the way, a trip to some of the alpine, glacier-hung valleys will soon convince you; for, in these deep recesses, high above timber line, tumbling ice-falls break in every direction through openings in the rock battlements and sweep in broken cascades of crystal ice to the morainal flats below. Following the path of the mountain goat from crag to crag, until sky-line is reached, the eye wanders over fields of purest white, rolling gently in billowy mounds, broken only by islands and reefs of jagged rock. Many of these snow-fields are of considerable extent, varying from ten square miles in the Illecillewaet, twenty in the Wapta, and thirty in the Brazeau, to between one hundred and two hundred square miles in the Great Columbian snow-field.

In a new and as yet inadequately mapped country, such as Canada, it is impossible to do more than approximate the area that may be described as "alpine." Roughly speaking, it can be placed at 250,000 square miles. This area is embodied by the Cordilleran or Rocky Mountain chain, embracing four principal ranges of mountains and numerous sub-ranges and groups. Enumerating from east to west, we have the Rocky Mountain or Main Range, the Selkirk Range, the so-called Gold Range, and finally the Coast Range, lying along the Pacific Ocean. Each of these ranges has its own distinct characteristics.

Arthur Wheeler's introductory piece to the first CAJ *of 1907 is a cross between an exultation, a scientific survey, and a sales pitch, and such a hybrid might indeed sum up the initial existence of the Alpine Club. In this outline of the geography and history of Canadian climbing, the love for the mountains by the Club's first president is as clear as the alpine sky he describes.*

– GP

13

In the Main range, the rocks, generally speaking, belong to the Paleozoic period, and consist for the most part of grey and blue limestones, sandstones, quartzites, slates, shales and conglomerates. They have been carved, by the processes of erosion and weathering, into many and varied styles of architecture, rising in such a profusion of fantastic towers, minarets, spires and obelisks as to delight the eye of the most exacting seeker after the picturesque. In these limestone rocks, of the Silurian and Devonian series, are seen fossil sea-worms and shells, and other relics of the low order of life in a bygone age. They are found even at the very summits of some of the peaks, at an altitude of 10,000 feet above the level of the sea — their former home. At the other places, beds containing fossilized species, closely allied to the trilobite, are to be found. One of these, on the slopes of Mount Stephen, at an altitude of 7000 feet, has become famous. In this range, the valleys are wide, owing to the susceptibility of the rock formations to the erosive power of ice and water. Their sides, clad with bronze green pine and dark blue spruce, sweep upward to open parklands, dotted with golden larch; then, to sunny alplands, where the ground is soft with a carpet of pink heath and white heather and where other alpine flowers of rare beauty and brilliance grow. Hidden in the recesses of these forests and high aloft, surrounded by snow, ice and rockfalls, are lakes of magic hues, like quaint jewels in rare old settings; turquoise green, in Hector, Bow and Emerald lakes; turquoise blue in Peyto Lake; transparent emerald in Yoho Lake; bright cerulean blue in McArthur and Turquoise lakes; royal blue in Lake Louise; even brilliant yellow may occasionally be seen. It is a land of leaping waterfalls and rushing torrents, of fierce sunlight and black shadow, of rosy alpenglow and purple twilight, a land of enchantment, where extremes meet; for it is but a step from grim, gaunt and cruel rocks to sunny alps, brilliant with the bloom of rare, exquisite flowers, and teeming with animal life, quaint and uncommon as the surroundings.

The Selkirk Range lies west of the Main Range. It is practically a vast island of rock, ice and snow, insulated by giant loops of the Columbia and Kootenay rivers. The material composing it is of a much older and harder formation, consisting chiefly of Archæan rocks: grey, pink, green and white quartzites, glittering mica-schists, argillites and rocks of gneissic character. The valleys are narrow, and the mountain masses rise swiftly up, their sides scored and seamed by giant scars. The fantastically carved limestone shapes of the Main Range are lacking.

The two most striking features of the range are its impenetrably luxuriant forests, filling up the valleys, and the immense accumulations of snow and ice stored in its mountain recesses, high up among the clouds. The former contribute much to the seeker after the picturesque in Nature, and the latter are a source of joy to the true alpine enthusiast. Both effects are from the same cause, viz.: the large amount of precipitation deposited in the form of snow, accumulating from year's end to year's end until the entire cap of the range appears in perspective as an endless succession of snowfields, with precipitous black faces of rock rising at intervals from their midst, where the sheer is too steep for snow to lie. Nor is this to be wondered at when it is considered that the average snowfall at the summit of the range is thirty-six feet, with an additional rainfall of thirteen inches; making in all an annual precipitation of fifty-seven inches of water. In comparison may be mentioned the annual average snowfall of about fifteen feet, and annual precipitation of about thirty inches, at the summit of the Main Range.

The excessive precipitation in the Selkirks is due to the fact that it is the first high range of mountains to intercept the moisture-laden clouds borne eastward from the Pacific Ocean by prevailing winds. The decreasing pressure, as this current is deflected upward over the range, causes a rapid cooling of the air and a consequent deposit of the large bodies of snow found in these mountain fastnesses. Where, in the Main Range, the slopes are clad with pine, spruce and larch, according to altitude, in the Selkirk Range, Douglas fir, hemlocks, cedar, giant spruce and balsam take their place. These forests of green, so deep in color as to appear almost black, rise grandly to the snows, and often amidst the trees may be seen crystal cascades of ice, tumbling in a wild confusion of seracs down rocky beds.

The Selkirk Range is remarkable for the number, purity and picturesque formation of its glaciers. In size they may not compare with the ice-rivers of other ranges, but what they lack in size, they more than make up in their wonderfully crevassed surfaces and in the grotesque seracs that are formed where they break over cliffs and rock ledges. Specially beautiful are the hanging and confluent glaciers, high up on the mountain sides, dropping tons of crystal ice daily to the trunk streams below. Splendid examples of these may be seen above the Battle glaciers at the head of Battle Creek, and in the hanging valley of Cougar Creek; also, in the Main Range the narrow gorge, known as "The Death Trap," leading between

14

Mounts Victoria and Lefroy to Abbott Pass. During the warm summer days the roar of ice falling from these upper glaciers is incessant.

The Coast Range, reaching into the far northland, is cut and intersected by many inlets from the sea. These inlets are often narrow and enclosed by precipitous sides of rock, over which cascades fall hundreds of feet to tide-water, below. The steeps are clad with forests of tropical luxuriance, through which it is only with great difficulty a passage can be forced, and giant trees of fir, cedar and balsam grow nearly to the summits of the mountains. As you proceed northward, the timber-covering becomes more scant until, at length, it is found only at the bottom of the lower valleys.

There can be little doubt that the characteristics outlined above, furnish not only a worthy field for an alpine organization, but a field of immense magnitude, and one that will continually offer something new for many years to come. It is true we have not the great height of other mountain systems of the world. Mont Blanc, the giant of the European Alps, is 15,780 feet above the sea; Mount Tacoma, in Washington, is 14,526 feet; Popocatapetl and Orizaba, in Mexico, are 17,500 and 18,300 feet; Mount McKinley, in Alaska, is said, by a recent explorer, to be 20,300 feet; and the Himalayas reach the enormous altitude of 29,000 feet. Against all this, except in a few isolated cases — Mount Logan, 19,500; Mount Hubbard, 16,400; Mount Vancouver, 15,600; Mount Augusta, 14,900, and others in the Yukon Territory, with Mount Robson, 13,700, and Mount Columbia, 12,700, in Alberta — we can only boast a general altitude of 10,000 to 12,000 feet; but, for primeval forests, beauty of glaciers and labyrinthine organization, the Rockies of Canada cannot be surpassed.

Up to the completion of the Canadian Pacific Railway in 1885, there was no thought of mountaineering in Canada. Prior to that date, by one year, attention was first called to the claims of the Canadian Rockies as a field for alpine work, and the great attractions they offered to mountaineers, by the Honorary President and Patron of our Club, Sir Sandford Fleming, K.C.M.G., who had the year before made a journey on foot through this rock-bound wilderness, along the route it was proposed to lay the rails. In his book, *England and Canada, a Summer Tour between Old and New Westminster*, he frequently refers to the massive, snow-clad peaks and crystal ice-falls of the Rocky Mountains as affording a suitable field for mountaineers.

In 1888 the Royal Geographical Society, represented by the Rev. William Spotswood Green and the Rev. Henry Swanzy, made explorations and rough topographical surveys in the vicinity of Glacier, near the summit of the Selkirk Range. They then made the first ascent of Mount Bonney (10,200 feet), at that time an arduous two-day climb from Glacier station. As a result, Mr. Green's able and instructive book, *Among the Selkirk Glaciers*, appeared in 1890, giving a delightful and humorous description of the range and of his climbs and surveys. It was in 1890 that the region was visited by representatives of the English and Swiss Alpine Clubs: H. W. Topham of the former, and Emil Huber and Carl Sulzer of the latter. Both parties realized that, at that early date, the most accessible alpine material lay in the Selkirks; so they made their headquarters at Glacier and, joining forces, accomplished many splendid climbs together. This year also, Professor Charles E. Fay of the Appalachian Mountain Club of Boston, visited the Selkirks and was so impressed with what he saw that he not only repeated his visit but brought many others with him, the result being: first, the formation of an Alpine section of the Appalachian Club, and eventually the organization of the American Alpine Club, of which Professor Fay is now President. From 1890 on, *Appalachia*, the organ of that Club, set forth the conquests made by its members in the Canadian mountains, and furnishes much instructive and interesting reading.

An account and map of the expeditions of Professor A. P. Coleman and Professor L. B. Stewart of Toronto University, accompanied by L. Q. Coleman, to the headwaters of the Athabaska River, by new and unmapped routes, will be found in *The Geographical Journal* of January, 1895. These trips, made in 1892 and 1893, resulted in the discovery of Fortress Lake, lying directly upon the Continental watershed, and in the dethroning of Mount Brown, on the west side of the Athabaska Pass. The mountain was climbed by Professor Stewart and L. Q. Coleman and the altitude fixed, by barometric readings, at 9050 feet instead of over 16,000 feet, as it is, even at the present date, shown in standard geographies and on published maps. At this time, eight peaks over 9000 feet above sea level were climbed, and three over 10,000 feet. A later expedition in 1903 resulted in the mapping of the Brazeau snow-field, never before visited by white men.

In 1894, W. D. Wilcox, S. H. S. Allen and two other young college men visited Lake Louise, of which the striking beauty had already been realized to such an extent that the Railway Company had built a small chalet on its borders to accommodate a few visitors. On this occasion, they discovered Paradise valley, where the Club will camp during the present summer. The explorations then made and, the following year, to the headwaters of the Bow River, resulted in Mr. Wilcox's artistic and beautifully illustrated book *Camping in the Canadian Rockies*, which has since been amplified and brought up to date as the author pushed his investigations farther afield, both north and south, accompanied in the latter direction by Henry G. Bryant of the Philadelphia Geographical Society.

The late Jean Habel of Berlin, a noted explorer and enthusiastic mountaineer, explored the Yoho valley in 1897, and it was due to his representations that it first attained notoriety. Again, in 1901, he travelled to the headwaters of the Athabaska River, visited Fortress Lake, and gazed upon the mighty Mount Columbia, which he designated in his records as "Gamma." Subsequently, we have records of explorations and first climbs, in 1897, 1898, 1900 and 1902, by Dr. J. Norman Collie, Hugh E. M. Stutfield, G. P. Baker and Hermann Woolley in the mountaineer's paradise on the north side of the Blaeberry River, along whose banks lay the old Howse Pass route of early fur-trading days. These have been embodied in a splendid book: *Climbs and Explorations in the Canadian Rockies*, written jointly by Mr. Stutfield and Dr. Collie. Accompanying the book is the only existing detail map of the region. In 1901, and following years, came Mr. Edward Whymper with four Swiss guides.

The same year, the Rev. James Outram captured Mount Assiniboine, and, in 1902, he made his big killing in the north country, first explored by Collie, Stutfield, Woolley, and Baker. Mounts Columbia, Bryce, Lyall, Alexandra and many others succumbed to his attacks, a truly wonderful mountaineering record for one summer. Mr. Outram has set forth his achievements in a well-written and charmingly descriptive book, entitled, *In the Heart of the Canadian Rockies*. Each year two or three travellers penetrate into the wilderness of snow-clad peaks and rushing glacier torrents, described in the works named, and some publish accounts of their impressions, but they follow only the beaten paths of the pioneers and see the sights they have seen.

Minor explorations have been made of valleys and passes opening from the main routes along the Bow and Saskatchewan headwaters by members of the Appalachian Mountain Club, among whom may be named: C. S. Thompson, G.

M. Weed, Rev. H. P. Nichols, C. L. Noyes, and H. C. Parker, also, at the sources of the Beaverfoot River by J. H. Scattergood. Accounts of these investigations will be found in the various numbers of *Appalachia* appearing since 1890. There are but two deviations from the beaten line of travel that have given us mapped results: Collie and Stutfield's exploration of the Bush River and vicinity, on the western side of the Main Range, and Wilcox and Bryant's expedition to the headwaters of the Kananaskis River.

Notwithstanding the large amount of information contained in the books referred to, our absolute knowledge of alpine Canada is confined to a strip of little more than ten miles on either side of the Canadian Pacific Railway, possibly some five or six thousand square miles, and what may be seen by travelling the paths cut by Collie, Stutfield, Baker, Wilcox and a few others. The books published all cover, practically, the same ground, with the exception of the trips up the Bush River and to the Kananaskis headwaters. The region lying between the Columbia River on the west, the Blaeberry on the south, and the Saskatchewan on the east, is unknown territory except to the pioneers who have published its fame. The only map we have of it is the one accompanying Dr. Collie's book, and that is admittedly a "sketch map." This field alone, embracing from 20,000 to 25,000 square miles, the finest alpine country of the entire continent, is sufficient to supply an alpine club with work, both scientific and athletic, for many years to come. In the Selkirks, north of Mount Rogers and south of Mount Purity, lie unknown tracts, with peaks, towers, pyramids and pinnacles, rising from wide snow-fields, that are unknown, unnamed, and unmapped, and have only been seen from Selkirk summits near the railway and from the more distant Rockies.

The Dominion Government is steadily pushing its topographical surveys into the unknown territory, but these surveys are slow and costly and some adequate return must be in sight before they can be undertaken. The books, etc., published by the authors named have attracted a great many people to the region, and, to meet the demand, the Canadian Pacific Railway Company have erected a number of hotels at beauty spots along the line, which have been enlarged and modernized, until now the acme of luxury may be found in the heart of these wilds, where the many forces of Nature that contribute so largely to a civilized world are seen at work.

Albert H. MacCarthy and Basil S.
Darling on gendarme on east side of
Extinguisher Tower, Mount Robson
ACC Camp, 1913. Photo: Byron
Harmon. Whyte Museum of the
Canadian Rockies

Garibaldi Lake, Coast Mountains. Photo: Ray Kodama

1908 : THE FIRST ASCENT OF MOUNT GARIBALDI

A. T. DALTON

O n the extreme west of the Rocky Mountains system, hard by the waters of the North Pacific, is a mountain range little known beyond its own horizon. Its highest peaks do not compare in altitude with the giants of the Selkirks and Rockies, rising above valleys already at a considerable elevation, but they have the same alpine features of rock and glacier and snow, while their ascent involves climbing almost from the level of the sea. Moreover, they possess an added feature of beauty impossible to the ranges lying further east, their seaward slopes being indented with numerous fjords which find their way often into the very heart of the range.

The peak of greatest height is Mount Garibaldi — known locally as "Old Baldi" — which stands at the head of Howe Sound, some thirty miles in from the Gulf of Georgia. Every dweller in the lovely Valley of the Squamish, which this mountain overlooks, is as proud of him as he is proud of his country; yet, except to these good people, he is all but a myth.

Years ago a party attempted the ascent, but failed; and it looked, as time went on, as if Old Baldi were to crumble away in peace. But in that party were some who were "baffled to fight better," and this is why one stormy night, early in August, 1907, an adventurous group found themselves about a roaring fire in an old log house in the Squamish Valley, forty miles by water from Vancouver.

At six o'clock the next morning under a clear sky, we set out for the coveted summit, following the Tsee-Ki whose source is in Garibaldi's glaciers. At first the travelling was easy, for the rise was gradual and the country open; and in a few hours we were in the foothills, with the Tsee-Ki's milky waters boiling through canyons, and our mountain looming ever higher and more forbidding.

By noon we reached a place where the way by the stream was barred and we were obliged to begin the ascent by a ridge on the left. And now our toils commenced. For 1,000 feet we had some very awkward rock-work made risky by loose fragments; and beyond this, a laborious grind of 5,000 feet up a wooded slope at an angle of 45 degrees. For hours we toiled up that interminable mountainside with never a glimpse of a view to encourage us; until at last, when quite near the summit of the ridge, we "played out." We had been travelling for twelve hours. Camp was made in an open glade carpeted with heather, and with plenty of wood and pure water, we were soon comfortable for the night.

Early next morning we broke camp and continued the work of the previous day with keen anticipation. In a short while we were rewarded by our first panorama, for all at once we stepped on open ground and, looking back, beheld the whole Squamish Valley lying 6,000 feet beneath us with its roads, rivers and farms showing as depicted

This charming article on the first ascent of Mount Garibaldi illustrates how difficulty of access plagued early mountaineers on the west coast of Canada. This article also exemplifies the writing style of the day. While it is obvious that the climbing life was simpler at the turn of the twentieth century, those who wrote about it were often more articulate than the writers of today.
– R W S

upon a living map. Beyond lay Howe Sound stretching away to the open sea, and in the far distance Vancouver Island. We were feasting upon this scene when a shout from our amateur guides hurried us on. Almost before we knew what had happened, we found ourselves on the first crest with Garibaldi beyond in full view, and quite close. Towering heavenwards in one magnificent mass of rock, his precipices crowned with hanging glaciers, and all his upper heights wrapt in a mantle of fresh snow, he seemed some terrible monarch of the skies not to be approached by man.

A rising ridge in the form of a crescent connected our present point with the glaciers behind the mountain. A steep descent of some 300 feet brought us to its crest and along it we took our way. The whole ridge was clothed with fresh green grasses and blossoming heather, through which flowed here and there silvery streamlets of purest crystal. Clusters of trees were scattered about in reckless order, and gorgeous flowers in wild profusion made fragrant the air.

In Indian file we moved along, ever on our right the mountain, and far below on the left the Squamish Valley and the ice-clad range beyond. Once a deer went bounding past with swift graceful motion, and then some fleecy, clouds floated by. A few hours brought us to a commanding knoll, and here at timberline we pitched camp in a group of dwarfed balsams. We now had a view behind Garibaldi of a vast sea of unknown mountains, glaciers and lakes.

After a somewhat uncanny night we awoke to find ourselves enveloped in clouds, so dense that our knoll seemed a little island in mid-ocean. All morning was spent in camp in that heavy, silent fog, but in the afternoon two of us set off with one of our guides for the base of the peak. It took two hours to get to it, steadily tramping up slopes of shale and snow in the thick fog. And then we reached a point where there was no sign of vegetation, and from whence we beheld the wildest scene of the trip.

We stood on the top of a huge mass of rock, on one side was a precipice vanishing below in clouds, and on the other a very steep slope of trap rock, up which the clouds were surging from out the Tsee-Ki canyons. Within a stone's throw on the left darkly loomed the red walls of the dome of Garibaldi, and from a glacier at its base rushed a noisy little streamlet, the very head of the Tsee-Ki, which we had followed for 25 miles. Early next morning the whole party set out to make an attempt at the ascent; but when we reached the snowfield below the

peak, silent, desolate and trackless, the party would go no further. The fog gathered thickly and it was snowing; so, dejected, we returned to camp. Now happened what nearly ruined the whole expedition. Four of the party wanted to go home, and one of the leaders was willing, but the other bitterly opposed to it. The fate of that virgin peak hung in the balance. It was settled by the "youngster" of the party stepping alongside the "foolish" guide, as he was rated, and with him swearing to retreat not one step till more than mere clouds and snow flurries barred the way to the summit. It had been "do or die" sitting before a cozy hearth in town, so now the only way home was the Spartan one: with your shield or on it!

At sundown the wind veered to the north and in a few hours there was not a vestige of a cloud in the sky. Now we had cold to contend with, for an icy wind blew from the glaciers behind Garibaldi, and our supply of wood was ended. The break of dawn on the twelfth was the scene of a lifetime. All hands were up early and, just as the sun was tipping the surrounding peaks and tinting glacier after glacier, we set off for the third time up that mountain ridge. The peak showed clear but was clad with new snow and looked anything but easy. In a couple of hours we reached the base and here roped, with the two men of the former expedition as guides. Then we stepped out upon the glacier at an altitude of about 8,000 feet, and began to circle the peak — a pyramid rising 2,000 feet — by the north.

For an hour we walked steadily over new frozen snow of dazzling whiteness, constantly encountering ugly crevasses, the peak on our right, a wall of unscaleable precipices overhung by a glacier. For another hour we hurried on, gradually rising, the silence of those dismal wastes broken only by the sound of an alpenstock biting the frozen snow. Once the whole place was shaken by an avalanche which came thundering down the precipice on our flank. At eleven o'clock we reached the 9,000-foot level where began the final struggle.

Soon we were on one of the frozen faces of the pyramid, a slope of 45°, rounding off abruptly to where, far below, we had passed early in the morning. We made a horizontal traverse of this, negotiated two crevasses, and then began to climb the steep face of iced snow leading to an arête above, which would take us to the summit. Every step had to be cut, and the higher we climbed the steeper it grew. Then someone murmured, for the slope became nearly vertical and a merciless wind was whistling across it. Close above, however, was rock, so we worked to this haven. Decidedly unnerved we reached it at last, and clambering up its steep face, gazed over the saw-like edge. What we saw there sickened the bravest of us. We were on the edge of a thin toppling precipice of rotten lava, overhanging a horrible green glacier a thousand feet below, with empty space beneath it again. A cry was raised to return, but our guides were firmer now, and we had to go on.

The arête was about a hundred yards long, all cracked and crumbling, with its north face, on which we were, a mass of loose slabs of lava, coated with snow and ice. Under this was a bank of snow too steep to use, with two yawning crevasses stretching across it. To the south was the paralyzing "overhang." It took an hour and a half to make that course. Every piece of dislodged rock went either silently flying into dizzy space on one side, or whirring down the other to vanish with an almost human howl in the hungry throat of one of those crevasses.

In a kind of trance we at last crawled up a ridge of soft clean snow, and found ourselves standing on a flat, bare rock, with only the four winds about us and the heavens above us. One of our young guides planted a Union Jack; and we realized that a virgin peak was conquered — Garibaldi. The view from that point 10,000 feet above the sea must be left to the imagination of those who have been in like places. A cairn was built, and then we hurriedly roped, for there were only four hours till nightfall and it had taken eight to make the ascent. Clouds were whirling about us now, and a storm was evidently coming on.

How we made the nerve-racking descent of that arête, and how once the front of our line went into one of those crevasses and was rescued, cannot be related here. Let it suffice that after a mad race with night and fog over the glaciers, we returned to camp, exhausted. One more night, and the worst, was spent in that desert spot, for all the elements seemed running riot, and our firewood was used up.

In the morning we bade farewell to our never-to-be-forgotten camp, and set off home by the route we had come. Observation Point was reached, and then began the long tedious descent to the Tsee-Ki canyons. It rained in torrents, we lost our way and got entangled in a maze of cliffs. Several of these we overcame by sliding down our ropes, finally reaching the Tsee-Ki; and at 5 o'clock we stood on the Squamish road and were soon safe in our log house again.

Wednesday, the eighth day out, broke as clear and bright as ever a day seen by man, and we set off early down the country road on a farm wagon. Quietly we drove through that lovely valley, among its farms with their peaceful green lands and happy faces; above, the blue sky with a fringe of snow peaks. Ten miles brought us to the sea where the little steamer "Britannia" waited. Then we bade farewell to Squamish and her "White-headed Baldi," and were homeward-bound.

The next four hours were spent steaming down that grand old fjord, Howe Sound, and at sunset we entered Vancouver harbor.

Teepee on shore of Maligne Lake, 1924. Photo: Lewis Freeman. Whyte Museum of the Canadian Rockies

1912 : THE FINDING OF LAKE MALIGNE

MARY T. S. SCHÄFFER

In the summer of 1908, a party of six — three guides, three tourists — and twenty-two horses, left the well-known station of Laggan on the main line of the Canadian Pacific road, traversed the Bow Valley, over the pass of the same name, descended Bear Creek to its junction with the Saskatchewan, crossed that river not a day too soon (as the spring floods had already started), ascended the North Fork as far as Nigel Creek, travelled up Nigel Creek and across Nigel Pass, then down the main branch of the Brazeau River to the junction of that stream with the waters from Brazeau Lake; then ascending this last stream, crossed it at its exit from the lake. From this point the way was an unknown one to the entire party. The route, in spite of the rather lurid descriptions I have seen written of it recently, is a very travelled one, very easy and very beautiful. Every mile of it, barring the fire-swept district just north of Laggan (and that has been materially improved by leaving the old Indian route in the valley and following the eastern hill-slopes), a child could take. Having reached new territory (to us), it was in slow but steady marches that we left the shores of the Brazeau behind us — our only guide the word of a Stony Indian (Samson Beaver) that Chaba Imne (Beaver Lake) existed, and a grimy piece of paper on which the said Indian had traced his ideas of mountains, streams and passes to be followed. With the exception of an occasional prospector's deserted camp, Dr. A. P. Coleman's blazes were the only sign that a white man had ever gone that way before; he had followed the trail of the Indian hunter, we followed the footsteps of both, and learned by bald experience the length and breadth of Poboktan Pass with all attendant miseries of the same, learned the horrors of Poboktan Valley, and peered into every cross valley looking for our mythical lake.

About half way down Poboktan Valley, a few comparatively fresh blazes from an Indian's axe attracted us, we accepted the suggestion and mounted the hills across which they led. The following day we climbed yet higher, made our way across an unmapped pass, and looked down upon a beautiful unfire-touched, flower-strewn valley about twenty miles in length. Too tempting to ignore, we travelled by the banks of the eve- increasing stream for two days, and then:: Chaba Imne of the Stony lay before us.

What her length or breadth, in those days, might be, we had no means of knowing, though, after a partial navigation of her waters on a raft, we realized that she had been made on no mean proportions. That she was fair to the eye beyond all compare, all admitted, and her beauty haunted us long after we had said "farewell" to her — as we thought forever.

Having almost lost two horses at the lake's very quiet-looking outlet, and having learned that Maligne River (named these many years, and which empties into the Athabasca River opposite Henry House), headed not

Before established trails and reliable maps, most of Canada's early mountain explorers confined their adventures to the valley floors and to passes that accessed unnamed terrain. One of the earliest and best-remembered tourist explorers was a Philadelphia Quaker of independent means named Mary Sharples Schäffer, who first travelled seriously in the Rockies with her friend Mary Adams in 1906. A book-length account of her explorations, entitled Old Indians Trails, *was published in 1911.*
– RWS

from Medicine Lake, as it appears on McEvoy's map, but merely flowing through it, came direct from our "new" lake, all the party decided the river named the lake, and it has since been so recorded.

Ten days later, when we stood on the banks of the Maligne River at its junction with the Athabasca, its turbulent condition was reason enough to our minds why some old French half-breed trapper had called its thus — he forgotten, its troublous water never, as long as those waters flow.

At the suggestion of Mr. D. B. Dowling, of the Canadian Geological Survey, who himself would be working in the valley of the Athabasca during the summer of 1911, I again went to Lake Maligne that spring — not by the longer and beautiful route from Laggan, but entering the country via Edmonton and the then uncompleted Grand Trunk Pacific road. In my dufflebag reposed a log, compass, protractor, scale, lined paper and, most valuable of all, intricate and detailed directions how to use, what to me was at that time a set of very formidable weapons. I confess my doubts were grave indeed that anything seriously worthwhile could possibly result from an expedition of this kind in such unskilled hands, and if the knowledge brought back has any value, it must be owing entirely to the careful notes and instructions so patiently worked out and sent me by Mr. Dowling.

It was a trip of interest from beginning to end; from the moment we left the last semblance of a railroad behind us and followed miles of country where men, like ants, were preparing the way to carry the new transcontinental road on its last lap to the Pacific Ocean; left the Athabasca and her dusty dunes behind us, and, surmounting the high intervening hills, with clothing, food and sixteen-foot timbers for a boat to ply the Maligne waters, fought our way through the still deep snows of a high pass and at last stood on the shore of that lovely sheet of water.

The boat was built at the lake's outlet. With doubting heart, forth came the long hidden paraphernalia and it was solemnly studied; but there was no sense of elation as, with the log securely attached to the stern of the boat, the surveyor took her first readings of the compass to the next visible point of the lake, stepped aboard, tossed out the log and was silently rowed to the site in question. The nervous sensation that something important might be forgotten, was great enough, but the rowing of that clumsy boat was equally bad. To sit hour by hour, with nothing to distract the mind from the rower's weary task but to guide the rudder

with a piece of frazzled twine taken from a side of bacon, was nothing short of painful; for the readings quickly became a mere matter of moment.

When three days had been consumed working from the lower end of the lake as a base, a day was taken for drafting. With figures and sketch obtained (trifling details too small for the log to be used were noted), the novice poured for hours over the result — drawing, re-drawing, going over and over each measurement — something was found to be wrong. What was it? Who was to blame? Again and again Mr. Dowling's notes were studied — they had been followed to the letter, but that shore line was incorrect.

Blunders are usually suppressed in print, I think, but should this case of mine reach the eye of even one who has the temerity to attempt to use such unaccustomed tools, I am willing to sacrifice my pride and expose my stupidity. No amount of juggling the figures obtained, righted the matter, we were forced to look elsewhere for the trouble. The tripod used on the work was examined, it looked all right, but to make doubly sure, the compass was read first from it, then from a stout post driven into the ground — the secret was solved. A steel screw in the brass head of the tripod had been the undoing of three days' hard labor. The entire sighting of the compass after that, was done from a stick of wood driven into the ground at every landing. Three readings were always taken, and the average was used.

The length of the lake and our clumsy craft combined, called for three bases of work. Our camp lay just within the Narrows — Samson Narrows as we called them — quite under the shadow of Mounts Unwin and Charlton. Here we were detained for two weeks by a prolonged storm, often so violent that it was scarce safe to be many feet from shore even in the punt — wonderful as its ability to weather any sea was warranted to be by its builder. Life, however, was far from stupid. The scenery at that point is magnificent, and the storm accentuated the beauty by flinging wonderful rainbows across the lake, tossing blankets of snow over the peaks and over our little home. One day we had the excitement of beholding a waterspout (probably two hundred feet high) sweep round the bend, tear madly up the middle of the lake, sucking up the water as it came, then die before us with such rapidity that we wondered if we had been dreaming the moment before.

Besides the desire to obtain a sketch-map of the lake, we were also in quest of an old trail which the Indians said lay between Maligne and Brazeau Lakes. When the low clouds lifted sufficiently one morning, we explored the valley back of our camp — Sandpiper Valley (so called as the alluvial fan at the mouth of the stream was a wonderful breeding ground for the sandpiper). It proved a blind valley: a valley for goat, or sheep, or bear, but with all the respect I have for an Indian's pony's capabilities, I saw no chance for a footing in the upper reaches of that valley. To its furthest limitations the distance is about five miles, with a fine, double-headed peak (snow and glacier-crowned), which we called Mount Maligne. Signs of goat and bear were numerous.

At the upper end of the lake we made our third camp. At that point the scenery is positively dramatic. Waterfalls: the grand cliffs of the Thumb,:avalanches thundering down on hot, sunny days; hundreds of wild duck skimming with pathetic little quacks across the glass-like lake; and in the distance, upon the green meadows of the Pixie Hills, little white dots (goat) moving, all combined to make a picture worth many a troubled hour to reach. Here the days were as fine as in the Narrows they had been dull, and with our log and compass work completed, we searched the valleys for the lost Indian trail. Behind, or east of the double-headed mass of rock and snow known as Mount Warren, we found a stream leading from large icefields about two miles distant, and from the mountains on either side of her course, innumerable waterfalls adding their quota to her flow. The first view of this valley looked very promising for the lost pass, but we followed it to its highest limitations — the glaciers — and there was no sign of other footsteps than the ever-present mountain goat. Hundreds of rocks, perched on end just below the ice-line, reminded us of guardians to some vast,

wild haunt, and thus suggested the name Pixie Valley. We returned to our teepee home late in the evening still wondering where the trail to the Brazeau lay.

Fagged with that day's trip, our guide tried what was apparently the only other available valley the next day, and at night reported "Bear Valley as a horse-shoe of glaciers at its southern-most end." Personally I have my doubts if the Indians ever came to the upper end of the lake with horses; first, there is not enough feed to hold a horse more than a couple of days, and second, we never saw a sign of a camp. Lower down the lake we found many a decaying wickiup, little shelters where the hunter had crouched from the bitter blasts of winter, as he laid over at night, while making the round of his traps. It is the lower end of the lake where we found teepee poles in every stage of decay and, in the meadows beyond, as well as on the Opal Hills, an inexhaustible supply of feed. Doubtless the little brown jacket of the marten had attracted the hunter, for we saw several of them playing about our camps. The beaver, for which the Stoneys had named the lake, had long been completely destroyed. Only a very few, old rotting stumps remained — to show where the busy workers had lived — and stood there, sad pathetic reminders of the improvidence of the Indian hunter. With our entire measurements completed, we spent one day drafting results, and by drawing a line directly through the centre of the lake, we had a length of eighteen miles. This is probably crude and will bear more scientific inspection; but no science, no other plotting can ever rob each mile of its great charm and beauty.

Lake Maligne, in its altitude of about 5,000 feet, surrounded by picturesque mountains, glaciers and falls, must ever remain one of the Chosen Places.

Yoho Glacier, 1906. Photo: Vaux family. Whyte Museum of the Canadian Rockies

1913 : REPORT OF THE 1912 CAMP

In 1905 the Dominion Government had carried the photo-topographical survey of the railway belt of British Columbia to the headwaters of the Vermilion River; and in 1904 the first ascent of Mount Ball was made by the Club's Eastern Vice-President, J. D. Patterson. These facts, in conjunction with the construction of a scenic motor road from Banff to Windermere, crossing the main divide by way of Vermilion Pass, brought forward the suggestion that the Club's annual summer camp should be held in the vicinity of the pass. A magnificent site was found on the British Columbia side of the pass, about a quarter of a mile from the summit, at an altitude of 5,100 feet. It was in every way ideal as a campground, but was it too low an altitude to give the best facilities for reaching the surrounding peaks, and necessitated a somewhat lengthy tramp through virgin forest before the actual climbing above timber line was commenced.

The dining canopy and official square, consisting of director's quarters, secretary's quarters, committee tent, press tent, tea tent, and cooks' quarters, was pitched in an open glade from which fallen logs and forest debris had been carefully removed. The square occupied the centre of an island surrounded by two branches of the headwaters of Vermilion River. Immediately outside the square, on the right looking down stream, was the fire circle, where each evening the campers gathered in force and spent the hours between supper and bedtime in song and story and many other kinds of entertainment. Directly beyond, amongst the trees along the western branch of the stream, were the ladies' quarters. On the other side of the square, across the eastern branch, also in the woods were the gentlemen's quarters, reached by a natural bridge of a couple of trees from bank to bank, across which at intervals the camp carpenter had nailed slats. Will anyone who has negotiated this crossing after dark forget the "Cawsway"? Indeed, at that time of night, a favorite method was to cross it on all fours. On the island also were situated the scouts' tent, the guides' tent, and the tent relegated to ladies for drying their clothes; while just by the trail at the entrance to the camp, but beyond the stream, were the store tents where that prince of caterers, young in years but old in the ways of the camp, Dr. Fred Bell, held sway with machine-like precision, and weighed each lot of baggage as delivered by the packers — relentlessly chalking up over-weights for double charges on a bulletin board, for future treatment by the treasurer.

The whole was gay with bunting, and the flags of the various nationalities represented flew from poles erected at points of vantage. Mount Castle, a flag station of the Canadian Pacific Railway seventeen miles west of Banff, was the stopping place of visitors to the camp. Here was a base where a number of tents were pitched to accommo-

Through the history of the Alpine Club of Canada, mountaineering camps have been held each summer, and have been the backbone of club activities. In the early years, camps mounted would result in numerous first ascents and significant explorations. This illustration of the 1912 camp held near Castle Mountain in the Rockies gives a sense of the major expedition feel, but also the genteel nature of the early camps, with their sermons, tea tents, porters, and Oriental cooks brought in by packtrain.
– GP

date people arriving too late to reach the Camp the same day. There were sleeping tents for ladies and for gentlemen, a baggage tent and a kitchen tent with a man in charge. Here also were the packers' headquarters, in charge of our old and genial outfitter, Jimmy Simpson, "Sunny Jim" of the Rockies.

The main camp was situated eight miles from Mount Castle. Of this distance, part was constructed wagon road and part pack trail, or road in various stages of construction. Some forty pack and saddle ponies carried the supplies, baggage, and some of the people to the main camp. The transportation was a somewhat difficult problem owing to the fact that there was no feed for the horses at the camp, necessitating a return of the pack train each day to Mount Castle — a trip of sixteen miles. As the ponies could not stand this every day, only half the number were available, day about. With the excellent managing ability for which Jimmy Simpson is noted, all difficulties were promptly and effectually met, and transport machinery moved on well-oiled wheels.

The cooks' quarters were in charge of the veteran, Jim Pong, who has officiated at all the Club Camps except one. With a competent staff at his back, he kept the tables loaded and, no matter at what hour parties returned, they were promptly fed and made happy. The tea tent was in charge of Miss E. Savatard, the Chatelaine of the Club House at Banff. Ready and cheerful assistance was given by the ladies of the camp, notably Mrs. Henshaw, Miss Vaux, Miss Feilman, and others; and, judging by the crowd that gathered here during the afternoon hours, and the quantities of tea consumed, this popular feature was much appreciated.

The Camp was in charge of Arthur O. Wheeler, director, assisted by the executive of the Club, among whom Dr. A. P. Coleman, president, J. D. Patterson, vice-president, and Mrs. J. W. Henshaw, honorary secretary, were present. Mrs. J. W. Henshaw was in charge of the ladies' quarter and the domestic arrangements and, assisted by Miss Vaux and Mrs. McWilliams, the excellent and charming administration made this section of the machinery a perfect sample of tactful skill.

OTHER CLUBS REPRESENTED

The Alpine and Mountain Clubs represented were: the Alpine Club, England, Swiss Alpine Club, American Alpine Club and Appalachian Mountain Club.

The following gentlemen were honoured guests of the Club: W. W. Foster, Deputy Minister of Public Works, as representative of the Government of the Province of British Columbia; J. B. Harkin, Commissioner of Dominion Parks; and R. H. Campbell, Superintendent of Forestry, as representatives of the Dominion Government.

CAMP FIRE

The great fire circle represented the altar of worship of the Camp, its fetish, and here gathered nightly all who were in Camp. Mrs. McWilliams acted as chairman of an Entertainment Committee, and each evening a full programme was on hand. An effort has been made to have the various local sections of the Club provide a previously prepared programme for the respective nights. This feature was now initiated and carried out to some extent. Winnipeg produced an excellent mock trial, at which the Hon. Mr. Justice Galt was the prisoner at the bar, accused of grand larceny of camp property. The trial exhibited a most distressing case of justice on the rampage. There was no doubt of guilt, as the goods were found on the person of the prisoner, even while at the bar; and yet, alas, for frailty of human nature, the majority of the jury being of the fair sex, the prisoner was declared far too good looking to be adjudged guilty, and the verdict of "not proven" was rendered.

Vancouver Island also produced a good evening, and something was done by New York. It is hoped the idea will grow and become an annual feature. An excellent lecture by Dr. A. P. Coleman gave a graphic illustration of the manner in which the mountain architecture of the Canadian Rockies had been formed. The audience was delighted with the simple and picturesque manner in which this most interesting of all subjects to mountaineers was set forth. R. H. Campbell addressed the gathering on the subject of forestry, and gave his hearers a clear insight into the value of the work he and his branch of administration are doing in preserving and developing this tremendously important asset of the Dominion of Canada. He also expressed his appreciation of the objects and aims of the Alpine Club, and hoped that all its members would co-operate with the efforts of the Forestry Branch to preserve the existing timber areas of the mountains.

J. B. Harkin gave a most instructive address upon Dominion parks, their boundaries, administration, and ultimate objects. He expressed himself on behalf of his Government as fully in accord with the good work the Alpine Club was doing towards the development of the Canadian Rockies as a world-playground.

W. W. Foster, in a stirring address, dealt with the mountain scenic features of British Columbia, and the policy of his Government to open up the same and make them accessible to the world by means of the creation of provincial parks to embrace the best of such scenery and the construction of motor roads winding through its midst. He touched upon the beauties of Strathcona Park in the centre of Vancouver Island, and described the magnificent picturesque scenery that would be opened to the public on the completion of the Banff-Windermere road. Finally, he stated that his Government was fully in accord with the excellent results attained by the Alpine Club, and particularly with its expedition to the grandly spectacular region of Mount Robson, to which expedition his Government had been pleased to contribute financial aid, and considered the results attained had been very satisfactory.

On Sunday morning, service was held around the camp fire, at which the Rev. J. J. Robinson, formerly Dean of Belfast, officiated. The Dean's sermon was undoubtedly inspired by the magnificent surroundings of snow-clad peak, towering precipice, rushing torrent, and forested valley. Standing at an impromptu pulpit, draped with the Union Jack, in simple, picturesque language he carried his hearers to the heights and placed them closely in touch with the wonders of creation in these mountains and forests, and reverently dwelt upon the omnipotence of the Great Creator of all things. It was with a feeling of regret his audience realized that his all too short sermon was finished. The thanks of the Camp are due to Dean Robinson for his very successful assistance in entertaining the members on several occasions when rain held the majority in camp. He was the life of the party, and all voted him a jolly good fellow.

Ice Cave, Illecillewaet Glacier, circa 1907 Photo: Elliott Barnes.
Whyte Museum of the Canadian Rockies

Mount Robson, with the Kain Face on the left and north face on the right. Photo: Greg Horne

1914: THE FIRST ASCENT OF MOUNT ROBSON, THE HIGHEST PEAK OF THE ROCKIES

CONRAD KAIN (TRANSLATED BY P. A. W. WALLACE)

O n reaching the Robson Glacier after the ascent of Mount Resplendent, I went down to the timber at 6,700 feet. Here I met my *Herren* for Mount Robson. Both were busy about the fire, Mr. Foster (Deputy Minister of Public Works for British Columbia) with cooking, Mr. MacCarthy with gathering wood. After a good supper, we went up, laden with firewood, to the foot of the Extinguisher. The rock bears this name on account of its form (candle extinguisher). On the moraine we made our shelter beside a wall of stones, over which we stretched a piece of canvas and crept under it like marmots into their hole.

I awoke early next morning and felt pain in my eyes, and for a long time I could not open them. It felt as if my eyes were filled with sand. My snow glasses were no good. I saw a starry sky, which was more than we had expected. I applied cold poultices for half an hour and the pain in my eyes began to abate. I lit the fire and wakened my *Herren*. Both were delighted at the sight of a cloudless sky.

At 4.30 a.m., after an early but good breakfast, we left our bivouac. We followed the route of the previous day (ascent of Mount Resplendent), over the glacier. Before we came to the Pass, we swerved to the right. From this point began the real climb of Mount Robson. We climbed up an avalanche trough, then under some dangerous ice bridges to the right. The snow was in bad condition. We proceeded without any difficulties towards the steep snow-slope that descends from the Dome (10,000 feet) and reached it at 7 a.m. We took a rest and deliberated over the route ahead.

Two years ago I spent hours studying this route, and did not take the bergschrund very seriously. From the Dome, one had a nearer survey of the bergschrund. We approached it over the glacier, which is here not very steep. A rib of rock comes down almost to the 'schrund. Over this rock I planned to ascend, but after every possible attempt we were forced to give it up, for at this place the glacier breaks off sheer. For about two hundred feet we followed along the bergschrund to the right. Here was the only possibility at hand of overcoming it. After long chopping at the ice, I stood on its 65° slope. Across the 'schrund I made more steps. Then I let both *Herren* follow.

A thin layer of snow lay on the ice, and, owing to the melting of the snow, the ice was in very bad condition for step-cutting. I made the steps in a zig-zag. Mr. Foster counted 105 steps to a ledge of rock. The rock, when seen from below, promised good climbing and a rapid advance. But it turned out otherwise. We climbed up an icy wall, and then to our disappointment had an ice-slope before us, fifty or sixty meters high. I kept as well as I could to the rocks that protruded here and there, which saved me a few steps. At the top of the slope we had another wall

No collection of Canadian mountaineering lore could be considered complete without the tale of the first ascent of Mount Robson, by the renowned guide Conrad Kain and his Herren, *Albert MacCarthy and William Foster. Kain's own telling, from the 1914* Journal, *gives a deceptively simplified account of the technical demands of the climb and the controversy surrounding its certainty as the first ascent of the mountain. Most of all, however, it simplifies the realities of Conrad Kain the man, who was truly extreme talent, drive, a vision of the future of climbing and an enigma rolled into one soul.*
– GP

of rock, and above that an almost hopeless ice-slope. One could see the tracks of falling stones and avalanches. On this slope I made 110 steps. It was a relief to climb on rocks again, though they were glazed with ice. But unfortunately the satisfaction was short, and for several hundred meters we had to climb again upon a slope of ice and snow. The snow here was in danger of avalanching. For safety, I lengthened the rope on the dangerous slope.

At last we reached the shoulder at twelve o'clock noon. I do not know whether my *Herren* contemplated with a keen alpine eye the dangers to which we were exposed from the bergschrund. In the year 1909 this route was attempted by Mr. Mumm and Mr. Amery with the guide Inderbinen from Zermatt. The party were in danger of their lives from an avalanche. I spoke with Inderbinen: he said, "I never before saw death so near."

On the shoulder we took a mid-day rest. There came a snowy wind that wet us to the bone. We pulled out all the clothing stowed away in our rucksacks. We found the shoulder less broad than we expected. It was a snow ridge, on the northeast side of which were overhanging cornices fringed with long icicles glittering in the sun, a glorious picture.

For a few hundred meters we had to keep to the southeast side. The snow on this side was in good condition, so that we made rapid progress. There was on each side a splendid view into the depths below (*Tiefblick*). The more beautiful view was that of the Robson Glacier, Smoky Valley and Mount Resplendent and the Lynx Range opposite.

From the shoulder to the peak, the route was no longer so dangerous, but complicated by the loose, powdery snow. It was as if we were on an entirely different climb on the southeast side. The complications arose from walls of snow. Never before on all my climbs have I seen such snow formations. The snow walls were terraced. The ledges between the walls were of different widths, and all were covered with loose snow. I often sank in to my hips. There were forms on the walls like ostrich feathers, a truly strange and beautiful winter scene. Unfortunately we had no camera with us. Some of the walls were fifteen to twenty meters high. It was difficult to find a way up from one terrace to another. At one place I worked for over half an hour without effect. We had to go back. A very narrow and steep couloir offered the only possibility. I warned my *Herren* that the piece would take considerable time to negotiate. Both had a good stand and kept

moving as much as possible in order to keep warm. The wind was so bad here that I often had to stop. The steepness alone, apart from wind, made step-cutting very hard work. For a number of steps I had first to make a handhold in the ice, and swing the axe with one hand. I do not think I need to describe this method any more fully, for everyone who has ever been on the ice, knows that cutting steps with one hand is a frightfully slow process. I know that in such places it is not pleasant either for those behind. As soon as I was convinced that I could make it, I called to my *Herren*: "Just be patient, the bad place will soon be conquered, and the peak is ours." Mr. MacCarthy answered: "We are all right here, we are only sorry for you. I don't understand how you can still keep on cutting steps."

When we had the difficult place behind us, the reward was a fairly steep snow-slope, with the snow in good condition so that we could all three go abreast. At the top of the snow-slope was another wall, which, however, could be outflanked without difficulty.

The last stretch to the summit was a snow-ridge. I turned to my *Herren* with the words: "Gentlemen, that's so far as I can take you."

In a few seconds both stood beside me on the peak. We shook hands with one another. I added my usual Alpine greeting in German, "*Bergheil.*" Of course, I had to explain the word *bergheil* because both knew no German. There is no word in the English language which has the same meaning as *bergheil*.

On the crest of the king of the Rockies, there was not much room to stand. We descended a few meters and stamped down a good space. It was half-past five o'clock. Our barometer showed exactly 13,000 feet.

The view was glorious in all directions. One could compare the sea of glaciers and mountains with a stormy ocean, Mount Robson is about 2,000 feet higher than all the other mountains in the neighborhood. Indescribably beautiful was the vertical view towards Berg Lake and the camp below. Unfortunately only fifteen minutes were allowed us on the summit, ten of pure pleasure and five of teeth chattering. The rope and our damp clothes were frozen as hard as bone. And so we had to think of the long descent.

As far as the steep couloir, all went well. The descent over this piece was difficult. All the steps were covered with snow. Except for this, we had no difficulties till the shoulder. As it was late, I proposed to descend by the glacier on the south side, for greater safety. Besides the question of time, it seemed to me too dangerous to make our descent over the route of ascent. As a guide with two *Herren*, one has to take such dangers more into account than do amateurs, for upon one's shoulders rests the responsibility for men's lives. Also as a guide one must consider his calling and the sharp tongues that set going on all sides like clockwork when a guide with his party gets into a dangerous situation. It was clear to me that we must spend a night on the mountain. The descent was not quite clear to me. I was convinced that on this side we could get farther down than by the way we came up. My bivouac motto is: "A night out is hardly ever agreeable, and above 3,000 meters always a lottery."

After the shoulder, we had a steep snow-slope to the glacier. I made about 120 steps. Once on the glacier, we went down rapidly for a few hundred meters until a sheer precipice barred the way. So far and no farther. In vain was my search for a way down. We had to go back uphill, which was naturally no pleasure. Between rocks and glacier was a very steep icy trench which offered us the only descent. I examined the icy trench for a few minutes, and the ice cliffs overhanging us. I saw the opportunity and, of course, the dangers too. Mr. Foster asked me what my opinion was, whether we could go on or not. I answered, quite truly: "We can; it is practicable but dangerous." Captain MacCarthy said: "Conrad, if it is not too dangerous for you, cutting steps, then don't worry about us. We'll trust to you and fortune."

That made matters easier for me, as I could see that both *Herren* had no fear. I lengthened the rope and left the *Herren* in a sheltered spot. I made the steps just as carefully and quickly as I could. When I had reached a good place I let both *Herren* follow. Mr. MacCarthy went last, and I was astonished at his surefootedness. This dangerous trench took a whole hour to negotiate. The rock was frozen, but the consciousness that we had such terrible danger behind us, helped us over the rocks. In greater safety we rested beneath the rocks.

Below us was the glacier which, seen from above, promised a good descent almost to timberline. I remembered that the glacier had still another break-off and knew that we must camp out. However, I said nothing of this to my *Herren*, but the opposite. I pointed with my axe to the woods with the words: "It will be a fine night down there in the woods beside a big fire." Both chimed in, for the word "fire" makes a very different impression when one is standing in soaking clothes upon ice and snow; from the word "fire" when one is aroused by it from a sound sleep.

We did not find the glacier as good as we expected. We searched our way through ice debris in an avalanche bed. Here on the glacier the sun bade us good night. The sunset was beautiful. It would have been even more beautiful to us if the sun had been delayed one hour. It was a melancholy moment when the last glow of evening faded in the west. We rested and spoke on this theme. Mr. MacCarthy said: "It is as well that the law of nature cannot be changed by men. What a panic it would raise if we succeeded in delaying the sun for an hour! It is possible that somewhere some alpinists will to-morrow morning be in the same situation as we are, and will be waiting eagerly for the friendly sun."

Despite the approach of darkness we went on. About ten o'clock in the evening we reached the rocks. It was out of the question to go any further. Our feet felt the effects of the last seventeen hours on ice and rock, and so we were easily satisfied with a resting place. A ledge of rock two meters wide offered us a good place to bivouac. We made it as comfortable as we could. We built a little sheltering wall about us. Our provision bag still had plenty of sandwiches, and Mr. MacCarthy, to our surprise, brought a large packet of chocolate from his rucksack. We took our boots off. I gave Mr. Foster my pair of extra mitts for socks, so we all had dry feet, which is the important thing in camping out. The *Herren* had only one rucksack between them, into which they put their feet. Both *Herren* were roped up to a rock.

I gave a few hints on bivouacing, for there are some tricks in sleeping out on cold rocks that one can only learn by experience. Fortunately the night was a warm one, threatening rain. Clouds were hanging in the sky, which, however, the west wind swept away to the east. In the valley we saw flickering the campfire of the Alpine Club and of the construction camp of the Canadian Northern and Grand Trunk Railways. I was very tired and went to sleep without any trouble. A thundering avalanche woke me from a sound sleep. I heard Mr. Foster's teeth chatter as he lay beside me. I uttered no word of sympathy, but went to sleep again.

Later I was awakened by a dream. I dreamed that we were quite close to a forest. I saw wood close at hand, and dry branches ready for kindling. In the dream I reproached myself what the *Herren* would think of me, sleeping here in the forest with firewood, but without a fire and almost freezing. With these reproaches I awoke and sat up to convince myself whether the forest and firewood were really so near. But I saw only a few stars and in the east a few gray clouds lit up with the dawn. I could not get to sleep again, but lay quietly and listened to the thunder of the avalanches which broke the almost ghostly silence of Nature. At daybreak it became considerably warmer, so my *Herren*, who had spent a cold and sleepless night, now fell sound asleep.

At six o'clock the friendly beams of the sun reached us. I wakened my *Herren*. Both sat up and described the pain in their eyes, which they could not open. The eyes of both were greatly swollen. It was not a pleasant sight. I thought both were snow-blind. Snow-blind, at a height of 9,000 feet, and in such a situation — that might have an unpleasant ending. After some cold poultices, the pain abated and both were able to keep their eyes open.

I told my dream. Both *Herren* had dreams of a similar nature, which had reference to the cold night. Mr. Foster dreamed that a number of his friends came with blankets and commiserated the barren camping ground, and no one covered him. Mr. MacCarthy, in his dream, implored his wife for more blankets, and his wife stopped him with the curt reply: "O no, dear, you can't have any blankets. Sleeping without any is good training if we want to go to the North Pole."

I searched for a descent over the rocks. After a quarter of an hour I came back. "Yes, we can make it without further difficulty." At 6.45 a.m. we left the bivouac, which will certainly remain in our memory. We did not get down so easily after all. We had to get around sheer walls. The climbing was difficult, and at some places the rock was very rotten. This was very unpleasant for my *Herren*. They could only see a few steps through their glasses and swollen eyes.

At last we had the most difficult part behind us, but not the most dangerous. We had to traverse a hanging glacier. For ten minutes we were exposed to the greatest danger. I certainly breathed freely when we lay down to rest under some overhanging rock. Our barometer showed 8,200 feet, time 10:15 a.m. That eight hundred feet had taken three hours to negotiate. I said to my *Herren*: "I am happy to be able to inform you that we have all dangers behind us. We shall reach the green grass in the valley safe and sound even to our swollen eyes."

We crossed loose stone to the southwest ridge. This ridge should be the easiest way up to the peak. From here we had a beautiful view of Lake Kinney below. Without further difficulty we descended through a wild, romantic gorge to the lake. In the gorge we had a slide over old snow. At eleven o'clock we took a long rest and devoured everything eatable we could find left in our provision bag. Then we followed the newly-built trail to camp.

About five o'clock in the afternoon we came, hungry and tired into camp, where we were hospitably received by our fellow campers with food and drink and congratulations.

From what Donald Phillips himself said, our ascent was really the first ascent of Mount Robson. Phillips's words are as follows: "We reached, on our ascent (in mist and storm), an ice-dome fifty or sixty feet high, which we took for the peak. The danger was too great to ascend the dome."

Phillips and Kinney made the ascent over the west ridge. The west side is, as far as I could see, the most dangerous side that one can choose. Kinney undertook the journey from Edmonton alone with five horses. On the way he met Donald Phillips who was on a prospecting tour. Mr. Kinney persuaded Phillips to accompany him. Phillips had never before made this kind of a mountain trip and says himself that he had no suspicion of its dangers. They had between them one ice-axe and a bit of ordinary rope. They deserve more credit than we, even though they did not reach the highest point, for in 1909 they had many more obstacles to overcome than we; for at that time the railway, which brought us almost to the foot of the mountain, was then no less than 200 miles from their goal, and their way had to be made over rocks and brush, and we must not forget the dangerous river crossings.

Mount Robson is one of the most beautiful mountains in the Rockies and certainly the most difficult one. In all my mountaineering in various countries, I have climbed only a few mountains that were hemmed in with more difficulties. Mount Robson is one of the most dangerous expeditions I have made. The dangers consist in snow and ice, stone avalanches, and treacherous weather.

Ever since I came to Canada and the Rockies, it was my constant wish to climb the highest peak. My wish was fulfilled. For this ascent I could have wished for no better companions. Both *Herren* were good climbers and Nature lovers, and made me no difficulties on the way. Each had a friendly word of thanks for my guiding. In this country people are much more democratic than with us in Europe, and have less regard for titles and high officials; but still it was a great satisfaction to me to have the pleasure of climbing with a Canadian statesman.

Martha McCallum on Mount Robson. Photo: Larry Stanier

Below the East Ridge of Bugaboo Spire in winter.
Photo: Pierre Lemire

1917 : FIRST ASCENT OF NUMBER 3 PEAK, OR "BUGABOO SPIRE"

ALBERT H. MacCARTHY

On August 29th, the day after our traverse of the Sextet Ridge, Mrs. MacCarthy, John Vincent, Conrad (Kain) and the writer left camp at 4.30 a.m. for a try on No. 3 Peak, which we erroneously imagined was the one on which Dr. Hickson, of Montreal, had made an unsuccessful attempt during the latter part of July. Later we learned that, with Edouard Feuz, he had tried the main ridge of spires, ascending the north arête but was driven back on account of snow conditions after reaching the base of the last big gendarme. The weather was not promising, but by the time we reached the saddle between Nos. 2 and 3, the clouds had broken and we were favored with sunshine for most of the day.

Crossing the eastern glacier close along the cliffs of No. 2 Peak, they presented a most forbidding aspect, as if trying to scare us from any search for a vulnerable spot that may possibly lie on the southwest side of the mountain between its main mass and a low lying shoulder.

The lower reaches on No. 3 above the saddle, for about 1,200 feet, varied at angles from 30 to 60 degrees, with two thirty-foot chimneys and one smooth slide, the whole stretch affording every possible kind of interesting rock work. Up the easier parts of these stretches Conrad set a fast pace with John trailing close behind him, while Mrs. MacCarthy and I, following close behind her to avoid the necessity of using a rope, took a more leisurely gait.

The *pièce de résistance* that took nearly two hours to negotiate was reached at an elevation of 10,000 feet, and here the laggards again rejoined Conrad and John, who sat below it nonplussed at the sight of a veritable bugaboo, which immediately suggested to our minds the appropriateness of the name "Bugaboo" for this spire. Our route was completely blocked by a most formidable gendarme, whose base completely spanned the width of the ridge. Its wall on the west side ran up in prolongation of the mighty cliffs that rose from the glacier far below, and its top edge rose sharply like a horn to the point where it joined the high sheer east wall. The side to the west was blocked by the cliffs, and on the east side a broken section led down directly below the east wall for about forty feet to a ledge four feet wide that ended with a 2,000-foot drop; while above this ledge, although the face was broken, there seemed to be no safe line of ascent, and Conrad finally decided that the face of the gendarme offered our only hope. Relieving himself of his rucksack, he gradually worked up this face by means of several diagonal cracks until he succeeded in getting both arms over the top edge, and here he stuck for a long time, feeling about and looking for some little thing that might afford him a hold long enough to pull himself over. At last he found it, although it was not apparent to us when we followed, and slowly crept over the edge, much to our relief, for we supposed the difficulties were ended, but they had really just begun.

Albert MacCarthy's tale of the first ascent of Bugaboo Spire is an endearing homage to the talents of Conrad Kain — both as a climber and an inspiring leader. Kain's tackling of the infamous gendarme pitch on the route — long felt to be the hardest lead on the continent — is spelled out by the author with a gentle trust in Kain that belies the difficulty of the route, and a selfless modesty about the collective abilities of the whole team. The greatest beauty in this story of the 1916 climb is found in the comradeship of guide and client.

– GP

Half an hour we waited while Conrad's body disappeared and reappeared at the edge; after each disappearance we expected to hear a shout that we could prepare to follow, but each time Conrad's fingers would slowly creep into sight and then he would appear again to survey the situation and make a fresh start. The whole trouble, he explained, was due to the lack of any sort of hold or footing on the steep, smooth face for a distance of six feet to a crack beyond. As it was impossible to throw the rope over anything to give him support and the ice-axe had proven unavailing, he was forced to depend entirely upon himself with no certainty as to what position he might find himself in when once in the crack. It was evident from his persistent efforts that he was determined to make it, and all we could do was to tend the useless rope, giving him slack and pulling it in again when he came back into view.

Just how he finally got into the crack is a mystery to us but, after a dozen reappearances, he smiled and said: "I make it," and soon began to call for rope, until about sixty feet had run out and he called from the top of the ridge above the gendarme. We then bent on two spare ropes and with the aid of a double rope went up, one at a time, fully realizing, as we passed over the top stretch and up the broken course above, that the real climb on a mountain is the one made by the guide, who often must take his chances without assistance from any helping hand. We also felt confident that Conrad would not descend over such a stretch if any other possible route could be found.

The distance from here to the first summit was short and ended with a good climb up a right angle corner at the junction of two rough walls, and John led us to the summit at 12:45, the barometer reading 10,250 feet. We levelled across to the other summit, lying a few hundred yards to the northeast, which appeared to be a few feet higher. After having a snack and building a cairn for the record, we started for the second summit, soon to be stopped by the sudden termination of the top mass which had run along on a level for a short distance and then dropped a little until its side cut sharply back for thirty feet or more, thus leaving the ledge pointing out into space over the glacier far below.

Twenty feet down, where the receding side again joined the vertical cliffs underneath the overhang, a sloping slab lapped the cliff a few feet; so, with the aid of a double rope passed over a convenient rock, we dropped down to this level,

the rope being left for use on the return trip. Horizontal cracks on the slab carried us to a broken causeway with sections of it only a foot or two wide, which were topped with a rounded edge, making a straddle the only safe method to negotiate them. Three or four sharp rises and a short irregular chimney landed us on the summit at 2:40; forty minutes of work to find the barometer reading exactly the same as on the first peak, 10,250 feet, and the first peak now appearing a little higher than the second one, a trait that nearby peaks seem to have to lure one on. The trip back to our rucksacks was easily made, each going up the double rope hand over hand to show that he was fit for the return journey, and at 3:20 we started down, all interested to see what was to be done at the gendarme.

Fortunately we had three ropes along, two of eighty feet and one of a hundred and twenty feet; so, after a survey of all sides, a route down the cliffs back of the gendarme was chosen and a double rope was passed over a projecting rock with Conrad's coat underneath to serve as chaffing gear for the loop and for the lowering rope. Halfway down the eighty-foot stretch and a little out of line with the hanging rope a small ledge projected from a side wall, which offered a chance for a rest, but, as this and the narrow sloping ledge below were insignificant edges above a 2,000-foot drop, no one cared to linger on the rope, but came down as quickly as possible, taking a turn of the double rope around a leg and pinching it between the feet to relieve the strain on the single rope. Conrad being the last to come down did not have the aid of a lowering rope and had to depend entirely upon his hands and the turn around the leg; but so long as the rope was kept securely pinched between the boots there was little danger, for a slight pressure on it will hold the weight of the body and relieve the strain on the arms.

The broken section carried us up forty feet to the base of the gendarme with just one hour spent in getting down its forty feet of height, and this gave us ample time to enjoy the many good short stretches that had annoyed us with delays during the morning. We also deflected from our route to try a short cut to the glacier, but were driven back by an unbroken row of cliffs that rise along the east side. Camp was reached at 8 p.m., and the next day we reluctantly turned our backs on the many spires whose intimate acquaintance we had not made, but with a resolve to return to them at the first good opportunity.

The Bugaboos. Photo: Roger Laurilla

Mount Bryce, north face. Photo: Ray Kodama

1921-22 : OLD TIMES IN THE CANADIAN ALPS

CHARLES E. FAY

The Director has kindly invited me to write an article for the *Journal* on the old times of mountaineering in the Selkirks and Rocky Mountains. While chronological periods are wont to be of a vague and more or less conventional character, there is usually some convenient event that is regarded as epoch-making, which forms a dividing line between a past and a present. For our purpose the founding of the Alpine Club of Canada furnishes the notable event and the old times here to be treated will antedate its formation in 1906.

Fifteen years does not seem a very long period to traverse, yet so much has happened in those just passed that they seem a lifetime. The phenomenal growth of the Club is another reason why the old times seem so long ago. Previous to 1906 the interest of Canadians in their splendid alpine heritage, if anywhere existent, had failed to manifest itself. It is hardly probable that a dozen men could have been assembled in the entire Dominion who would have been eligible for membership in the Alpine Club of Canada as it exists today, and perhaps not one for that of the mother club in London. Possibly half a dozen might have been enrolled in the Club across the International Boundary, had the early plan for a Canadian Section of that organization been carried into effect. The thanks of all everywhere interested in alpinism are due to the patriotic protest and energetic initiative, in response to which an independent organization was called into being.

As a nearby observer of the extraordinary exhibit made by the Club at the International Congress at Monaco in 1920, and of the high place it won in the estimation of all the delegates, the vigorous life of the Alpine Club of Canada was to no one a source of more sincere pleasure than to myself. It is a joy to have been permitted to watch its growth from the beginning, and another to have known the superb region that was to call it into life for a period as long preceding its formation as the time that has elapsed since.

For my first visit to the Selkirks and Rockies was made in 1890, on my way home from southern California, where I had been with a long tried friend of the Appalachian Mountain Club on a mission to select, if possible, a mountain top as a site for a station of the astronomical observatory of Harvard University. This was, of course, in the very first days of mountaineering here. The C. P. R. had been open for traffic only three years. It was but two years since the Rev. W. S. Green had made a beginning with ascent of Mount Bonney, and had only just published his *Among the Selkirk Glaciers*. That very year, and only a few weeks previous to our arrival at Glacier House, Huber and Sulzer had made the first ascent of Sir Donald. Indeed, we had unconsciously passed our Swiss friends headed westward, as our train, eastbound, crossed theirs at Westminster Junction!

A great number of pioneering ascents had already been made in Canada before the Alpine Club of Canada and its famous journal came into being in 1906. The Canadian Alpine Journal *recaptured this missing historical terrain by encouraging important early mountaineers to reminisce at length within its pages. Charles Fay was president of the Appalachian Mountain Club and later the first president of the American Alpine Club when the latter was formed in 1904. Fay was with Philip Stanley Abbot that terrible day in 1896 when Abbot fell to his death on Mount Lefroy, becoming the first mountaineering fatality in North America.*

– RWS

Things at Glacier were then very primitive, with only the little hotel of the original pattern adopted for the several dining stations of the railway; but, under the genial management of Mr. Perley, whose mantle of whole-souled hospitality was to descend upon a line of equally admirable successors, it had already begun to be the delightful place of sojourn for lovers of the grand and beautiful that it has increasingly remained. Of improvements only the excellent foot paths to Marion Lake and to the Illecillewaet glacier, and perhaps a casually indicated trail up the Asulkan Valley, so far as I recall, as yet existed. Several of the neighboring peaks were still unnamed, and the majority of course unclimbed; among them Rogers, Dawson, Donkin, Castor and Pollux, and the lesser ones of the Asulkan ridge.

Edmands and I had not come to climb, but merely to see and to admire, and our stay here was limited to a single day. Less than my own was my companion's normal aspiration for the high places stirred by the inspiring scenery. Consequently I had to make alone my forenoon's climb to the top of the screes at the base of the sheer rise of Sir Donald previous to continuing our journey. The unforgettable impressions of Glacier House, however, and of that initial scramble found expression some three years later in an article in *Appalachia*, entitled, "Up to the Crags of Sir Donald," called out by the first article on the Canadian Alps that ever appeared in that magazine: "Back Ranges of the Selkirks" by the Rev. H. P. Nichols, an account of the second ascent of Mount Fox.

Four years later (1894), I repeated that long, roundabout journey, this time with another friend in the Appalachian Mountain Club, Mr. R. F. Curtis, with whom it was my good fortune to make several subsequent trips to this region. Not this time either had we had serious climbing in view, nor were we in any way properly equipped for it. Nevertheless we did not confine ourselves to mere gazing and wishing, but ventured forth to test our powers in a limited way. Taking in Mount Abbott, I was tempted farther to the summit of what now bears the name of Afton — and to a sitting glissade down its steep northern slope. The next morning we set forth — of course with no expectation of being the second party on Sir Donald — and advanced by Huber and Sulzer's line of approach to a point some distance beyond my turning point of 1890. Deterred from further progress in that direction by the crevassed glacier, we turned about in the hope of at least making a traverse of Eagle Peak. The story of our failure to reach that summit, of

our being overtaken by night high up on its steep eastern face, of our long watch until daylight on a narrow ledge and our hour's long search for the elusive way of escape, of the beauty of the moonlit alpine landscape and the glory of the sunrise, is narrated in *Appalachia* under the title "Our Bivouac on Eagle Peak." All the experience of that remarkable day, particularly certain of the more perilous ones, were not there rehearsed in full. Even now I do not recall them without being reminded of Sir James Outram's comment in his *Heart of the Canadian Rockies*. After his generous praise of the pioneers, he says: "In perusing the records of the earlier climbers one is struck by the very special Providence that has watched over their initial efforts." Little or no change had taken place in the surroundings of Glacier House since my previous visit. Perhaps the zig-zag path up the cascades in front of the hotel had been constructed meanwhile. Mr. Perley was still in charge and the hospitable traditions of the place were growing.

On our way east we stopped a day at Field and climbed high up on Mount Stephen; but the complete ascent was deferred for a year. At Laggan we paused only long enough to make the trip to the little chalet, then just finished to take the place of the short-lived original one destroyed by fire; but it was our good fortune to meet there the party of Messrs. Wilcox and Allen, just coming in from the first ascent of Mount Temple. The latter was still fresh enough to join me for a row on the lake, during which he proposed that I should delay my journey long enough to try conclusions with Mount Victoria. An inelastic itinerary forbade acceptance, even had I felt competent to what at the time seemed to me a most hazardous undertaking. I little realized that the pleasure of its first ascent was in store for me.

With the year 1894 there began for me a series of annual visits which continued, with a single interruption, until 1908, when I had the pleasure of attending with my son the Club Camp at Rogers Pass. That omission (in 1900) was in a way compensated by two visits in the summer of 1903. In 1895 Mr. Curtis and I, whose visit of the previous year had this possibility in view, brought out with us a party of twenty members of the Appalachian Mountain Club, the majority of whom were ladies. Among the men were two whose names were destined to become fatefully linked with the region, the alpine glories of which were now for the first time revealed to them — Abbot and Thompson. The former was undoubtedly the most experienced alpinist among American lovers of the sport, he having had experience not only in Mexico and California, but as a close student of the methods in the Swiss Alps. For Thompson it was, I believe, his first introduction. Both became at once enthusiastic lovers of the Alps of Canada.

Making a brief stay at Banff, we hastened on to Lake Louise, and took complete possession of the Chalet. It is interesting to compare the Chalet of 1895 with the grandiose Chateau of the present day; still more to have watched its development. In its initial stage the little structure — a single storey with a hip roof — contained in all only eight rooms including the principal one, whose plate glass windows looked out on Mount Victoria, not as yet named, and the changeful lake. It served as office, dining room, drawing room and even bar, and on this occasion one of its corners furnished my sleeping quarters; for our party of twenty quite exceeded the Chalet's capacity, several being relegated to tents. Remaining in possession for several days, it is hardly too much to infer that for the general C.P.R. tourists of that year we were most unpopular.

While the rest of the party were enjoying the minor climbs about Lake Louise, Abbot, Thompson and I, accompanied by Tom Wilson as far as a bivouac by Hector Lake, made our first virgin ascent, accomplishing the easy conquest of Mount Hector. A few days later from Field we were the first party to follow McArthur's two ascents to the top of Mount Stephen, which he had occupied as a topographical station.

With Glacier House as a base our whole party was quite active. The C. P. R. having detailed two men for a day's service, I employed them in cutting out the steep original trail up Glacier Crest from the first bridge over Asulkan Creek. My "day" proved longer than theirs, and with a few hours' overtime labour, I succeeded in locating the upper portion nearly to the edge of the timber. The passage of some fifteen persons over it on the following day proved all that was needed to complete a very clearly marked line of approach to this unusually fine view point. The party signalized the occasion by following over the crest and descending with an exhilarating glissade from its western end to Illecillewaet glacier, by the left moraine of which the return was made to the hotel.

It was on this occasion that names were bestowed on several of the near-by peaks: Glacier Crest, Overlook, Uto, Afton, The Rampart, The Dome, Castor and Pollux. One glorious day's climb, begun as late as nine o'clock and with no intention of attempting anything beyond the usual trip to Mount Abbott, brought Abbot, Thompson and myself successively over Afton and the intervening summits of the Asulkan ridge and culminated in the first ascent of Castor. Thompson charmingly tells the story of that day and of our descent of the then practically pathless Asulkan valley in the darkness of the night, in the same issue of *Appalachia* that contains Abbot's article on Mount Hector. Success did not attend our party's attempt on Mount Rogers, the weather turning bad just as we reached the real climbing. Better fortune was in store for the attempt of the following year. A novel feature of the day of our failure, and one which made it seem the more deplorable, was the fact that we had laboured long and hard at the cranks of a hand-car in transporting ourselves and our belongings up the heavy grade of the railway and beyond the watershed to the point from which we took to the timber. In some respects this would count as the most memorable of my early visits. Those of the next two years, however, were hardly less so, one for its tragedy, the other for its international interest.

On one of the afternoons while our party of 1895 was tarrying at Lake Louise, our more ambitious trio advanced up the glacier as far as the so-called "Death Trap," our object being a reconnaissance of Mount Lefroy, with a view to a possible attempt upon it. The large snow couloir visible from the Chalet, broad at the base and tapering upward almost to a point, was so alluring to intimate inspection that, late in the day as it now was, we could not forbear to ascend to the little 'schrund that cuts off a fragment of its upper end. The chimney beyond seemed inviting, and we returned to the Chalet with minds made up to try Lefroy on the morrow. The day dawned none too propitiously, but it was our only chance. The clouds hung ominously low when we reached the base of the couloir and the snow was softening, for which reason we left it high up for a promising lead on the rocks to our right. By this time it had actually begun to rain and miniature cascades were soon drenching us from the overhanging upper edge of our chimney. Evidently the Fates were against us, and we withdrew, with a feeling that Lefroy was our debtor.

To secure the cancellation of that debt was the prime object of our return to the Rockies the following year, our trio being increased by the addition of Professor G. T. Little of Bowdoin College. A slight abrasion below my right knee, received on the summit of Mount Chocorua, which developed a mild case of blood poisoning, made my own attendance somewhat doubtful; but as the cure seemed likely to progress as favourably on the train as in regretful restlessness at home, I set out on my only westward journey in which pain overmastered pleasure. We proceeded at once to Glacier, to allow me more time for recovery and the opportunity for practice climbs for the others. It was in one of these that the first ascent of Mount Rogers was secured, with Little in my usual place on the rope. From here we returned to Lake Louise and the renewed attempt on Lefroy was my first alpine climb of the season. The sad outcome of that third day of August is told in detail in *Appalachia* and need not here be rehearsed. Thus ended the brief expedition of 1896.

That of the following year had a brighter sequel, and a stone-man on Lefroy was set up as a memorial to our lost companion on the anniversary of the tragedy. It had been Abbot's hope that his friend, Professor Dixon of the Alpine Club, with whom he had climbed in Switzerland. would join us for the attack on Lefroy and what other climbs might follow it, but the conjunction did not prove feasible for that season. This year, however, moved in part by the knowledge that Mr. Abbot, senior, was interested in having the feasibility of the climb proved, Professor Dixon made arrangements not only to come himself, but to bring with him not only Dr. Collie and Mr. G. P. Baker of the Alpine Club, but also Peter Sarbach, of Saint Niklaus, the guide that he and Abbot had employed in Switzerland, who thus became the first professional guide to visit the Canadian Alps. The party was further increased by three others from the United States: Messrs. Michael, Noyes and Vanderlip. Such was the composition of our notable Anglo-American party of 1897. Its alpine experience was rather extraordinary. Nearly all were more or less familiar with the Swiss Alps. Baker had visited also the snow peaks of Norway, while Collie had ranged as far as the Western Himalayas. It was therefore with no slight pleasure that we witnessed their undisguised enthusiasm over this region, that had so completely captivated us.

Dixon was first to arrive, accompanied by Sarbach. Collie came a few days later, joining us at Glacier, which we had again chosen for our training climbs. A delightful week was spent here, to the alpinistic and social features of which full justice is accorded by Professor Dixon in a paper read before the Alpine Club. Mr. Baker was unable to join the party until the start for the trip to capture Mount Balfour. We celebrated Sarbach's fiftieth birthday on Glacier Crest. We made the interesting ascent of The Dome on its east side by a snow arête ending at a notch, above which were a few feet of rock-work declared to be "more difficult than anything on the Matterhorn." Our long return on the western side of the ridge and over Mount Abbott made it 10:30 p.m. when we entered the hotel. Miss Mollison met us with an assumed austerity, which banished all hope of the warm supper which for some hours we had been enjoying in anticipation; yet a few moments later we were revelling in a repast surpassing our fondest imagination.

On another day we traversed Castor and Pollux, thus making a first ascent of the latter. The air was very clear and from these summits we caught sight of an unusually fine peak in the north, to which provisionally we accorded the name "Mount Victoria." Doubtless it was Sir Sandford of present nomenclature.

My brief notes show that we left Glacier for Field, August 1st. They read: "Left on No. 2 Locomotive with Collie and Dixon." On the 2nd: "From Field to Laggan. Freight to Hector, handcar balance. Walked to Chalet. Met Mr. Niblock on the way." These items chronicle a form of travel quite in vogue with us of the "old times," when infrequent trains and slower schedules made it most convenient and agreeable to accept the hospitalities offered by the sympathetic management of the C. P. R. Mr. Niblock's name properly finds record here, as the representative of that management on the mountain division. The entry for the 3rd comprises two words: "Ascended Lefroy." That for the 5th reads merely: "Ascent of Mount Green." This is the name under which for a short time the glorious peak that closes the vista at Lake Louise was known, given in honour of the author of *Among the Selkirk Glaciers* in which is reproduced a sketch of the mountain over the title "Mount Lefroy." As a memorial of its first ascent in the Queen's Jubilee year, we substituted the name which had a few days previously been proposed for Sir Sandford. We also did our part in stabilizing the name Lefroy, which had been quite peripatetic since first bestowed by Hector, in all probability on Number One of the Ten Peaks.

The story of these two glorious days has been so fully recorded elsewhere as to call for no further mention here (*Alpine Journal*, May, 1898). A few days later, Mr. Baker having now joined us, we set out for the proposed ascent of Mount Balfour. We straggled into the camp at Hector Lake, that "Bill" Peyto had prepared to receive us, at a late hour of the night, our British friends getting under these most unfavorable conditions their first experience of muskegs. This expedition was undertaken at the suggestion of Thompson and myself. Balfour had seemed to us the year before, as our trio saw it from the summit of Hector, a very inviting summit. Indeed, we had actually started for its ascent on the following day from our bivouac at the lake; but the broad, rushing stream had proved an insuperable obstacle.

On this occasion we subordinated, perhaps unduly, our completer knowledge of the topography, which naturally calls for an approach from the head of the lower lake, to the greater general mountaineering experience of our new companions, and changed our camp to the upper lake to make the attack from there. It gave us a very interesting introduction to territory new to us, and an exciting day in our quest for Balfour. It added to the list of virgin climbs that of the peak we christened "Mount Gordon" (the family name of the then Governor-General, Lord Aberdeen) from the summit of which we saw Mount Balfour rising some miles to the south, and quite beyond our reach for that season.

The most exciting episode of the day was not Collie's leading the unmarried men of the party down into and across one of the large crevasses of the glacier by which we ascended from above the lake, but when, proceeding unroped along the dry glacier that here forms the backbone of the continent, Thompson broke through a seemingly safe snow bridge and, notwithstanding a fall of fully sixty feet to where the crevasse narrowed, miraculously escaped practically uninjured.

Another incident of the day was the sight of the famous Twin Fall of the Yoho Valley that, although fully five miles distant, fairly forced itself upon the view immediately on our reaching the summit. Habel had visited it only a few days previously, and to him its introduction to the public is due, though Tom Wilson is said to have made its earlier acquaintance. From here we returned to Lake Louise and our delightful party was broken up. Collie and Baker, however, retaining Sarbach, made another trip to the north, in quest of a fine peak that we had seen and supposed was Mount Murchison, but which proved to be Mount Forbes. So far as this mountain is concerned, their trip was a disappointment; but it proved the lure that brought Collie back to a success the year following, and so began that notable series of expeditions which connects his name indissolubly with the Rocky Mountains of Canada.

A similar sentiment regarding Mount Balfour was what brought me back with my friend Curtis the next year. Attaching to ourselves, as general helper in camp and as a third on the rope, a young schoolmaster of Banff, we attacked it by the way of the Sherbrooke Valley, at that time apparently unexplored, though the surveyor-general later sent me the contour map of it which illustrates his work on "Photographic Surveying."

A morning thunderstorm delayed our departure from our far-viewing camp on the day optimistically planned for our conquest. Once under way, we plodded hopefully on over the miles of névé along the Divide. At length the snow became so soft that my stout companion was sinking almost to his waist. Declaring himself out of it, he urged Campbell and myself to keep on for the now imminent prize. We two were soon on the northern arête and were crossing a well-marked notch, when in climbing its farther wall, my ice-axe slipped from my hold and fell a few yards, yet was easily recovered. At this moment "Bob" (for it was this well known "old inhabitant" of nowadays, then making his first trip on the snows) called my serious attention to the fact that he had a wife and children at Banff. I looked at my watch. It was 5:30, the very hour, and the day was August 3rd.

Our trip was not, however, entirely fruitless, for, during our brief stay in that secluded valley, we captured the peak to which we gave the name of Mount Niles. A few days later we made the first traverse over Abbot Pass. For the third on the rope on this occasion we had a lively boy of perhaps fifteen years, whom we called "Jim." Today you read his name almost everywhere in Banff, on stages, garages, stores and I know not what not. A little later another party consisting of Messrs. Thompson, Nichols, Weed and Noyes, who had come out seeking adventures up the Pipestone and down the Siffleur, from the old camp at Hector Lake, succeeded in winning the prize of Mount Balfour.

But my lengthening article warns me that I must be briefer with my reminiscences. The following year, 1899, was notable for the coming of the first Swiss guides, brought over by the C. P. R. Their first climb of a virgin peak on this continent was made, accompanying Parker and myself on a two days' trip, to the top of Mount Dawson. In commemoration of this event the names of Hasler and Feuz were bestowed on the two minor peaks that combine to form that summit. 1900 was the year I missed, but it brought into the game Outram and Scattergood, with whom in 1901 I enjoyed a delightful week of exploration about the Ice River valley, which we entered from that of the Ottertail, taking in Mount Vaux on the way. By a niggardly hundred feet or so we failed of making the south tower of Goodsir. We climbed out of the valley by ascending the fine many-peaked ridge that parts it from the Beaverfoot. Three of these we traversed, but were foiled in our attempt to close the series that same day with the Chancellor. A week later this peak was captured by my two companions, accompanied by Mr. G. M. Weed, who owed that opportunity to the disabling accident that meanwhile befell me in a reconnaissance our trio was making for the capture of Mount Biddle. This was the year of the first visit of Mr. Whymper with his retinue of four Swiss guides, and of the advent here of the man destined to surpass all others in his contribution to our knowledge of the topography of the Selkirks and Rockies, to say nothing here of what his later life-work has meant for mountaineering in the Canadian Alps. I think, however, it was not until my next year's visit to Glacier House (1902) that I first had the pleasure of meeting Mr. Wheeler, with whom the casual acquaintance was in the next years to ripen into a cordial friendship. In 1903 Parker and I with Hasler and Christian Kaufmann entered the Ice River valley by the usual route and succeeded in completing the first ascent of Mount Goodsir. A few days later Parker with the Kaufmanns made the first ascent of Hungabee and,

joined by Dr. Eggers, with the same guides, successfully attacked Deltaform and Biddle. Meanwhile, with two new-comers to the region and with Hasler and Bohren, I satisfied a long-felt curiosity by ascending Mount Daly from the Sherbrooke valley, descending over the Takakkaw glacier and by a somewhat sensational negotiation of the cliff on the left (south) side of the great cascade.

My more recent visits were so brief as rather to deserve the name of calls. Indeed, as compared with more modern expeditions, or even with several of the contemporary ones, nearly all in which I participated were limited in time, and seldom beyond the utmost reach of the whistle of the locomotive. But the old times furnished grand opportunities for first class ascents at short range from the hotels, and, so far as the peaks themselves are concerned, what ones of the remoter giants have afforded richer sport to their victors than Lefroy and Victoria, Deltaform and Hungabee, Goodsir and The Chancellor, Rogers and Dawson, to the pioneers of the elder day?

An early Alpine Club trip to Mount Aberdeen, circa 1924. Photo: Brian Wyvill. Whyte Museum of the Canadian Rockies

Mounts Ermatinger and Hooker. Photo: Glen Boles

1921-22 : A TRAGEDY ON MOUNT EON

ALBERT H. MACCARTHY

The Jubilee Encampment of the Alpine Club of Canada, held at Mount Assiniboine in 1920 offered a large number of members an opportunity to get good views of Mount Eon from the summits of Towers, Terrapin, Magog, and Assiniboine, and the sight of this magnificent virgin peak stirred the ambition of many of them to make an attempt on it; however, owing to the excellent and varied climbs near at hand only one party of three members made an attempt that year, and they were defeated by the cliffs high up on the northeast shoulder. The Walking Tour Camp at Assiniboine in 1921 again offered excellent facilities for another attempt and, after the several discussions I have had with Doctor Winthrop E. Stone concerning its formation and probable best lines of approach, I was not surprised to receive word from him, upon his arrival at the Club House at Banff early in July, that, if weather permitted, he and Mrs. Stone intended to make a short trip in to explore Eon after they had conditioned themselves on the trail; for he had made a careful study of the peak in 1920, had consulted Mr. Wheeler and the members of the former expedition, and felt confident that a feasible route could be found on the southeast or south side, and he and Mrs. Stone would like very much to "crown a big one this year."

After a short stay at the Club House and several days on the trail, they set out from the Assiniboine Camp on July 15th for a four days trip, having sent in their dunnage and provisions to Marvel Pass by the Walking Tour packer, Ralph Rink. Crossing Wonder Pass and the valley of Lakes Gloria, Terrapin and Marvel, they ascended Marvel Pass and made a bivouac near one of the small lakes in the pass, a short distance south of the col that divides the east face of Mount Gloria.

The next day was spent in prospecting the pass and the lines of approach to Mount Eon, and, the sky being clear on the morning of the 17th, an early start was made over Mount Gloria by way of the col, but upon reaching the morainal basin between Gloria and Eon instead of taking the route up the northeast shoulder of Mount Eon tried by the 1920 party, they worked to the south and, gaining the first broad ledge at 7,800 feet elevation, passed around the southeast arête to the base of its wide south face where at its east end a yellow capped outlying tower on a level with the ledge served as their "key" to the mountain, for the tower and the summit of the mountain are clearly visible from each other as is also almost the entire 3,300 feet of slope, ledge, couloir and chimney elevations between them.

With this tower as their point of departure, they first ascended three slopes and broken-down ledges of easy gradients for an elevation of about 800 feet, followed by steep ledges and couloirs of excellent firm rock for another 500 feet or more and then ledges with broken faces which made them fairly easy but very interesting to negotiate

Though it is surprising how relatively few fatalities there were in the early years of mountaineering, accidents did happen. The agony of Mrs. Stone is surely one of the most harrowing stories told in the literature of Canada's mountains. Albert MacCarthy's unadorned account is straightforward, complete and riveting.
– RWS

and which carried their route over to the southeast arête at about 9,500 feet. This arête they followed more or less closely but always on its south side until they reached the snow band that completely crosses the south face at 10,300 feet and lies at an angle of about 50°; but the snow being in excellent condition and firmly annealed to the underlying ice, they were able to kick secure steps and mount to the ledge above by way of a slight rock cut near the central point of the band and directly below the summit. Above this band the route rises up broken ledges and short couloirs of unstable rock to a final wide, steep, irregular chimney that opens with dangerous sloping top sides on to the summit.

They had made excellent progress throughout the whole day, were both in first class condition and, upon reaching the base of this chimney at about 6 p. m., felt that they were near their goal; so, after placing Mrs. Stone in secure footing in its base and clear of any possible rock falls, Dr. Stone ascended it until he could see over the top slopes but was still unable to determine whether or not a higher point lay beyond. In response to Mrs. Stone's enquiry if they were near the top he replied he could "see nothing higher" but that he would go up and make sure; that the rock was very unstable and to be careful and keep under cover.

Dr. Stone then climbed out of the chimney and disappeared for a minute or so and shortly afterwards, without any warning, a large slab of rock tumbled off from above, passing over Mrs. Stone, and was closely followed by Dr. Stone, who spoke no word but held his ice axe firmly in his right hand. Horror stricken at the sight, Mrs. Stone braced herself to take the jerk of the rope, not realizing that the Doctor had taken it off in order to explore beyond its length.

The first fall was for about sixty feet to a narrow ledge and then the body descended from ledge to ledge until it seemed to Mrs. Stone it must have gone completely to the bottom of the mountain side.

Dazed and rendered inert by the disaster, Mrs. Stone had not sufficient strength to move for a long time and when she was able to control herself it was then too dark to attempt to descend, so she was forced to remain at the bottom of the chimney, only forty feet from the summit, throughout the night. With the first rays of light in the morning she began working down, looking as she went in the hopes that she might find her husband alive, but realizing such a thing could hardly be possible.

Fortunately, by recognizing various prominent features of the formation, she was able to keep more or less to the line of ascent and made fair progress during the day, but owing to the delay in search, lack of food, and her unstrung condition, she was unable to reach the lower ledges before darkness set in, and so was forced to seek shelter under a rock for the second night.

The next morning early she began the descent again, searching each ledge and keeping in view the yellow capped tower which she finally reached at about mid-day; but in her haste to find her husband's body or to get down from the mountain to secure assistance, she became confused and mistook the route here, descending to the cut between the tower and the broad ledge instead of staying on the ledge and so worked along the lower narrow ledge to the eastward until it broke off sheer for a hundred feet or more. Then realizing she had gone astray, she retraced her steps for a short distance and seeing a scree slope that seemed to carry up from timberline to the ledge below the one she was on she decided to try this line and, securing her rope around a rock, let herself down a broken chimney until she was about ten feet from the ledge. Here the rope ended and she was forced to drop to the ledge, soon only to find that it broke off at both ends in smooth faces, and did not connect with the scree slopes below, thus completely trapping her; for she could not climb the chimney unaided and the end of her rope was out of reach. Her efforts to build up a pile of rocks by which to reach her rope's end were unavailing and her strength was not equal to the task, so here, on the narrow sloping ledge, she was forced to remain without food or shelter and with no clothing other than the flannel shirt and knickerbockers she had been climbing in until she was rescued on Sunday the 24th, eight days after the accident.

It was providential that she discovered a small seepage of water coming from a crack under the cliff, for by scooping out two small holes about the size of a watch and directing the trickle to them she was able to get a swallow from each every four hours. To this supply of water, the fact that her narrow ledge was on the south side of the cliffs where they and she received all the warmth of the sun during the daytime and her firm balance of mind, causing her to wind her watch and to thus regulate her hours for taking her meagre supply of water, she can ascribe her coming through the terrible ordeal alive.

When Dr. and Mrs. Stone failed to return to the Assiniboine Camp on the 18th, as planned, it was thought that some unforeseen difficulty had delayed them, as is not unusual on such expeditions; but when they did not appear on the morning of the 19th it was feared that an accident might have happened and Mr. Raiman of Brooklyn, N.Y., set out with some provisions to try and locate them, but being unable to make Marvel Pass he continued on to Trail Centre Camp. While en route there he met Mr. Waterman of Summit, N. J., and Dr. Gilmour of New York City, and reported to them the missing of the Stones, and his failure to locate them. They immediately pushed on to the Assiniboine Camp and, finding that no news had as yet come in, they urged that assistance be sent for and the next morning, the 21st, set out with the packer, Reno Fitten, and a supply of milk for the Wonder Pass Trail Gang's camp, where they interviewed Frank Gombert and Jack Betteridge and learned of the location and condition of the Stones' bivouac as the latter found it on Sunday the 17th. With Gombert they then ascended Marvel Pass and found the bivouac just as it was found four days before, and so felt certain that a serious accident had occurred and that the situation called for the best assistance possible, for their careful search failed to disclose the route taken by the Stones. Returning to Assiniboine Camp late that evening they were gratified to learn that Mr. Burnett had already dispatched the packer Childs to Banff to secure, if possible, the services of a Swiss guide and that he, with Messrs. Gooding and Elmer, had gone with an extra supply of provisions which they left at the Stones' bivouac, and then returned to the Assiniboine Camp at ten that night.

The next day, the 22nd, Reno Fitten, Frank Gombert and another member of the Trail Gang, ascended Marvel Pass and, working around the south shoulder of Mount Gloria, explored the basin between Gloria and Eon, but save for a few indistinct prints that seemed to resemble those of a boot, they found nothing to indicate the Stones' route; however, upon their return to the Assiniboine Camp, they found Rudolph Aemmer and Bill Peyto of Banff, who had made the forty-five mile trip out in one day, and Fitten gave them an account of his day's trip and drew a sketch of the route he had taken, and all agreed that the south side of the Eon was the most promising place to begin the search.

Messrs. Waterman and Dr. Gilmour volunteered their services to Rudolph in whatever capacity they could serve, as well as did all others present, but, as it was now four days beyond the time when the Stones were to have returned, it seemed evident that an accident had occurred that must have resulted fatally to both and Rudolph decided it best to take but a limited number who were in con-

dition for heavy work, as he knew the men of the Trail Gang were available to pack in provisions for them.

Accordingly, on the 23rd, he set out with Peyto, Childs, and a member of the North West Mounted Police, furnished by Mr. Stronach, Superintendent of the Park. Ascending Marvel Pass they found the Stones' bivouac still undisturbed and the next morning, taking Fitten and Gombert's route around Gloria into the basin, they worked up to the broad ledge of Eon and out to the summit of a south spur at 7,800 feet elevation that commanded a good view of the lower reaches of Eon's south face. After a long and careful scrutiny of the mountain side with field glasses they were about to give up the search for the day, as it was growing late, when they were startled by hearing a call from a point to the westward, and they discovered Mrs. Stone on a ledge almost a quarter of a mile away and 300 feet below them. Quickly firing a shot to notify her that rescue was at hand, they worked around the mountain side and were soon on the ledge above her. Rudolph then descended with the aid of a rope and, by the use of a rope from above and Rudolph's assistance below, Mrs. Stone was raised to the broad ledge; but the eight days of exposure with no food had rendered her too weak to walk, so Rudolph, strong and resolute, carried her on his back around the base of Eon for about a mile up and down and along this much broken and unstable ledge and then down the morainal basin to timber line where they made bivouac for the night.

Here, fortunately, they were soon joined by Dr. Fred Bell of Winnipeg, who immediately took charge of Mrs. Stone and, from the supplies brought in to the lower bivouac, gave her such food as her condition would warrant. During the two days here, while she was gaining strength, the weather was bad, but Rudolph and his men made a careful search of the lower reaches of the mountainside without result. By the use of an improvised stretcher, Mrs. Stone was then carried to a bivouac in Marvel Pass not far from the bivouac she and the Doctor had started from eleven days before. Here another rest was taken for two days while the Trail Gang slashed the trail from the pass down through the valley of the three lakes and up to join the Wonder Pass Trail. With this work completed, members of the Trail Gang assisted in carrying Mrs. Stone out on the stretcher for fourteen miles to the Trail Centre Camp where Miss Brown, manager of the Camp and Mrs. Fred Bell, did everything possible for her comfort.

This heavy work in bad weather had seriously told on all the members of the rescue party, and especially so on Rudolph, the leader, who bore the responsibility and had not spared himself in the work; and it was realized that all must have a rest and that a fresh party must be organized to continue the search.

During all this serious time, Mr. Wheeler, Director of the Alpine Club of Canada, and also of the Walking Tours, had been in the north on his official survey work, but upon his arrival at Banff, he promptly took charge of affairs and on August 2nd, set out in charge of the new party which consisted of Rudolph, Edward Feuz, Conrad Kain, Lennox Lindsay, Mrs. MacCarthy, the writer, and Ralph Rink in charge of the transport. Pushing through as quickly as possible on saddle ponies, the Trail Centre Camp was reached late that afternoon where all were gratified to find Mrs. Stone making rapid improvement, Dr. Stone's younger son, Richard, having joined her there two days previously.

Mrs. MacCarthy remaining in camp to care for Mrs. Stone, the rest of the party, accompanied by Richard Stone, left the next morning with a pack outfit and made camp that night in Marvel Pass about half a mile from the Stones' last bivouac. During the night and early next morning a storm swept the pass and left a blanket of fresh snow on all the peaks, so the work for the day was confined to a reconnaissance trip to the northeast shoulder of Mount Alcantara, from which point a complete view was had of the south face of Eon down to the broad ledge.

Early on the 5th of August, under the guidance of Rudolph, Edward, Conrad, Mr. Lindsay and I circled the shoulder of Gloria and reached the "key" tower at about 10 a.m. As the former search had covered the lower sections of the mountain with no results, and, as the stretches for 1,500 feet or more below the summit are much broken and rough and it seemed probable that the body must have become lodged in a couloir or depression higher up than was at first supposed, it was decided to follow, as nearly as possible, the Stones' route to the summit and to make the search on the way down; thus giving us an opportunity to learn, if possible, the cause of the accident, and also to recover the Doctor's ice-axe and rucksack.

All five members, therefore, went on one rope, with Edward leading, and after a short search their trail was picked up and followed by the foot prints in the scree patches and the nail marks on the rocks almost continuously to the base of the chimney at the summit. Upon reaching the 10,000 foot ledge at the southeast

arête at 1 p.m., Edward sighted the body lying on this ledge about 300 yards to the west of us and directly below the summit. Realizing the heavy task that must be accomplished, a short rest was taken and an attempt was made to eat some luncheon but with little success, so we continued the climb. Considerable time was required to negotiate the snow band as there was but a light covering of snow over its ice base in places, thus requiring the cutting of a number of steps at its lower and top sections. A short distance above its upper line Conrad discovered and recovered the Doctor's ice-axe. From here to the summit the formation is badly broken and great care was required by all members to avoid starting rock-falls; and instead of mounting by way of the final chimney, a slight deflection was made to the westward up a badly broken line until the summit was reached at 3 p.m. and the Doctor's ice-axe planted where it was apparent to all of us he had carried it twenty days before.

An examination of the chimney from above, opening onto the summit with its sloping top sides strewn with large unstable slabs, made it evident to us that in climbing out of the chimney and disappearing for a minute or so Doctor Stone had stood on the summit of the mountain and walked a short distance to make sure that there was no higher point beyond, then upon returning to the chimney he had stepped on a loose slab of rock near the edge that had slipped from under him and carried him over the cliff.

A cairn was built by all hands at a spot on the summit, where it could best be seen from the surrounding valleys, and the following placed in it:

FRIDAY, AUGUST 5TH, 1921

This monument was built by the undersigned in tribute to their comrade of the mountains, Doctor Winthrop E. Stone, President of Purdue University, LaFayette, Indiana, U. S. A.; who, on July 16th, 1921,* with his wife, virtually completed the first ascent, reaching a point not more than 50 feet from this spot. Dr. Stone's ice-axe crowned this monument. Albert H. MacCarthy, A.C.C., Lennox Lindsay, A.C.C., Edward Feuz, Rudolph Aemmer, Conrad Kain.

*At the time this inscription was written the actual date of the fatal accident was apparently not clear to the party who erected the cairn. It occurred on Sunday, July 17th.

The summit of Eon is somewhat irregular but all on practically the same level and the spot chosen for the cairn was perhaps a hundred feet in a horizontal line northeast from the top of the chimney, and it was thought that in climbing out of the chimney the Doctor had gone directly north from it for about fifty feet until he could assure himself that he was on the summit and then when returning to report the good news he slipped and fell.

After taking a picture of the cairn, Conrad led off and we descended by the southwest arête and the slopes and ledges on the Aye side of Eon to the 10,000 foot ledge which is about 20 feet in width and slopes about 20° from the horizontal. Traversing the ledge to where the body lay, we were gratified to find that, owing to the high elevation and the proximity of large snow patches, thus making the nights cold, the body was in a good state of preservation with no sign that any animal had molested it. It was evident from the large scalp wound across the top of the head that the Doctor met death instantly upon striking the first ledge in his fall of 850 feet.

After careful preparation of the body by the use of medical supplies, oiled silk, blankets, canvas, and lashings, all supplied by Mr. Wheeler, two one-hundred foot climbing ropes were bent on and a start made from the cliffs at 6 p.m., and Conrad, Edward and Rudolph did heroic work on that perilous mountain side, until 9 o'clock when we reached the 9,400 foot level and it was too dark for such work. So the body was placed in a secure, sheltered spot and we descended to 9,000 feet and made bivouac under a large rock that had slid from its base and so lodged as to give excellent shelter on three sides and from above, with a small stream running near one side. At 9,600 feet Rudolph found the Doctor's rucksack intact, containing Mrs. Stone's sweater, Kodak, and a small supply of provisions.

All hands were ready for the start when the first streaks of light came at about five in the morning for the little stream had frozen solid, the ledges were covered with ice and the rarefied air was penetratingly cold. The best route for the lowering was down the open exposed stretches of the mountain side which called for as rapid work as possible and, save for short intervals when shelter was sought behind boulders and ledges, during occasional rock falls from above, no rest was

taken until 1 p.m., when the scree slopes above the broad ledge were reached; here a halt was called and the few crumbs that remained from the small sandwich breakfast were devoured.

By the use of a shoulder pole and guy lines, the slopes and lower ledges were traversed and the bivouac at timber line in the basin between Eon and Gloria was reached at 5:30 p.m. with every member of the party completely exhausted from their heavy labour and lack of food, and it was realized that before further work was possible all must have a comfortable night's rest; so a return was made to the Marvel Pass Camp which was reached at 8 p.m. just in time for a good hot supper that in some mysterious way Mr. Wheeler seemed to know we would need and would come for, and he had prepared for us.

In the morning Mr. Wheeler and Richard Stone left for the Trail Centre Camp to report to Mrs. Stone the recovery of the Doctor's body, while our party returned to the bivouac at nine o'clock and, after constructing a skid of small green logs, the final descent of 1,500 feet to the bottom of Aurora Creek was completed and here we were joined by Rink with one of his strongest pack horses. After luncheon a trail was cleared up the many long, rough, tree-grown rock slides and ledges and the Marvel Pass Camp was reached at 8:30 p.m.

At 8 a.m. Monday, camp was broken and good time was made down the new trail cut out by Rink to join the Wonder Pass trail and, after a short rest at the Trail Gang's camp and another at Trail Centre Camp in mid-afternoon, camp was made for the night at 7 p.m., near the Walking Tour's Fishing Camp. An early start from this point next morning with relay pack horses brought us to the Eau Claire Camp at noon, Tuesday the 9th, where we were met by Doctor Stone's brother, Harlan F. Stone, and the Doctor's elder son, David, who took charge of affairs thereafter.

On Wednesday evening, the 10th, the Stone party left for LaFayette and we bade good-bye to the earthly remains of our fine comrade of the mountains whose last conscious thought probably was one of satisfaction in having conquered a magnificent virgin peak.

Amethyst Lake and the Ramparts with Mount Geikie in the centre. Photo: Ray Kodama

1923: MOUNT GEIKIE

CYRIL. G. WATES

P uns are the cheapest form of humour. Despite this dictum I have had a pun upon my conscience which is now set forth for the first time and the manner of its birth was thus. One summer morning ten years ago a little party passed through Jasper on the way to Mount Robson, a district then almost unvisited. It was their first glimpse of the Canadian Rockies and in the mind of one of them Jasper was henceforth "J'espére". A decade was to elapse before hope blossomed into realization but the hope lived on, fed by tales of such wonder spots as Tonquin Valley and the Circus, Maligne and Fortress Lakes, the rock cliffs of the Ramparts and the ice fields of Mount Edith Cavell, until one morning I awoke to look out upon the Athabaska, a river of quicksilver, the crests of its ripples turned to elfin gold by the rays of the rising sun, its distant reaches winding their way into a soft blue haze of peaks, like a mysterious road leading into the fairyland of heart's desire.

A glance at the map in the guide to Jasper Park published by the Department of the Interior, will show that Mount Geikie rises to the height of 10,850 feet at the western extremity of the Ramparts, seventeen miles southwest of the town of Jasper, but nearly forty miles by trail. To make a homely comparison, the Ramparts are like a train of giant freight cars, of which Mount Geikie forms the locomotive and Mount Barbican the cow-catcher.

Mount Geikie is a supreme example of a Canadian rock peak. Rising to a height almost equal to that of glacier-hung Mount Edith Cavell, it bears upon its extreme summit a cap of ice; but aside from this and a few snow-filled couloirs on the southeast face, Geikie's mighty cliffs are entirely bare, unless we include a small tributary ice stream which feeds a glacier on the northern slopes of Mount Barbican.

Roughly, Mount Geikie forms a three-sided pyramid, its faces lying north, west and southeast. In our preliminary reconnaissance, we passed entirely around the mountain at heights varying from 6,500 to 7,200 feet, with the exception of the col between Mount Geikie and Turret Mountain to the east. Mr. A. O. Wheeler, whose advice proved invaluable throughout our trip, had summed up the north face in one word — "impossible" — and our view of it as we tramped down the valley of Tonquin Creek into British Columbia, amply confirmed this verdict. The black cliffs rise smooth and unbroken from base to summit, like a great wall, and although, after reading Harold Raeburn's comments on the exaggeration of the steepness of rock faces, one hesitates to express an estimate of the angle in degrees, I do not think that anyone seeing this splendid face from the north will question the correctness of the classification, "unclimbable."

The west face, below which we camped, resembles the north face in being almost flat and very steep, but it

This description of the 1922 attempt on Mount Geikie in the Ramparts near Jasper is a classic piece of period writing, well-illustrating the "conquest of the impossible" feeling that makes up so much of the mountain literature of the '20s and '30s. The melodrama, however, mustn't prevent the reader from understanding that the attempt, and the eventual ascent of the peak by Mr. Wates two years later, was a significant achievement in a remote setting. Geikie is still a challenge for the few parties who travel in the Ramparts and use the hut named after the author.
– GP

is more broken in character. The lower portion consists of vertical cliffs, slightly buttressed and terminating at a height of about 9,000 feet in a more or less continuous ledge which we referred to as the "Great Traverse." High up, the west and north faces meet in a smooth and tremendously steep arête which, lower down, eases off in a series of gendarmes and buttresses to the Geikie-Barbican Col at an altitude of about 8,100 feet. The southeast face is by far the most rugged and broken part of the mountain. Two great gorges cut into the heart of the peak, each carrying at its foot a black tarn, surrounded by precipitous cliffs. These are the lakes which Dr. Bulyea has described under the name of the Ink Wells. Between the west and southeast faces is the south arête, which has weathered to such an extent that a great slide descends through the forests right down to the floor of the Geikie Valley, 2,000 feet below. Between the two gorges is another arête, the southeast, and between the east gorge and the north face is another very steep arête, running down easterly to the Geikie-Turret Col. This concludes the circuit of the peak and our observations showed three main facts: the impossibility of the north face, due to its smoothness; the doubtfulness of the west face, except as a last resort; and the attractiveness of the deeply eroded gorges and arêtes of the southeast face.

Our optimism was somewhat damped by a curious phenomenon, that all the aretes are deeply notched at an elevation of about 9,500 feet, making a direct attack impracticable, but we ultimately decided to circumvent these notches by following a snow-filled couloir in the western gorge, hoping in this way to reach the arête at a point above them. This failing, we reserved the steep west face above our camp for a second attempt.

THE FIRST ATTEMPT

On the evening of August 7th we rolled ourselves in our blankets at a bivouac camp on the shores of the western Ink Well. The full moon floated in a clear sky and all promised well for the morrow. We planned to rise at 3:30 but when the alarm waked us it was still pitchy dark. So we snatched another hour of sleep and left camp at 5:30 skirting the west shore of the lake over great rock-slides and reaching the foot of the snow fan below the couloir at about 6:15. Easy progress up the snow talus made us optimistic but our hopes were sadly dashed upon entering the couloir, for the snow proved to be badly crusted, making it necessary to use the axe at every step and calling for more care with a party of two than would have been necessary had the snow been in good condition. The couloir is winding and steep, while down its entire centre runs a U-shaped trough carved out by the rush of falling stones from above. At two points we were crowded to the walls of the couloir by this trough and were obliged to cross it; no easy task for two. The trough was about twelve feet deep and twenty wide with perpendicular walls; a place where deep steps and careful anchoring were at a premium. Fortunately the day was yet young and the stones slept.

At about 8,700 feet the couloir became steeper and the snow changed to ice. Luckily, the rocks on the east side, which had hitherto been smooth, became more broken at this point and we attacked them, alternately climbing and traversing on steep, solid rocks until at 12:30 we reached the top of the couloir, well above the last notch on the southeast arête.

We were standing in a col formed by the junction of the two gorges and we were surrounded by scenery, wild and savage in the extreme. Looking down the east gorge we could see the eastern Ink Well, like an oval of black glass. Directly facing us rose the last thousand feet of Turret Mountain, closely resembling the well-known Watch Tower in Cataract Valley. Beyond, through a haze of smoke, shone the snow-fields and glaciers of the group known collectively as Mount Fraser.

Turning once more to our task we attacked the broken cliffs and shelves of the east arête. Our progress though slow was continuous until we encountered a gigantic block of stone, perched on the arête and split from top to bottom, the upper part of the cleft being jammed by several chock-stones. The cleft was just wide enough to admit us and was backed by steep ice. Having cut my way to the top of the ice, I was still far below the first chock-stone. Here I spent half an hour of fruitless struggling between the smooth walls and at last retired baffled and exhausted to give the Doctor a chance to try his luck. While I rested, I was treated to as pretty an exhibition of knee and back work as anyone could desire and ten minutes later, aided by a friendly haul from above, I joined the Doctor on the first chock-stone. From here our work was easy until we emerged from the crack to find ourselves on a ledge overhanging the Tonquin Valley which lay 4000 feet below us in all its beauty. Now more than ever, we anathematized the dense smoke obscuring a view which would have extended to Mount Robson and perhaps beyond to Mount Sir Alexander.

We had been forced out on the north face and to regain the arête it was necessary to make a short traverse over a little ledge of snow plastered precariously upon the rock wall, which overhung about four feet above the snow, making it impossible to stand erect. So, having scooped out a channel with our axes, we lay down and crawled across, passing over holes in the snow ledge through which we could catch glimpses of the valley and Moat Lake far below. We were unpleasantly aware of the steepness of the north face.

Again we followed the arête and at last stood at the foot of the summit mass. The watch read 6:15, the aneroid 10,300 feet, and we were confronted by sheer, smooth cliffs, black with running water from the ice cap above. On the right was the impossible north face; on the left a series of descending ledges broke away to the south arête. To try the latter route would involve a long descent and far more time than we had at our command and without any assurance of success. Regretfully we turned back and, unroping, began the descent with all the haste that safety allowed. Darkness was drawing on as we reached the Col and a flurry of snow warned us that a night on the mountain would be anything but pleasant.

We roped and continued the descent, hoping that we could reach the couloir before it became too dark to see our route and with the expectation that we might make our way down the steep snow by aid of the moonlight, but at 9:00 o'clock it was so dark that farther progress would have been extremely hazardous for the last man on the rope. We selected the only possible place to spend the night: a ledge so narrow that lying with our heads against the cliff our feet overhung the ledge.

Neither of us will soon forget that night. Fortunately the snow flurry had proved a false alarm but we were at 9,000 feet altitude and the wind blew keen and bitter up the couloir. The first hour was spent in collecting all the loose stones we could find and piling them up to form a little wall a couple of feet high and enclosing a space no larger than a dining table. Here, roped to a projecting crag, we snuggled down and tried to sleep, only to be awakened by the clatter of rocks as one of us straightened his legs and pushed a portion of our wall into the gulf below, an accident not unwelcome, since it gave the excuse for some added exercise in rebuilding the barrier more securely. For fifteen minutes in the hour we would doze and then wake shivering to sit up and engage in violent but restricted motions to arouse the sluggish circulation. Our surroundings added to the strangeness of the experience. The black cliffs fell away into mysterious gloom. Far below, we could see the faint outlines of the snow; while facing us, a portion of the opposite couloir wall was lit with a ghostly radiance by a yet invisible moon. In this lighter space loomed what seemed to be a black cave containing a figure which the Doctor stated was his Satanic Majesty gloating over our sufferings.

And yet — so unaccountable is human nature — when we woke from uneasy slumber to find the sky greying with the first promise of day, we stretched our stiffened limbs and began the descent with a feeling that was almost regret at leaving the perilous ledge with its little wall which had been our home for the night.

An hour brought us to the snow and, having doubled our hundred-foot rope for added security, we began the descent. The procedure was this: each in turn would cut a large step and anchor, belaying the rope around a buried ice axe while the other man descended. Once we tried glissading the length of the rope, but the bad condition of the snow and the sudden jerk of the rope soon made us abandon it. We were in no mood for talk and for hours our conversation was confined to: "End of the rope!" from the man above, and "All right, come ahead," from the man below.

At last we emerged onto the snow talus and unroped. A wild glissade, followed by a tramp over the boulders by the lakeshore, and we reached our bivouac at 11:30 having been on the mountain exactly thirty hours.

THE SECOND ATTEMPT

Our permanent camp being situated within a few hundred yards of the cliffs of the west face, it was natural that the various features of that aspect should occupy much of our attention and such phrases as the "Great Traverse," the "Snow Patch," and the "Geikie-Barbican Col" were constantly coming up in our conversation. Even at such close range the dense smoke almost obliterated all detail and a proposal to ascend Mount Barbican, in order to make a closer study of the upper part of Mount Geikie, was vetoed for lack of time.

As far as we could make out, the portion of the west face lying above the buttressed cliffs is practically smooth, with the exception of one shallow couloir, but whether this couloir is bounded by distinct arêtes, we were unable to distinguish. The only snow on the entire face lay on the Great Traverse at the bottom of the couloir and was known by us as the Snow Patch. The problem finally simmered down to this: could we reach the Snow Patch and if so would any practicable route present itself from there to the summit? The only answer to these problems was to go and find out for ourselves.

Two days after our first attempt we left camp at 5:30 and made our way over grass slopes and rock slides towards the Geikie-Barbican Col. The buttress to the east looked impracticable, so we bore to the right before reaching the col and, roping up, tackled a succession of pitches and traverses, aiming always at the foot of the gendarmes. Our choice of route was unfortunate as we wasted two hours of valuable time, being finally driven back to the col. A traverse of the north face then became ours by choice of necessity, a choice which proved in the event a happy one, affording us some very interesting climbing. After climbing some easy rocks we came to a fairly steep piece of ice, the tributary to the Barbican Glacier of which I have previously spoken. At this point the ice stream is about eighty feet wide and step cutting cost us an hour's time and a mass of broken blisters. We were using a sixty-foot rope, which necessitated our being on the ice together, a fact which had a sinister significance in the light of later events.

Once across the ice, we made our way up a series of chimneys until, at about 11:30, we reached the foot of the gendarmes and, sitting upon some great, flat slabs in the sunshine, we indulged in a second breakfast.

Much as we regretted the loss of time in trying to climb the south side of the buttress, we were well satisfied with our progress. The end of the Great Traverse lay before us, an easy route to the Snow Patch, and now that we could see the west face in partial profile we began to have great hopes that it would go.

Starting again we skirted the two gendarmes, one of which has a rectangular window pierced in the upper part, and stepped upon the end of the Great Traverse, which runs like a giant wagon road around the west face above the buttressed cliffs. At this point we made one of the most interesting discoveries of our whole trip. A great ledge of pure white, milky quartz lay exposed to sight, glisten-

ing in the light of the noonday sun. Presently, among the debris, the Doctor picked up a little rock crystal like a hexagonal pyramid of clear glass and about as large as a man's thumb. There was nothing very remarkable in this, but, a moment later I found another equally perfect and weighing over two pounds. This crystal lies on my book case as I write and its facets cover my extended hand.

But the Doctor, not to be outdone, discovered another crystal fully thirty inches in circumference and later we unearthed two others of equal size. For the most part the ascent of the mountain was forgotten in admiring these gigantic gems and we determined that the finest of them should repose in the Club House at Banff.

Having placed our specimens where they could easily be found on our return, we followed the Great Traverse to the Snow Patch, which proved to be the usual pile of dirty debris, half snow and half ice, left from the avalanches of the previous spring and undermined by a little stream flowing down the couloir. But what interested us far more than the Snow Patch was the fact that to the south of it rose a distinct arête, tremendously steep but perfectly practicable.

Now followed more than a thousand feet of really grand rock climbing. We had encountered uniformly good rock upon Mount Geikie, firm and solid with no trace of rottenness, but this little west arête will always stay in my memory as one of the most enjoyable climbs in my experience. Alas, that it was not to prove the key to our hidden treasure house!

As we climbed higher and higher it seemed as though we could reach out and touch the summit which loomed up through the haze on our left. But suddenly, when within 300 feet of our goal, after climbing a particularly steep pitch, we halted on a ledge and faced another pitch, perpendicular for fifty feet and actually overhanging at the top. The arête had narrowed to a knife-edge with vertical faces and it was forward or nothing. And the verdict was, "nothing."

Many times since, I have looked back and wished I could stand on that ledge again. The fact is that we were both worn out with the constant strain of difficult climbing. There had been hardly a moment throughout the day, with the exception of the Great Traverse, when the use of hand-holds could be dispensed with. We were confronted with the most difficult pitch at a time when we were least able to deal with it, and I have the feeling that under more favorable circumstances our opinion of its impossibility might be reversed. If so, and our route proves a feasible one, the climb of Mount Geikie by the west face will be one of the cleanest and sportiest rock climbs in the Rockies.

Our return by the arête was marked by an incident so disgraceful that I should hesitate to describe it, but for the fact that memory assures me that I am in good company.

I must explain that we had donned our tennis shoes before tackling the arête and that Dr. Bulyea, whose rucksack was somewhat small, had given me one of his boots to carry. As I descended the last pitch to the Great Traverse it was necessary to face out and my bulky rucksack embarrassed me. Slipping out of the straps, I passed it down to the Doctor. How it happened neither of us know, but next moment I helplessly watched the precious sack rolling slowly across the shaly slopes of the Traverse until it vanished over the cliffs into the valley.

As the rucksack disappeared I had a vivid mental image of eighty feet of sixty-degree ice to be covered in tennis shoes with a sixty foot rope.

We paused at the crystals long enough to convince ourselves of the impossibility of carrying even one without a rucksack and then continued past the gendarmes and down the buttress. We had been doing some deep thinking and when we reached the ice I had about made up my mind that it would be necessary for one of us to go out and excavate a huge "step" at the centre, in which he could stand securely anchored, while the other crossed over. But the Doctor voted for an attempt on the rock wall first and with the aid of his single boot we crawled up the edge of the ice, climbed a little chimney, traversed a narrow ledge and emerged at the top of the ice, which we straddled and rode across arriving at the col just as the light failed us.

We stumbled down the last thousand feet of rock slides in the dark, reaching camp at 11:00 o'clock.

The result of our two attempts on Mount Geikie may be summarized as follows: The broken southeast face would probably offer several alternative possible routes to the summit mass, but it remains very doubtful whether the last 500 feet can be climbed from this side. The west face, on the other hand, presents no apparent difficulties at the summit and the quality of the rock, freedom from snow and directness of attack all combine to make it by far the more attractive of the two. Good luck to the next assailants of this noble peak.

The summit of Mount Lefroy, circa 1902.
Whyte Museum of the Canadian Rockies

Mount Resplendent. Photo: Greg Horne

1924: FIRST ASCENT OF MOUNT ROBSON BY LADY MEMBERS

PHYLLIS MUNDAY

The return from a climb is hardly the time one expects a grand surprise. This was my experience on returning from Mount Mumm, when Mr. Wheeler told my husband to be prepared to go to the high camp on Mount Robson next morning and, in spite of the prevailing impression that no women would be allowed to attempt the "big climb," I found I was to go also. Our companions were to be: Mr. Lambart whose company we had enjoyed on one climb already, and Mr. Drinnan. Shortly before starting we found our number increased by Miss A. E. Buck and Mr. Porter; Joe Saladana, a guide employed by Donald Phillips, completed the party.

I found the heat and the choking dust of the long nine miles to Lake Kinney nearly the most trying part to the whole trip. Our lengthy rest there after lunch seemed merely to give the slope of Robson added time to heat with the afternoon sun. On the steep climb of 3,500 feet to High Camp not a drop of water was to be found. This was extremely trying with heavy packs, as we had to take up food from the cache at Lake Kinney. Having seen my lady companion's pack lightened, unbeknown to her, of the supplies she was going to carry, led me to guard mine closely. The upper part of the climb was mostly on rocks, and in one place a fixed rope saved time and effort up shelving ledges.

High Camp, in charge of Herbert Newcomb, was surprisingly spacious and comfortable, consisting of three tents, one provided with a stove, plenty of cooking utensils and bedding. This wooded shelf was practically at timberline on this slope. The first climbing party of the year had not returned when we arrived at 8 p.m. Herbert served us the excellent soup intended for them, but before it was cool enough to drink we heard a shout from the cliffs above, so poured it back in the pot and impatiently awaited their arrival. On seeing only two weary men out of six return we had visions of disaster. The two had turned back at 11,000 feet. The last they had seen of Conrad Kain, Mr. Moffat, Mr. Geddes and Mr. Pollard, was close up under the peak at 5 p.m., still ascending. Therefore the hope of their returning that night was slight, which meant we could not climb on the morrow.

We were awakened about 4 a.m. next morning by Conrad's well-known yodel, and had time to prepare their breakfast before they arrived, tired, hungry but radiantly victorious.

We had to resign ourselves to a precious, perfect climbing day — rare enough on Mount Robson — in camp, and so a quarter of a mile of trail was built to a tributary of the Grand Couloir, the nearest water supply. Bathing parties then proved popular. We were fortunate in seeing the whole front of the Whitehorn glacier break off, yet the great ice cap on Mount Robson, visible 5000 feet above us, seemed strangely silent, although the night before we had listened to an almost terrifying description of ice avalanching across the route of ascent.

The names of Phyllis and Don Munday are best known through their connection to exploration of the Waddington Range of the Coast Mountains, but Mrs. Munday's contributions were far broader in scope — both geographically and personally. The Mundays were strong members of ACC camps over the course of many years, with pioneering ascents in several ranges, and Phyllis served for years as the editor of the CAJ. In this account of the "all-ladies" ascent of Mount Robson, she shows the dignity which hallmarked all of her many endeavours.

– GP

Three times during the night we were roused instantly by the ominous patter of rain on the tents. When Conrad woke us at 2:30 a.m. our section of the sky was cloudless, much to our joy. At 3:30 a.m. we were on our way. For a thousand feet the shelving ledges were about as steep as one could stand on; then came a wall seemingly without a break, which Conrad had not wished to attempt to descend in the dark on the previous trip. On surmounting this we had a chance to study the immense cliffs dipping to the shore of Lake Kinney — Mount Robson is one mountain which loses nothing on close approach. We reached the crest of the ridge just in time to see a great slice of ice front tip slowly outward and crash down toward the valley of the Little Fork. Mounting the rocks beside the glacier we soon came to the point where it breaks over the crest of the ridge, and overhangs the top of the couloir which supplies High Camp with water. The rock was sound and the ledges good so we crossed rapidly under the menacing ice without having to rope up.

At 9:30 we lunched on the rocks, about 10,500 feet, in sight of the great ice wall about three hundred feet in height, which cuts completely across the glacier and caps the ridge diagonally upwards until it meets the Wishbone Arête, this wall furnishing the chief danger point of the route. For the greater part of the climb so far, the peak had been in plain view, a gleaming horn of ice against a blue-black sky — incredibly far away if we believed Conrad's estimate of the time to reach it.

At the edge of the glacier above this point we roped up for the first time, following along the crest of the ridge to the ledges under the ice-wall. Here Conrad paused to give us all demonstrated instructions regarding the special handling of the rope in such a dangerous situation. The huge hundred and fifty foot wall towering its threatening, overhanging ice above us was most impressive. It was silent — too silent! I could almost imagine I heard it creaking, ready to give way when we started. "Are you ready?" Conrad asked. As we answered, he said "go," and we went. Never before had I travelled so fast under such circumstances. The ledges being from one to four feet wide and good travelling, barring the remains of recent avalanches, we lost no time in getting across. Waiting on the ledge to watch the second rope traverse under the wall, I had time to realize that it was about two hundred yards we had travelled on this horseshoe ledge, with an 8,000-foot precipice below. The second rope followed in safety. It was a relief to us all, and I'm sure more so to Conrad, for he felt the added responsibility of the second rope.

All together again, we climbed from ledge to ledge and up small cliffs to a place in the wall where the ice had broken away. Leaving the second rope on the rocks till we reached a place of comparative safety, Conrad cut steps to a ledge in the wall where we were able to stand together. From here a narrow shelf in the ice traversed out and over the big white wall. He cut the steps along it with one hand, steadying himself by handholds cut in the wall with the other. Surmounting this, we were at last on the glacier above the huge ice wall. Conditions were heavy for the leader, the snow being very soft. To relieve Conrad, Joe took the lead for a while, following the tracks of the former party. Nearly an hour was lost rescuing Joe's ice axe from a crevasse when a treacherous ice bridge gave way under his weight, in spite of his careful testing. Additional time was lost finding another place where the crevasse could be crossed — there was no way round.

Once across, we soon reached the top of the long ridge running out toward Mount Resplendent, whence the icy summit looked so near, and yet so far, the huge ice terraces of the final slope appearing like monster breakers on a rough sea. This formation was beautiful in the extreme. Under the graceful folds of each of these "breakers," were fantastic, glistening icicles which shattered the sunlight into every colour of the rainbow. It was very interesting travelling under, round, and on top of the "breakers." The snow was inclined to avalanche, and masked crevasses, often rendering them troublesome. Some of them we crossed by lying down and wriggling over.

It was now 4:30 p.m. While we mounted the last lap, which was none too easy, we left the second rope waiting under the summit cornice as there was not room for more than one rope on the top at a time. The face was very steep and brittle with an awkward crevasse to negotiate. It was a slow job as only one could move at a time. Surmounting the shoulder of crumbling ice, the last fifty feet was somewhat spectacular, as the narrow summit ridge was broken ice covered with snow.

"Conrad's on top, thank Heaven!" I thought, for he was gathering up my slack fast. As I stepped up beside him he held my rope and said in a very satisfying tone, " There, lady! You are the first woman on the top of Mr. Robson." I said out loud, "Thank Heaven!" for it was a four-year-old ambition at last achieved.

No permanent record can be left on the summit, but we found the film pack tab from Mr. Pollard's camera stuck in the snow on top. The view in some respects was disappointing, although I might have expected it as I have been on high mountains before. Everything else was dwarfed as we were 2,000 feet above the next highest mountain. The névé of the Tumbling Glacier seemed at our very feet. The Helmet, which looks so impressive from Berg Lake, appeared flattened out, so all sides of it were visible. The wee, white specks of the tents of the Main Camp on Robson Pass made "home" and comfort look a long way off. Range upon range of mountains were spread out beneath us, beckoning and tempting.

The hour now being very late and the atmosphere frosty, we took a last good look at the magnificent surroundings and said *au revoir* to the summit.

We passed the second rope and kept on down while they continued the ascent. Fortunately the frost had greatly lessened the dangers, by freezing our foot-steps more solidly, making the descent easier than I had expected. No particular difficulty was encountered crossing the big, broken crevasse although extreme care had to be taken. On the glacier below we found our tracks all obliterated by heavy avalanche snow. The ice wall reached again, I felt somewhat like a spider as I turned with a twist and lowered myself slowly over the edge to feel for the first foothold — not such an easy task when backing down. Both ropes passed under the ice wall again in perfect safety. This made one feel as if all troubles were over. Not so for us, though, as we later found.

At the edge of the glacier we unroped and started down the rocks. In the dusk it was slow work and not easy with such a large party. With the gathering smoke from a bush fire and a thunder storm in the west, darkness was approaching faster than usual, so Conrad decided to take to the glacier again. He left us at the edge of the rocks to rope up again in readiness while he cut steps with wonderful speed, then returned and we were all soon on the lower glacier. For my part I was very glad as we could travel so much farther down by the reflected light from the snow and ice. I had noticed in the morning that this glacier couldn't be badly crevassed, as it was really nothing but an avalanche chute of the ice-cap above, so all big crevasses would be filled up.

The most thrilling part was getting off the glacier — just above the lower ice wall, back to the rocks again. Conrad unroped and found the only possible way, I believe, then came back for us. It was necessary to cross a six-inch wide bridge. A few feet further was a black hole to be crossed by a leap to an unseen foothold in the higher opposite wall. The grunting and the vibration of the ice around us was all too unpleasant in the darkness. Conrad personally assisted the crossing of each person. All this was on the very brink of the lower ice wall. Steps were cut down again to a rock ledge where we decided to stay for the rest of the night, at an elevation of 9,500 feet. It was now about 10:30 p.m. We finished the rest of our food, changed into dry socks, and tried to sleep in spasms between the rolling echoes of falling ice from the glacier wall we had so recently outflanked.

We were mighty thankful there was no rain or snow, as clouds were down on the glacier and all the shoulders and cliffs of the mountain were hidden.

Groans were heard from nearly every member of the party as we started our cold, stiffened limbs into action at about 3:30 a.m. After all we had experienced, the passage under the lower ice wall made little impression on us, although the ledges were covered with newly-fallen ice. On arriving in camp at 5 a.m. we found the ever faithful Herbert Newcomb and the next climbing party (Miss Gold, Mr. Lindsay and Mr. Montgomery) had prepared a delightful breakfast for us.

Knowing if we stayed in High Camp any length of time we should require another meal, and not wishing to deplete the precious provisions, we left about seven and reached Lake Kinney Camp a little after eight, where we prepared a good second breakfast. Shortly after we started the long, long trail to Main Camp which we reached about 2 p.m., having been on the go almost thirty-five hours since 3:30 a.m. the previous day, with the exception of the five hours rest on the rocks the night before.

We were touched by the warmth and sincerity of the welcome received from all those in camp.

One is denied opportunity of studying the many interesting details of such a magnificent mountain when roped together, so that my ambition was then, and still is, to climb Mount Robson again.

Bute Glacier. Photo: Pat Morrow

1931 : SEVEN DAYS IN THE COAST RANGE

FRANK SMITH

> *All that survives of a climb is seldom more than a sediment of small incidents. In our less exalted valley humour we find them as lees in our glass of memory and stir them diluted into a tale.*
>
> —G. Winthrop Young

"You may as well put away that map of Asia," said Bill. "I've only got a week and that's not enough for Everest, besides these are hard times." So as usual, Time and Money, the gods who preside over a poor mountaineer's destiny, compelled us to seek less distant and expensive ranges on the North American continent, which, by a process of elimination, narrowed down to some point within a hundred and fifty mile radius of Vancouver. At the northeast corner of this circle, to be Irish, there appeared on the only available map, a small dot marked Kwoiek Needle, surrounded on all sides by nice blank spaces and removed about thirty miles from the Canadian Pacific line through the Fraser canyon. It was virgin territory from a mountaineering standpoint, although there was a rumor that Mr. J. P. Forde of the Canadian Alpine Club had many years ago climbed a peak to the north called Skihist. The question of location was therefore settled.

My companions were to be Jack Betts and Bill Henderson of the B.C. Mountaineering Club, and after anxious negotiations we finally found a week which would suit the three of us. Then came the grub list which was arrived at by writing down all the things one had ever eaten or heard of anyone eating, and then striking them off until sufficient was left to support life over a given period without making it necessary to pack the weight of a grand piano to an elevation of 6700 feet.

I was to leave Vancouver on the morning train of August 16th, which arrived at Keefers, our jumping-off point, early in the afternoon, so that I might interview the local inhabitants to find out if perchance there might be a trail leading in the general direction desired, and to obtain any other information regarding the flora, fauna, geology, weather, and whatnot of the district.

At last, after everything had been checked and double checked in the approved style of Amos and Andy, the morning of the 16th dawned and together with my pack, ice-axe and boots I was ushered into a Colonist car by a porter who eyed me and my equipment with a certain degree of suspicion, perhaps not altogether unwarranted. The Fraser canyon and Keefers, a hundred and ten in the shade, eyed me with more suspicious looks as I clattered down to the platform. I sought the post office and general store as the most likely source of information and discovered there was a trail which would take us part of the way. So, after obtaining directions I settled down to wait until

This piece was selected for its representation of the nature of the Coast Mountains and the demands of early exploratory forays, and also because it has such a nice touch of facetiousness — a good attribute to bring along on any trip into the range!
– GP

2:30 a.m., when my companions were to arrive.

While engaged in this strenuous occupation I was treated to a demonstration of a scheme which might be used to advantage in any large office and I take this opportunity of disclosing its secret to those interested, without charge. Into the store came an old fellow who looked like the kind of a man you think of when the term "Forty-niner" is mentioned. He had several letters in his hand and, going to the wicket, bought some stamps. He then placed the letters on the counter, removed his hat, drew the gummed side of the stamps over his bald head, replaced his hat and affixed the stamps to the letters. A fortune awaits anyone who can produce a breed of bald headed office boys.

A bed was kindly placed at my disposal but, since the night was hot and I was excited, I arose about 1:30 a.m. and crept outside to a grassy spot alongside the track where I could lie and look up at the stars. All was quiet save for a muffled roar from the canyon below where the great river quickened its pace as if anxious to reach the not-far-distant sea. At last a faint "chug chug," and a light flitting from side to side of the canyon walls, warned me that the eastbound transcontinental approached. She slowed down and from an open door, with a great clatter of boots and ice-axes, two forms descended followed by two huge packs. "Shish shish" went the air signal, a platform banged, the ghostly sleepers glided by and the tail-lights disappeared round a bend. "Well," said a voice out of the darkness "we're here and I have a devil of a pack, when do we start?" "Right now," I replied.

Just as the first faint indication of dawn appeared, we started off down the track to a point a mile distant where we crossed to a road leading up over the pass to Nahatlach River. We travelled in silence, each one trying to think of something they had forgotten. Alas, as the day wore on it became all too apparent that our troubles arose from having remembered too much. We reached the pass at daybreak and turned north into the woods on a trail which would take us up a ridge between the Fraser and Nahatlach. Here we paused and inspected our packs. We seemed to have everything except the kitchen stove. Some kind friends had given Bill a large bag containing about fifty plums and one or two dozen pears. We tried to eat them all in order to distribute their enormous weight, but were unsuccessful and regretfully left the remainder for the squirrels, if squirrels eat plums.

This is not the record of a pedestrian tour and no great interest attaches to elevating a week's board and lodging up a mountain, so we will pass over the rest of the morning and afternoon which were occupied in the drudgery of back-packing up steep grades. The climb was enlivened, however, by the remarks of Bill and Jack on the demerits of fancy pack-boards. They had been betrayed into borrowing what the owners claimed were the last thing in such equipment. They pretty nearly proved to be such, as, when loaded, the weight extended so far out from the back of the unfortunate wearer, that he had to maintain an unceasing struggle with gravity, and whenever he sat down to rest, it required the combined efforts of the rest of the party, aided by an ice-axe, to get him up again. If the hopes expressed regarding the future state of the inventor of this contraption are ever realized, his lot is not to be envied.

Fifteen hours out found all hands at an elevation of about 5000 feet, in a stretch of freshly-burnt timber, three hours from the last drink, and it was thereupon decided that the first water encountered in an unburnt district would mark the site of our camp, even though it was so steep that we should have to stand up all night. For a time it looked as if we would be forced to forego even these requirements, but at last on rounding a shoulder of the ridge we gazed into a draw up which the fire had not swept and soon came upon a lovely stream flowing through the heather. Dropping our packs we ascended the slope for a few feet and reached a small flat, dotted with ponds and surrounded by meadows, which formed an ideal camping ground. Packs up at last, we revelled in a cold plunge which drove out that tired feeling and put an edge on our appetites, soon appeased by countless cups of soup and tea reinforced by whatever was handy in the way of solids. Then the evening pipe round the fire and that feeling of contentment which only a good day's work can bring.

To the consternation of Jack and myself Bill, produced a new pipe and said he intended to take his first smoke. It was one of those patent abominations with a composition bowl set in the brier. One look at it and we sternly forbade him to make the attempt. The ordinary perils of mountaineering are sufficient, without adding thereto the disastrous results we well knew would follow such rashness. We drew such a horrible picture of his untimely decease that Bill gave up the idea, much to our relief.

A little moon witnessed three forms stretched out under the sky in the dreamless sleep of the hills. One recalls waking in the night and gazing at the stars which seemed to hang just above the tree-tops and later feeling the dampness of the dew which fell like rain. It grew colder before dawn and we awoke finally to find our bags white with frost. A quick breakfast and before the sun rose we were away again. We soon left the burnt section behind and all through the morning and well on into the afternoon wound our way across the ridges towards the distant Needle, now angling their ends, now making for a low point on their summit. Had it not been for our packs we should have enjoyed the climb, as we travelled mostly through meadows, past lakes and near running water.

Late in the afternoon, at a height of 6700 feet we gazed across at the final ridge which seemed to run right to the base of the north face of Kwoiek Peak. The sky had become overcast and rain was falling. The end of the ridge on which we were standing dropped sharply for nearly a thousand feet to a pass before the final climb, and there we hoped to find water and a camp site. Descending to the bottom we searched round for a stream, ignoring the fact that the top of a pass is a most unlikely place to find one. However, luck was with us and we discovered a spring issuing from the hillside near a clump of trees. It was now raining heavily, so, dropping our packs, we soon had the tent up, boughs cut for bedding and a rock fireplace built. The rain ceased and a beautiful sunset ended the day as, well fed, we stretched by the fire and watched the stars twinkle.

The dawn light disclosed clouds but as there were indications that the day might turn out fine, we made an early start in order to reconnoitre the approach to the peak, if nothing else. Climbing the ridge we reached its highest point at 7000 feet and looked across a series of bumps to the ice below the north face. The best route evidently lay along the top of the ridge, so down and up we went a number of times to its end. Here the weather became worse, as, with a roar, a deluge of wind and hail swept down upon us from the peak as if to try and turn us back. We crouched in the shelter of a rock but as the clouds remained high, decided to get up on the ice and look around. Roping up we ascended the bare ice to the lower side of a bergschrund which traversed the slope. Here the weather again changed, the sun broke through the whirling clouds and blue sky appeared, so taking this as a sign that the mountain had relented we carried on. Skirting the end of the 'schrund, we swung above it, but encountered a steep slope of ice which caused us to turn off to the foot of a buttress which sprang from the west ridge. Although steep, the rock proved fairly good and we made good time to the crest of the ridge from which point we gained our first glimpse of the country to the southwest. At the base of the peak nestled a little lake, jade green in color, while in the distance rose some well glaciated peaks, which form the source of the south branch of Kwoiek Creek.

Turning our attention to the west ridge, we were not so thrilled. To use one of Andrew Brown's expressions, it was a "mess." Rock towers rose and hung and overhung and double overhung without any visible means of support; in fact the flying clouds overhead gave one the illusion that the rock was actually tottering to a fall. However, there appeared to be no other way, so like expert burglars we silently crept round and under and up, afraid to speak lest our voices shatter the unstable equilibrium which was all too apparent. By that good fortune which sometimes protects the rash mountaineer, we passed the most serious obstacles and at last reached a point just below the summit.

Kwoiek Peak is slightly blunt, so arm in arm we three marched to its tiny top and gave vent to a long pent shout. We found the elevation to be about 8500 feet. It was Jack's and Bill's first ascent and the picture taken of them seated on top reveals two very broad grins.

As most of the peaks in sight are unnamed I am spared a tiresome recital. We discovered, however, that the existing maps are wrong and that we were cut off by deep valleys from a very fine group of peaks rising to 10,000 feet, which we had hoped to explore on this trip.

After building a cairn of suitable dimensions and depositing therein our record, we commenced the descent. Holding our breath we crept under the overhangs and reached the top of the buttress without mishap. Another scramble brought us to the ice-slope down which we faced in for a few hundred feet, contrary I suppose to good mountaineering practice, but when there is no room between one's back and the slope to admit a pack, who cares for good practice? We soon raced off the glacier below and started back along the ridge, reviling its successive humps which led up to the highest point. This having been attained and the worst part over, we strolled down towards camp as the evening light gave the green slopes an unearthly beauty, and that peace which follows a long, hard day of victory settled down on us, seeming to release the spirit from the body, which plodded along without thought or direction.

Since we had discovered that we were shut off from the further peaks, we decided to have a day of rest and next morning was devoted to removing four days' growth of beard and sundry other occupations connected with the wear and tear of mountaineering. In the afternoon we climbed a ridge to the northeast from which point we obtained a good view of an interesting country lying to the north of Harrison Lake.

The fifth day broke clear and we set out to cross the west ridge of the peak and perhaps descend towards its southern base. Rapid time was made to the ice by our previous route, where we swung off under the cliffs of the west ridge and made for a gap in its walls. Ice necessitated considerable step cutting, followed by a very nasty climb up rotten rock to the summit, which left us without much ambition to descend the other side, so we worked along the ridge to a little bump and decided to study the rest of the country with the aid of glasses rather than by personal contact. Bill insisted on calling the point we reached, Mount Henderson, saying that any explorer of note got things named after him, and he didn't see why he shouldn't. We warned him that he would probably be made an F.R.G.S. but he remained obdurate.

Homeward bound the descent to the ice proved worse than the ascent and removed highly important parts of our attire and sundry portions of our skin. Roping up we traversed round the glacier and, on stopping under the north face to take a picture, found that Jack had pulled the prize bonehead play of the series. Reaching to take off his pack he discovered that it wasn't there but was lying about a mile away where he had removed it in order to put on the rope. So we had to right-about-face, tramp back, recover it, and return, to the accompaniment of sundry remarks about people forgetting their heads, etc.

During the night a storm blew from the southeast. Our tent was pretty well protected from that direction and we did not bother about it until in a flash the wind changed round and blew in the tent door. Bill made a dive for the door and held the flaps together while Jack and I struggled into some clothes and went outside. Putting the sacred climbing rope to base uses, we made everything fast and added a few large rocks round the edges, whereupon the wind suddenly dropped and it was dead calm for the rest of the night.

The next morning we had a real thrill. We had just finished breakfast when there was a rumble and up popped a grizzly bear from a draw beside camp. It didn't look very dangerous so Jack got out his camera and, with the moral support

of Bill and myself, crept up and took a snap. As he did so, there was another rumble and a second bear emerged, quite a bit bigger than the first, evidently Mr. Grizzly himself. They stood about fifty yards away sniffing the breeze which was blowing from them to us and seeming to peer in a short sighted manner at our unusual forms. With commendable courage Jack advanced again and took another shot, but his movements startled Mrs. Grizzly who ambled off. The old man, however, was not satisfied so he climbed round above camp into the wind and stood looking down at us for some time. However, much to our relief, he evidently decided that since it was Friday he had better stick to fish and berries and so he followed his mate.

As there was now no longer any necessity for action we boldly discussed what we would have done had the bears come into camp, our theories ranging from a massed attack with ice-axes to crawling out on the face of a nearby precipice. I have since learnt that bears have been known to eat goats. It is a disquieting thought since anyone who has attempted to eat a goat will realize that a mountaineer, however tough, would be by comparison a very tender morsel. It is regrettable that the pictorial results of this visit are unsatisfactory. To our excited gaze the animals appeared at least as large as elephants and Jack stood almost in their shadow. In the pictures they appear to be the size of cats about a quarter of a mile away. They say the camera never lies. I doubt it.

Our last day dawned and regretfully we broke camp and prepared for the journey home. Despite the fact that we had apparently consumed mountains of food during the past week, our packs remained unduly heavy and the pack-boards continued to be a source of adverse comment to Jack and Bill. We had thought to break our journey at our first night's camp but made such good time that we reached it by noon. We then decided to push on to the end of the next ridge above timber line, but since we arrived there early in the afternoon we conceived the brilliant idea of going all out and trying to get the night train stopped for us. The down trail took on an unremembered steepness as we staggered along in the heat but at last the Nahatlach road was reached. Here it was necessary to halt in order to allow Jack to make some adjustments to his nether garments before returning to civilization. A rough road is not the best thing on which to finish off a long day, but we hobbled down it somehow, and after a final mile of tie jumping flung down our packs in front of Keefers store and called for all the drinks available. Jack had been packing round a flask all week in the emergency kit, to be used in case of accident. The only accident of the trip evidently occurred that evening when we reached Keefers and it must have been a very serious one, for it required the entire contents of the flask to cope with it.

It now remained to get in touch with the dispatcher at North Bend. The telephone at the station was one of those venerable things on which you crank out a number of dots and dashes in the form of a signal. We took turns in cranking with no response from North Bend. We said "Hello, Hello," till we got tired and began to leave off the "o," but finally when we had about decided to give it up as a bad job and go to bed, Bill gave a final crank and got his man. By representing that the Prime Minister of Canada, the President of the C.P.R. and the President of the Alpine Club were waiting at Keefers, we got the promise of the dispatcher to stop the westbound train for us at 2 a.m.

One more thrill remained. We had unrolled our bags on the platform and crawled in to get what sleep we could. During the night two freight trains and one passenger train dashed through the station and, since our feet were about a yard from the rails, it was a nerve-racking experience. From the distance came the sound of the approaching train; the headlight flashed on us; with a crash the very foundations of the earth seemed to totter; clouds of dust and small rocks blew over us; the cars lurched above our heads, as if about to collapse and we passed through all the mental anguish of being run over, before the universe once more assumed its customary stability and the clatter faded into the distance. Thrice we were shaken by this horror and as the sound died away for the last time, there arose from the pile which marked Bill's resting place a plaintive wail — "O damn those trains." It was the voice of an outraged mountaineer, who, returning from his free hills, finds himself once more enmeshed in the toils of civilization. By the same token we knew that our holiday was over.

Telemarking on Mount Grenville, Coast Mountains. Photo: Pat Morrow

Baiba Morrow on Mount Sir Donald, Rogers Pass. Photo: Pat Morrow

1933 : CLIMBS IN THE ROCKIES AND SELKIRKS DURING THE SUMMER OF 1933

KATIE GARDINER

After nearly two years absence, it was delightful to come back to Canada in the spring of 1933, and see the dear familiar mountains once more as the train sped on past Glacier, Field and Lake Louise to Banff. Arriving at the Alpine Club House was like coming home, and I felt myself lucky to have such comfortable headquarters for the summer. I had been fortunate to get Walter Feuz again as guide. He joined me for some climbing on June 27 and after a few days scrambling, we set out for the Vermilion Range, the ascent of Mount Foster being our principal objective. Walter very kindly lent me his car to drive over to Marble Canyon and accompanied by Ken Jones, a boy from Golden who was coming with us as cook, we set out on the morning of July 3, taking with us two silk tents and some stores. We had hoped to pitch our climbing camp near Floe Lake, but on reaching Marble Canyon found to our dismay that the bridge over Vermilion River had been washed out. However, the game warden informed us that there was another bridge higher up the stream leading to Numa Creek valley through which we could reach a pass just above the lake.

The Vermilion Mountains lie parallel to the Banff-Windermere road, behind a low line of undulating hills, which dips down into Numa valley at the foot of this magnificent rock range with its three outstanding peaks of over 10,000 feet. Mount Foster (10,511 feet) is named for Col. Foster, the well-known climber and explorer. It lies to the south and with the other more northerly peak (10,240 feet) had as yet not been climbed; the centre peak (10,060 feet) had already been ascended by a survey party. We spent the night at Marble Canyon auto camp and the following morning, leaving Walter's car in a sheltered spot down the woodland track to the river, we crossed the Numa Creek bridge with the water swirling below. The old trail which the game-warden had advised us to take on the left side of the creek scarcely existed, except for the blazes, and as we were heavily laden, we found it strenuous going. We had to ford the stream at one place and cross it in others on fallen logs and a very frail snow-bridge and then from time to time were forced to make our way through thick underscrub. The woods were full of aromatic flowering bushes and lovely flowers were blooming everywhere, one variety of white orchid having a delightful perfume like that of lily-of-the-valley. About four o'clock we came to a glade which was blue with forget-me-nots and larkspur. There we camped for the night, getting a good view of the centre peak up the valley.

The following morning the ground was white with frost although the altitude was only 4500 feet. The day was perfect, however, and after breaking camp we went on to the fork of the river, enjoying en route lovely views of Mount Foster. At this point we reached a good trail which went winding through the valley between the trees to the summit of Wolverine Pass under Mount Foster. Here a view of Floe Lake was obtained with all its ice and snow

This typically understated mountaineering article introduces us to three very significant mountaineers. Katie Gardiner and Lillian Gest became legends in the Rockies with their first women's ascent of both the giant Goodsir Towers in Yoho National Park. Mentioned in this article is a young guide named Ken Jones. Jones was the first Canadian-born fully accredited mountain guide. Jones would be an influence on Canadian climbing for the next sixty years.
– RWS

and a fine cliff-like mountain in the background. As the day was sultry and as steep banks of snow still covered the trail in places, our uphill grind wearied us and it was a relief to reach the pass. The range stretched away before us, a sheer wall of rock with the three peaks towering rather formidably above it. After looking round, Walter decided that it would not be advisable to attempt Mount Foster from the lake; but that it would be better to camp at timberline at about 7800 feet, below the pass on the south side of Numa valley, where some larches were just coming into leaf on knolls which formed little islands in the surrounding snow. As it was nine o'clock by the time we had pitched camp, we decided to make a late start next day on a reconnaissance trip to the centre peak in order to spy out a good route for Mount Foster. Accompanied by Ken, we set out at 8:45 and descending rippled banks of snow below our camp, climbed over snow and bare patches up to a saddle between Mount Foster and the centre peak, thus gaining the main ridge of the range. By traversing on the south side on shelving rocks we reached the southeast ridge. Here we lunched and enjoyed the magnificent view. The air was crystal-clear and the mountains looked unspeakably beautiful glittering in the sunlight. From this point we had some good climbing.

On the summit Walter got out his field-glasses and had soon worked out a suitable route of ascent for our expedition on the morrow. The top of the mountain was covered with snow and as this continued down on the southeast side we descended through it, noting that it would have made a good route of ascent. Then we climbed to our pass again, over ledges and rock pitches, getting quite near to a fine mountain goat as we crossed over towards Numa valley and were soon sliding down over the snow towards our camp.

After three such strenuous days we rested, on the 7th until the shadows were beginning to lengthen and only set out on our expedition at 5 o'clock. We first climbed to the saddle again and, dropping down into a large gully on the Kootenay side of the range, we descended over ledges on our right and then part way down crossed over to the far side to another snow-filled gully running up in the Mount Foster direction. Here swarms of mosquitoes beset us. We made a fire among the trees at timberline and as the night grew colder they all disappeared. It hardly became dark throughout the night but was so chilly that we were glad of the warmth and cheerful blaze by which to sit and doze. The morning of July 8 soon came and we were off again by 4 a.m., up the gully to a plateau and a half-frozen snow-surrounded lake. Ascending a steep hill on the far side of this we came on a fine view of our mountain, but found it necessary to descend to the snow on the other side of the hill to gain the main face of the peak up which Walter had planned our route of ascent. We soon scrambled down and climbing up by a waterfall, followed a central rock rib which ran up to the main ridge of Mount Foster, to within fifteen minutes of the top, over shelving ledges and rock pitches with intervals of very rotten snow. The ridge was narrow but we went along it without much difficulty and were soon, to our great joy, on the much coveted summit, Ken's first unclimbed peak.

From the snow-covered top the view was superb. One could see most of the great peaks of the Rockies and Selkirks, range after range fading away into the blue distance. After enjoying the beauty of it all for some time, we descended by the same route, with the utmost caution because of the precarious state of the snow. We tried to avoid some height by skirting round the steep hill which separated us from the lake, but in that way came in for some rather difficult climbing. However, we finally got to the plateau and down the gully again to our bivouac and having rested there, made our way back to camp over the pass. Unfortunately a heavy shower en route made the rock somewhat slippery.

We had a fine day for our return to Marble Canyon. As the snow bridge had gone, we had to cross the much swollen river on a log and in another place wade knee deep into the swift current. Walter found a much better trail however below the forks on the opposite side of the river. From the bridge we motored back to Marble Canyon where we enjoyed the comfort of the Bungalow camp after a day's strenuous back-packing.

The weather was too unsettled for us to climb again for the time being, so the following morning Walter drove us through Radium Hot Springs and the beautiful Columbia valley, with its woods, rugged peaks and picturesque farms, to Golden. Mrs. Feuz entertained me that evening with some very good homemade stout at their pretty house in the Swiss village. On July 11, Walter and I climbed Storm Mountain, bivouacking by a fire at timberline en route. From the summit we were able to spy out a route of ascent for the other unclimbed peak in the Vermilion Range.

I then spent a very pleasant fortnight in the usual friendly atmosphere of the Club House and Annual Camp at Paradise valley and was fortunate enough to climb Pinnacle from there and several other peaks. Also I had a delightful hiking trip over the five passes to O'Hara before setting off once more with Walter and Ken for another trip to Numa valley.

On July 29 we camped in the woods near the bridge. There was a great deal of fresh snow on the mountains and it rained during the night but cleared on the morning of the 30th, when with the help of two friendly road men we carried our belongings up to the forks. We pitched camp there near the river, which had fallen considerably.

We set off about 9 o'clock on Monday, July 31, hoping to ascend the other unclimbed peak in the Vermilion Range. After crossing the right fork of the river and following the Wolverine Pass trail for a short distance, we struck straight up the very steep hillside through the big timber below the mountain. It was very hot and the scrub and fallen logs made going slow and difficult. When at last we got up to timberline it was about 12:30 and too late to consider going further that day. Before us lay a lovely lake surrounded by open flowery slopes. A big hill beyond it hid the pass we wished to cross to make our ascent. We bivouacked just below the lake, among trees and large rocks and made a fire on a ledge in front of one of these which was slightly overhanging, with small trees growing on the top. This gave us some badly needed shelter during the night, when we had a thunderstorm.

Walter and Ken had made a reconnaissance trip the previous evening to spy out a route and as the morning of August 1 was again fine, we were able to set out to attempt our peak. We went past the lake, up over the hill and found that the pass on the south side of the mountain was quite easy to ascend and that it sloped gently down on the far side. The ridge of the peak towered above us on the right with quite impossible cliffs. We worked round on the western side, first on grass and then over ledges and scree until we came to a snow face which we ascended for some distance. Then, as the snow was bad, we climbed up over steep rock ledges to the south ridge which we followed, arriving at the summit at noon. The rising and falling mist had rather hindered and we were able to get excellent views of Tumbling glacier and the nearby peaks.

It was too cold to enjoy this for long and we soon moved on towards the lower snow top of the mountain. We dropped down along a snow and rock ridge to a saddle from which the second summit seemed quite a separate peak. As it was bitterly cold on the top of this peak, we soon started our descent, coming down from the col mainly in rotten, sliding snow on the top of ice, through which Walter had cut large steps. In one place we were on rock for a short time and then descended through the thick new snow of the previous day which had avalanched from above. When we came to a place a little below where we wished to recross the ridge, we struck over to our left along the ledges and were soon on our way up the slope to the pass again. From there it did not take us long to return to our bivouac rock, where Ken boiled the billy and, after a refreshing cup of tea, we went on down the hillside and through the forest, making camp by 7 o'clock.

On the morning of August 2, we were starting out about 10 o'clock to photograph some peaks from the heights on the Wolverine Pass side of Numa valley, when much to our astonishment four college boys suddenly appeared down the trail on their way to the Banff-Windermere road from O'Hara. They had intended to go on through Numa valley and strike the road over the Floe Lake bridge. Fortunately we were able to tell them to follow the creek leading to the other bridge instead. After they had left we set out once more on the trail by which they had come and spent a most enjoyable day going through beautiful country. We obtained wonderful views of Mount Foster and the whole range from the hillside opposite the peak we had just ascended, and were able to photograph the remarkable three tiers of Tumbling glacier on its steep side.

The sky was overcast the following morning and we just managed to take down our tents before the rain fell.

Earlier in the summer Lillian Gest had very kindly asked Walter and me to join Christian Hasler and herself on a climbing trip to the Ice River valley and by the appointed day, August 8, the weather had fortunately cleared again. Jim Boyce came with us as packer and cook and with him Bill Harrison to look after the fourteen horses. We met at Leanchoil that evening, where Jim, who had already made camp some miles out by the Kicking Horse River, was waiting for us with his outfit.

On the evening of the 8th, we had motored to our camping place partly along a woodland track and on the following morning rode on along this for some miles and then over about three miles of trail before coming to the junction of the Kootenay trail. Farther on we passed an old mining camp and a little later pitched our tents at the foot of Zinc gulch in the Ice River valley itself. When wandering in the surrounding woods after supper, Lillian and I surprised a magnificent moose feeding nearby. As we approached, he dashed right through the camp giving the others quite a fright.

On August 10, we rode on along the trail which became rougher and had to be cleared a little. Soon we reached the river flats and finally a beautiful wide meadow at the foot of the majestic North Tower of the Goodsirs. Our camp consisted of two teepees and a supply tent. Jim did the cooking himself and gave us excellent meals.

The South Tower of the Goodsirs (11,686 feet) was our first objective. On August 11 we started off at 3:30 a.m. Going straight up through the forest undergrowth to grassy and shingle slopes on the face of the mountain and keeping to our left, we mounted over steep stone-covered ledges with a downward slope, until we came to a rib of rock leading up to the northwest ridge. This rib was narrow and of rotten rock slightly corniced towards the top. Here and there we traversed over to the face of the mountain to avoid a perpendicular bluff and also to gain time. In one place we had to rope off down a difficult pitch, after which the final summit rose steeply with an overhanging edge and a sheer drop below it. We gained the top in nine and three quarters hours and there found a cairn and records of previous ascents; Lillian and I were fortunate enough to be the first women to stand on the summit.

Dr. Hickson made the traverse of this peak with Edward Feuz up the southwest ridge in the opposite direction to that by which we had come. We in our turn descended in that direction, over a narrow, shaky, rock ridge, traversing to the eastern side of this on to a face of shelving stone-covered ledges and finally, over steep scree and grass slopes, came down by the usual route through the forest in Zinc gulch to the valley again. Here we followed an old mining trail, its overgrown condition impeding our progress somewhat. The horses were awaiting us beside the river and we were back in camp by 9 o'clock. We rested on the 12th, bathing and watching for moose, elk, deer and goats which abound in the district. At the end of the valley beyond a high cliff and extensive glacier rises a fine rock peak called Mount Hanbury (10,267 feet) which to our joy we found was as yet unclimbed.

On August 13 at 5:10 a.m. we set out on horseback for the head of the valley. Dismounting at the end of the track, we made our way through the scrub and trees up to the open rock face below the Vaux glacier. This is very steep and spec-

tacular, with beautiful waterfalls which form the beginning of the Ice River. The glacier stretching away towards Mount Vaux was mainly snow-covered with small crevasses showing here and there. Crossing this white expanse, we worked our way up the south face of the mountain over steep shelves with one or two small rock pitches, gaining the summit at 1:15, in two and a quarter hours. It was Lillian's first unclimbed peak and we built a large cairn on the top to commemorate the event.

The view was indistinct on account of forest fires. We descended by an easy route along the north ridge to the glacier, which we recrossed, and then went on down the cliff-like sides of the waterfalls to the horses awaiting us in the valley below. We were back in camp by 7:15. After another lazy day we set out on the morning of August 15 at 5:15 to climb Goodsir North Peak (11,565 feet). Avoiding the bush we ascended through one of the steep meadows which run up from the river towards the mountain, and were soon on the grass and scree slopes and up on the southwest ridge which we followed to the height of over 10,000 feet. Here we found the relics of an earlier party in the form of a sardine tin and meat can. We then traversed over a scree band to the south face reaching a dangerous ice-blocked couloir up which Walter cut steps. From there we zigzagged from one to the other by steep rock pitches and reached the summit in 9 hours at 1:30.

On the descent we followed practically the same route, Walter being obliged to cut even larger steps in the ice of the couloir as it was in a most dangerous condition. Coming off the ridge we descended by way of a meadow rather lower down the valley where the going was somewhat better and then got into the main trail and were in camp by 8 o'clock. Two days later we left the camp at 5:30 a.m. to attempt the ascent of an unclimbed, unnamed peak on the northern side of the Goodsirs. This mountain was tent-shaped and although a good climb, apparently presented no great difficulties. The guides laughingly suggested that Lillian and I should change places with them, leading alternately. It was decided that, if we succeeded in taking them to the top, the mountain should be called Teepee Peak. We rode as far as a creek coming down from a little glacier on the northwest side of the Goodsir North Tower and dismounted at 6:10. Then after ascending the course of the stream through some scrub by way of steep slopes and ledges, over which waterfalls were coming, we came out onto the glacier up which we made our way to a gully. This gully led in a southerly direction towards a ridge which we reached after climbing over some steep ledges. The easy, gently-ascending ridge soon led us to the double summit which we reached by 12:15 in 6 hours.

After spending about two hours on top we descended by the same route, keeping as much as possible on the scree and soft snow and avoiding the glacier which was very slippery, by descending over the moraine. The horses met us at 5:30 and we were back in camp by six o'clock.

We rested on the 19th and that evening we had a thunderstorm, the weather not clearing again until the 21st. We then attempted the ascent of Mount Chancellor; unfortunately when we reached the ridge a series of gendarmes presented such difficult climbing that we saw we should be benighted on the mountain if we pushed on to the summit. After climbing a lower peak on the same range, we reluctantly retraced our steps to Ice River valley. That was the last day of our enjoyable stay in that lovely spot and the following morning we rode back to our first camping place near the Kicking Horse River. Our party then broke up, Lillian going to Lake Louise and I, after a short interlude in Golden, to camp near the old hotel site at Glacier with Walter and Ken. Mr. Binnie joined us for a few days and we were fortunate enough to get the traverse of Mount Sir Donald and some other good climbing before the weather again broke. For me at any rate that put an end to the season's climbing and a week later, after visiting Banff once more, I was on my way to Vancouver and another summer's climbing in New Zealand, carrying with me many pleasant memories of two very happy months in those beautiful surroundings and of the unfailing kindness and hospitality of the Canadian mountain people.

Mount Sir Donald, 1898. Photo: Vaux family. Whyte Museum of the Canadian Rockies

Mount Waddington. Photo: Pat Morrow

1936 : THE FIRST ASCENT OF MOUNT WADDINGTON

FRITZ WEISSNER

T he discovery of Mount Waddington (13,260 feet), its location and the ways of approach to it, and the previous attempts to climb it have already been well described in many articles in the *Canadian Alpine Journal*.

In March 1936, several of my friends from the American Alpine Club asked me to join them and try the mountain the following summer. At the same time, unknown to us until some weeks later, another party, made up of some of the best climbers of the British Columbia Mountaineering Clubs and of the Sierra Club of California, the latter of which had made a fine attempt in 1936 were also organizing for an attack. After some friendly correspondence both parties agreed that they should go through with their plans, and as the other party included climbers who had tried the mountain before, we agreed that they should have the first chance.

Our party consisted of Elizabeth Woolsey, W. P. House, and Alanson Willcox, and after all our preparations were made we left Vancouver on July 2 and reached by the Inland Passage the mouth of the Franklin River at the head of Knight Inlet on the morning of July 4. Twelve days later, with the help of the hunting guide Jim Stanton and his assistant J. Varley, we had transferred our 700 pounds of provisions and equipment to Icefall Point twenty-one miles distant. We were bringing provisions sufficient for five weeks, in order to be able to make a long siege on the mountain if weather conditions should demand it. This back-packing trip, which had to be done in many relays, proved very hard and unpleasant work during a period of almost continuous rain.

We made our first relay to the lower Dais glacier where we had planned to establish a base camp. Crossing Icefall Point, we had our first good view of the mountain. Only once before had Willcox and I, on one of our packing trips, seen our objective from the lower Franklin glacier during a short break in the rain. After the twelve day storm, the visible south face of the mountain showed very clearly, even from the distance its formation emphasized in all its details by the snow which covered all ledges and the less steep rock. It was then that we considered a couloir, leading down over the south face between the prominent tooth-shaped tower on the southeast ridge and the summit tower, the best possibility for climbing the mountain. The route would follow this couloir to the notch on the ridge and then up the summit tower either along the southeast ridge or on one of its sides. Also a good route might prove to exist, leaving the couloir about half-way up and then traversing into the south face on snow bands to the prominent snowfield in its middle part. From there a route might be found over the steep upper part of the

Though climbers share information and experience religiously, mountaineering can be highly competitive. A little friendly international competition may be all it takes to solve even the most difficult mountaineering problem. By 1936, primarily as a result of the efforts of Canadians Don and Phyllis Munday, Mount Waddington was recognized as a world-class mountaineering prize. Fritz Weissner was a heavy in the contemporary mountaineering world. His name was brought to world attention after the frightful and controversial attempt of K2 in 1939.
– R WS

south face. The couloir between the two peaks looked less favorable from here, but we thought it might prove to be the possibility which had been described to us in Vancouver.

The weather seemed now to have become stable, and judging from the high temperature that prevailed, we had every reason to believe that the rocks in the south face of Mount Waddington, after four or five days, should be clear of snow fallen during the storm. Our spirits were high at the time, and we were full of hope for a successful climb.

After crossing the spur of Icefall Point and paying a visit to the stone cairn erected as a memorial to Alec Dalgleish on a rocky promontory of the point, we again entered Franklin glacier. From here on, the glacier was still covered with winter snow and it became necessary to travel on the rope to be protected from hidden crevasses. We followed the glacier in a northwesterly direction. During our first relay we left the glacier below its junction with the Dais glacier and climbed to the ridge of Mount Cavalier group. This proved difficult and impractical, and we changed later to a route which led to the junction and then crossed below the last spur of the Mount Cavalier group, reaching the lower Dais glacier. By the 18th of July, we had established a well-provisioned camp on the lower Dais glacier. As at this point we were still some distance away from the foot of the rocky south face of Mount Waddington, we decided to establish another camp higher up, on a snow shelf of the Franklin glacier, just below the rocks of the south face.

The other party, under William Dobson of the B. C. Mountaineering Club and Bestor Robinson of the Sierra Club, had made fast progress with transferring their supplies from Icefall Point to the Dais glacier and had erected camp near us that same day. The next morning they started out on their first attempt, planning to climb as high as possible over the south face of the mountain, to bivouac on a band system, and then to climb the mountain the following day. We used the day to carry supplies up over the upper, steeper and crevassed part of Dais glacier, and established a one tent camp approximately 400 feet below the bergschrund.

As we realized that the mountain would offer a difficult climb, we decided that only two of us should make the first reconnoitering climb and eventually climb the summit, hoping that the two other members of our party would have an opportunity to climb the peak on a later day. Miss Woolsey and Alanson Willcox suggested that William House and I go together on this reconnoitering trip, while

they would carry more food to the high camp the next day.

When we arrived at the snow shelf we could see the B. C. and Sierra Club climbers, who were trying to climb the south face of the mountain with three ropes all at different places. Soon one of the ropes, which had planned to climb the mountain over the steep rocks between the main couloir and the couloir which leads down from the prominent notch in the southeast ridge, was forced to turn back. The other two ropes, which were working further away in the right part of the south face, could be seen most of the afternoon, working their way up to a snow ridge below a finger-shaped tower in the southeast ridge. Then they crossed along its base towards the couloir which leads downward from the prominent notch in the southeast ridge between the summit tower and the large tooth-shaped tower. The climbers found, however, great difficulties later, and also because of the rotten rock-structure, they considered it impossible to reach the summit over this route, so they turned back shortly before dark.

They reached our camp around midnight, and told us, as the first rope had done earlier in the day, that they felt we had given them every chance and that we should start to make our attempts. They went down to their camp on the glacier below, planning to have another try two days later.

On the morning of the twentieth, House and I left our high camp at 3:30 and after crossing the bergschrund proceeded to the entrance of the couloir coming down from the notch between the lower northwest and the main peak. We had decided to give this route the first try, as it looked the shortest and it seemed to offer an entrance to the upper, vertical-appearing summit rocks. We made fast progress up the snow and ice of the steep couloir, moving together on our Eckenstein crampons. The inclination of the couloir was between 50 and 55 degrees and going was easy, especially when we used the hard-frozen trough that had been formed by little snow and ice particles which rushed down continuously from the summit ridge. In the morning, clouds had formed over the Franklin and Klinaklini valleys and the temperature was relatively high, a weather condition which in more continental mountain regions usually brings storms. We had observed that here in the Coast Mountains these rules did not apply and that usually later in the day a cloudless sky would prevail. We now followed the couloir to a point approximately 270 feet below the notch and then tried to climb the vertical eastern wall of the couloir, and to reach a point on a ridge protruding in the south face. From there we hoped to be able to make a traverse into the upper part of the south face and to continue over its upper steep part to the summit. The couloir wall was in a very bad condition. As well as being nearly vertical, it had a rotten rock structure, and every little crack and unevenness was glazed by ice. We soon realized that there was no chance of climbing the 150 feet (approximately) of this wall under these conditions, so we descended the couloir, reaching our camp early in the afternoon. We were disappointed to find these conditions, especially the loose rock structure, which undoubtedly would continue through the whole south face. It had always been reported that there would be little loose rock on Mount Waddington and that the difficulties would be more of a technical nature, and probably in the ice-work once the ice-coated summit ridge was reached.

We decided to make another attempt the next day, over the route which we had considered to offer the best chance when we had seen the mountain the first time. It could be expected that the summit rocks, which clearly would offer the main obstacle in the climb, would be free of an ice coat, being under the rays of the sun most of the day. In the evening after a beautiful sunset the disappointment over our first failure had faded and we were both ready, mentally and physically, to make another attempt the next day.

On the 21st of July we left our camp at 2:45 a.m., crossed the bergschrund at 3:30, and soon had entered the somewhat hidden but large couloir which leads through the middle of south face to the notch between the summit tower and the wild-looking tooth-shaped tower in the southeast ridge. The inclination of the couloir ranged between 50 and 60 degrees. Again we progressed fast, moving at the same time and on crampons. Soon a short ice-fall, formed over a rocky step in the couloir, had to be climbed. Approximately 250 feet higher, the couloir sent out a branch to the left which, as we had seen from below, leads finally into a band system that connects with a large snowfield which is set in the middle of the south face.

We choose this branch for our further route and soon, following the snow bands, reached a short ridge on the base of a large tower projecting from the south face and at the left (east) of the large snowfield. A traverse over very rotten rocks led us to the snowfield and we crossed this in an upward direction to its end on the ridge. We were now near the point which we would have reached the day

before, if it had been possible to climb the wall of the couloir. In the middle of the steep snowfield a deep trough had formed, and we noted that occasionally rocks would come down here with the ice particles. Each of us well belayed by the other climber, we crossed this trough very quickly, ready to swing out of it on the rope if large fragments should break above.

It was 7 a.m. now and we were standing at the upper end of the snowfield. We were very well satisfied with the good progress we had made. Above us extended the last 1000 feet of the south face in sheer forbidding-looking rocks, but the possibility of climbing it could be detected by anyone looking at it with a trained eye. I knew that the objective dangers could be overcome, if this part of the climb was attacked intelligently and cautiously. Mentally and physically I was keyed up to the very high pitch which one reaches on certain occasions: at this time I knew that the summit would be ours. Determined, and feeling that today no obstacle of a technical nature could stop us, I started on the rocks.

From the highest point of the snowfield, we followed its left side, along the base of several ridge towers, crossing two snow spots. The climbing was severe, and soon I had to change to rope-sole shoes and rid myself of a 300-foot rope which we had taken along in case of long rappels, together with the ice-axe in order to get the utmost ease and balance. House was left now with the difficult task of following with this added load over the most difficult part, which still was ahead of us. Since we had left the snowfield the stances had become too narrow, and pitons had to be used to secure a safe belay. After four rope-lengths from the snowfield, we reached an ice chimney between the last tower in the ridge, along whose base we had climbed, and the final 500-foot rockwall which separated us from the summit. Crossing the ice chimney, well belayed by House, I succeeded in getting on to this vertical rockwall, and followed up it, using a chimney-like depression. For three rope-lengths the climbing reached the upper limit of the technically possible. Aside from the fact that the rocks of the depression had in general an inclination of 85-90 degrees, several overhangs had to be climbed. The narrow cracks which usually made this possible were coated with ice in many parts, and the lower part of the depression had an ice coat on most of its little ledges and roughnesses. Also great care had to be taken because of the rotten rock structure. House usually had to stand secured to a piton in a straight line below me, and any rocks which I loosened might hit him. Several hours were necessary to overcome this most difficult and precarious part of the climb.

Approximately 120 feet below the end of the depression, which was on the summit ridge, at a point 100 feet west of and below the summit, we traversed over somewhat easier rocks to the right (east) crossing a snow- and ice-filled couloir into a second depression. Here we found the first place in the last 850 feet where we could sit on a little ledge. We followed this depression to the summit ridge. It had looked easy from below but it also offered some difficult climbing. An overhang twenty feet below the ridge was the last obstacle the mountain put in our way, but we climbed it quickly and a few minutes later we stood on the southeast ridge twenty feet below the summit. One at a time and belayed by the other we climbed up over the narrow rock ridge which carried a layer of hard-packed snow crystals, to the highest point, a spot just large enough so that one man could stand on it. It was 3:40 in the afternoon, thirteen hours after we had left our camp.

We were rewarded with a grand view of the beautiful Coast Mountains which extended around us. Large smoke clouds covered raging forest fires in the interior of British Columbia. In the southeast and south, parts of the Inland Passage and the Pacific Ocean were visible.

We could not allow ourselves much time on the summit, as we realized that with the few hours ahead until nightfall we must decide quickly on the descent. Our hope to descend over the north face then traverse to the northwest summit and there reach easier going, did not prove encouraging, in view of the ice- and snow-crusted rocks of the north face of our peak. The rocks there are not vertical as in the upper part of our south face route, but the structure indicated that much loose rock might hide many objective dangers. The ridge leading down to the notch between the two peaks, with its many rock towers, each of them covered and plastered with a crust of hard frozen snow crystals, also offered little promise of a quick retreat. Much better looked the northeast face, a steep face dotted with rocks, but we had heard that this face further down becomes much steeper, and this seemed verified by the fact that we could not see very far down. So after erecting a little stone cairn at the point where we had left the south face and the only place where there was room for it, we thought it best to go down the same route which we had used for the ascent. We had a 300-foot rappel rope and our climbing rope of 125 feet. With the aid of these ropes we could make long rappels over the 1000 feet of the summit rock. These rappels had to be laid out very carefully in order to avoid loose rocks falling on us, and also to find stands in between, and places where we could attach rope slings or drive a piton. On many places we were rappelling in mid-air and realized again the sheerness of the upper rocks. Laying out of these rappels proved even more difficult than we had expected, and although each of them was done in an efficient way, it was getting dark when we reached the large snowfield 1000 feet below the summit. We crossed down to the snow bands, and descended in the dark into the couloir, now belaying each other and half-feeling our way down. Shortly before we had reached the main branch of the couloir we heard rocks break above and a few seconds later several pieces shot over our heads like shrapnel. A high wind, which had come up during the evening and which had increased the falling of snow particles from the summit ridge, had probably loosened larger lumps which, bringing rocks with them, were the cause of this. Shortly afterwards, we descended over the short ice-fall in the main couloir. At 2 a.m. we arrived at our little camp on the snow shelf of the upper Dais glacier, to be heartily greeted and congratulated by our two friends, without whose splendid cooperation we would not have had the excellent chance for climbing the mountain.

For repetitions of the climb I should suggest again a fast two-man rope, as a three-man rope would be slow on the upper 1000 feet where moving at the same time is not possible. Also the danger of falling rocks for the third man would be great. The climb should be started at midnight or even before that, as the couloirs and snow bands can be climbed very well in the dark. Much time and strength can be saved when crampons and ice-axes are left behind before entering the 1000-foot summit cliff. One pair of nailed boots should be taken along, for the last twenty feet of the snow-covered steep summit ridge. Pitons and caribiners are necessary, as we did not carry sufficient pitons to leave all the pitons that were necessary for preparing safe stands. However, pitons were left on the places where it was necessary to secure belays for the leader, and of course the pitons which were used for rappels, and several rope slings had to be left on the upper rocks. There may be possibilities of avoiding some of the very difficult parts of the chimney-like depression through traverses to the left of it. In general our route can be climbed safely by careful and intelligent going, after several days of warm weather. There will always be objective dangers and good timing and observation is necessary to overcome these. Stormy days should be avoided for the climb.

Mist Peak, Coast Mountains. Photo: Pat Morrow

Cathedral Crags, near Field, B.C. Photo: Roger Laurilla

1936 : NEW ROUTES IN THE ROCKIES

GEORGIA ENGELHARD

After a season in the Alps, it was indeed a pleasure to return to the Canadian Rockies, unmarred by civilization and unscarred by artificial aids, where the climber may find ample opportunity to make new routes on already ascended peaks. The summer of 1936 was an excellent one for such purposes, as the steady weather made it possible to concentrate on long and arduous climbs, without being forced to worry about oncoming storms.

One of the most impressive peaks in the vicinity of Field is Cathedral Crags, towering 6000 feet above the railway, and erroneously pointed out to tourists as Cathedral Mountain, which although part of the same massif is a separate peak, seen at its best from Lake O'Hara. The Crags (10,081 feet) had been ascended three times prior to 1936. The last ascent, in 1923, was made by Dr. Hickson with Edward and Walter Feuz who found considerable difficulty in getting from the glacier onto the peak itself, smooth vertical slabs necessitating a *courte échelle* in the ascent and a rope-off in the descent.

On July 2 Ernest Feuz and I left Wapta Camp at 5 a.m. and started up through the open, bushy slopes beneath Vanguard Peak. Following goat trails higher up over scree and easy cliff bands we reached the east glacier, which rises gradually to the base of the Crags, which from here present a sensational sight, reminiscent of Dolomite Peaks. Skirting the east base of the cliffs we followed a steep snow ridge which led us to a rocky platform, just below which we noted the piton and karabiner ring left by the Hickson party.

Being early in the season, snow conditions had obviously been in our favor, carrying us without difficulty over the troublesome pitch. On the platform we changed to sneakers and enjoyed fifty minutes of good rock climbing to the tiny, knife-like summit, a sensational spot indeed, for on three sides the tremendous cliffs are overhanging, and the peak is cleft by great vertical cracks, which appear unscalable. The descent to the col was easily made in half an hour, from whence we plodded in knee-deep snow to the summit of Cathedral Mountain, which boasts one of the most magnificent views in the district. An oncoming storm however drove us down; we descended straight to the valley of Cataract Brook, a route which is not altogether to be recommended, as the last thousand feet are marred by considerable dead fall. The ascent had taken six and a half hours, while the descent was made in three and a half.

On the 21st of July we started from the Plain of Six Glaciers and ascending to Abbot Pass, made the first north to south traverse of Glacier Peak, a pleasant and easy climb, offering a good opportunity for those spending the night at the hut after climbing Victoria or Lefroy, to do another peak en route to Lake O'Hara. Ascending a few hundred feet up the west face of Lefroy we reached a very prominent yellow scree band which leads continuously along this face to the northwest ice wall of Glacier Peak. Here we donned crampons and walked up the ice ridge and broken rocks to the summit in

It is all too simple to assume that mountains, like too many things, have been the domain of men, and that women's roles in the history of mountaineering have been restricted by chauvanism. In Canada, and in the ACC in particular, this was not at all the case, with women significantly involved in the club from the beginning, participating in several notable achievements in the mountain scene, and having a strong administrative voice. This modest report, on a summer season by Georgia Englehard and her guide Edouard Feuz, Jr., speaks well to the achievements and abilities of the early Canadian women.
– GP

about two hours from Abbot Pass. The magnificent view makes this climb well worthwhile and it is a good one for novices, accustoming them to traverses on loose rock and to the use of crampons. The descent however, proved more eventful. We descended the broken south ridge, with occasional traverses on the west face to the big snow couloir lying between Glacier Peak and Ringrose. It was extremely steep and we were carefully making our way down it, when a huge boulder came bounding toward us from the Ringrose side. The slope was too steep to allow us to move out of our steps, but fortunately we were spared by the margin of a foot. With this as a warning, we took to the rock and scree on the north side of the couloir, only returning to the snow near the bottom where we could glissade rapidly and avoid the continuous stone fall. This route is dangerous, and inspecting the peak from Lake Oesa we discovered a rock rib on the west face of the peak which would be feasible and far safer.

The next day we made the first traverse of Mount Hungabee, a venture which we had attempted in 1933, but in which we had failed, due to lack of extra rope in roping-off on the south ridge. This time we set off from Lake O'Hara well armed with two hundred and fifty feet of alpine line, pitons and extra slings. The Fynn route up to Ringrose Col and along the north ridge offers some pleasant climbing on moderately steep and solid rock, joining the regular route on the shoulder. We reached the summit in five and a half hours, and then hastened down the sharp south ridge composed of black rock with few holds to the point, about five hundred feet below the summit, where it breaks off in an overhanging cliff. A party some years ago, climbing up from Prospectors Valley had reached the base of this pitch and had even climbed a little way up it, leaving a fixed rope for descent which I could plainly see from my airy perch astride the ridge. It took us some time to arrange our alpine line, and so long and sheer was the pitch that it was difficult to see if the rope would reach to the great platform below. The first sixty feet of the rope-off (we figured the total distance to be about one hundred and thirty feet) are extremely sensational; the initial pitch being overhanging and for a good deal of the way you are free in the air. A convenient little platform gives a welcome resting place before you descend the rest of the way in a chimney, which required considerable cleaning out before it was safe to descend. The rope-off could be done in future with a hundred and twenty foot rope, as there is a good belay at the head of the chimney.

Thence we proceeded southwards along the platform-like ridge, it being our intention to traverse onto Wenkchemna Peak and down to Wenkchemna Pass. However, when we reached the gap separating Hungabee from Wenkchemna, we found it to be unclimbable, the bluffs being sheer and practically without holds. The descent to the gap could probably be made with the aid of several pitons, though the rock is not too secure, but the bluffs on the north side of Wenkchemna looked none too inviting.

So we retraced our steps a few hundred feet and then led off down the west face over a boulder slope, finally reaching a broad couloir, well broken with ledges, which however, were disagreeably wet from melting snow patches. The descent down the couloir seemed interminable. It became narrower toward the bottom, finally breaking off in a bluff, which forced us to traverse around a ridge to the left, bringing us out onto a big snow patch, where we unroped and sped easily to Prospector's Valley a little above the Eagle Eyrie. Two more hours of trudging in the afternoon sun brought us over Opabin Pass and back to O'Hara. This traverse is not nearly as enjoyable as that of Victoria, and the south ridge has little to recommend it beyond the sensational rope-off.

After a day of rest we set off for Field across Mount Stephen. In 1904 Miss Benham established a remarkable record, going from Lake Louise over Abbot Pass to O'Hara and thence via Mount Stephen to Field. I had no desire to repeat this gigantic feat, but the trip across to Field was appealing and new. We differed in our route from the Benham party; for where they followed the meadows almost to the base of Duchesnay Pass, thence ascending a snow-slope to the gap between Stephen and a subsidiary peak to the southeast, we struck directly for the southeast ridge and followed it throughout.

Crossing through the timber to charming Linda Lake, we made our way northwards through the alplands to the ridge which runs southeast from Mount Stephen. For a while the going was easy, along goat trails, the first obstacle to present itself being a prominent red tower. Two rather difficult pitches brought us within a couple of hundred feet of the top, but this last bit proved so sheer and excessively rotten that we retraced our steps and, traversing the tower on the west, regained the ridge beyond, which led easily to the small peak separated from the main Stephen massif by a gap below which lies the exceedingly steep glacier above the mine near Field. The descent to the col could not be made along the ridge entirely, which consists of a series of flat platforms separated by sheer drops of about twenty feet, however traverses on the west led around. The last thousand feet up the south ridge of Stephen presented unexpectedly nice rock climbing, similar to the pitches on Mount Collier. The summit was reached in seven and a half hours from Lake O'Hara. It is an interesting trip, the climbing being pleasant and the views excellent. Our destination, the Field beer parlor, being extremely alluring, the descent was made by the usual route to Field in less than three hours.

A few days later, Eaton Cromwell, Francis North and I made the first ascent of Wenkchemna Peak by the entire south ridge from Wenkchemna Pass. The main object of the climb was to reconnoitre the Wenkchemna-Hungabee gap from this angle; we had an idea that the climb itself would not be of much interest; in this surmise we were mistaken. Three easy hours from Moraine Lake up through the beautiful flowery meadows of Larch Valley brought us to the pass where we roped up. The first part of the south ridge is easy, but increases in steepness besides being very long. We struck no actual technical difficulty, although a good deal of care had to be exercised on the rotten rock, until about five hundred feet below the summit. The first obstacle was about a forty-foot pitch, extremely sheer and in one spot almost overhanging. At the top of this slab we found a piece of rope which had been used in 1931 by a Belgian party, who had unsuccessfully attempted to lasso the rock and had finally resorted, after some time, to a traverse on the east face along uninviting dirt bands. Above this we arrived at a slabby chimney with few holds and most of them rotten. After pulling out a good deal of rotten rocks, Cromwell had to take a back-stand in order to reach the slabs above an overhanging pitch in the chimney. I am afraid that this chimney can never again be ascended without the aid of a piton, as North and I pulled out the last remaining holds and relied a good deal on the rope. Above this, slabs with infrequent holds led to the summit. I consider the final part of the ridge to be one of the hardest pitches in the Canadian Rockies, being far more delicate and difficult than anything on either Mount Louis or the southeast face of Castle Tower.

The ascent having taken us eight hours we lolled luxuriously in the warm sun on the spacious summit. An examination of the Hungabee-Wenkchemna gap confirmed my suspicions of its impracticability. Reluctantly we roped up to descend, roping off twice on the two difficult pitches. This was a very time-consuming occupation, for as soon as we would start to hammer in a piton (there being no safe rocks to use as belays) the surrounding slabs would flake off, and we literally had to reach bed rock before we found any secure material. On the occasion of the first ascent in 1923 the entire ridge had not been followed, traverses on the east face avoiding the difficulties we encountered. As is so often the case in the Canadian Rockies, this peak will be much more pleasant when freed of much of the rubble by repeated ascents. As a farewell to the Rockies, before leaving for the Selkirks, Cromwell and I made the first traverse from Abbot Pass to the Plain of the Six Glaciers, of Mount Victoria, Mount Collier and the south and north shoulders of Popes Peak, descending by the "Pope's Nose."

It was a long but delightful day, full of fine and varied rock work. The Victoria traverse, with its airy ridges, jagged pinnacles and sensational pitches is by far the best climb of the district, comparable to some of the good routes in the Alps and although, to quote Val Fynn "*nur fur schwindel free*," offers no real technical difficulties. All was plain sailing until we started to descend the Collier ridge toward Popes Peak, when we struck an unexpected stretch of ice, entailing time-consuming step-cutting. Again descending from north Popes Peak to the platform above the "Nose," we were confronted by a ridge of glare ice, the extraordinarily warm, dry season having melted down the usual snow. This forced us to do a rather ticklish traverse on loose rock, which however, was far preferable to at least an hour of step-cutting. The descent down the "Nose" was an interesting one, and at the bottom we encountered extremely smooth slabs, once covered by ice. The glacier has receded tremendously in the past few years, exposing these slabs, which were descended best by trusting to the seats of our pants. Just as the light was failing we reached a platform to the right of the glacier, and roping down a narrow chimney in the sheer black cliff-band, we reached the long boulder-filled gully leading to the trail just as the full moon rose above the sharp triangle of the Mitre. The tour had taken sixteen hours (including halts) and was one of the most enjoyable I have ever made, one of its outstanding features being Cromwell's consistently smooth and well-timed leading, while the clear weather not only made the rock warm and pleasant to climb on, but greatly added to the scenic beauty of the trip. It was indeed a fitting conclusion to a very satisfactory two weeks, and not to be rivalled by any of the fine climbs which we made thereafter in the Selkirks.

Mount Assiniboine. Photo: Craig Richards

1941 : MEN, MOUNTAINS AND MOTIVES

Cyril G. Wates

"How do you get that way?" This question every mountaineer is called upon to answer from the day that he makes his first climb until wheelchair and crutches take the place of ice-axe and rope. In our youth we tackle the problem with a great deal of enthusiasm, quite confident of our ability to explain to our non-climbing friends the attractions we feel in the heights, and we are more than a little puzzled by their obtuseness and lack of horse sense. As we grow older, our explanations, so far from getting clearer, are apt to become diffuse and less facile, and when we pass middle age we shall, if we are wise, abandon the attempt altogether, or substitute some jocular remark such as: "We climb the peaks to keep the cairns in repair!" Our friends are hardly to be blamed if they decide that there is "something lacking" in the cerebral equipment of all mountaineers, since we disagree so widely among ourselves in our estimation of the motives which take us to the hills.

They — our friends — are in the position of the blind men who were examining an elephant. One, who touched a leg, declared that an elephant is like a tree. Another, who handled the trunk, insisted that an elephant is like a snake. A third who ran into the beast's side ruefully proclaimed that an elephant is exactly like a house. All were partly correct, but none could be said to have given a complete description of the "tidy pachyderm." This little parable has its parallel in the problem of mountaineering motives. Each of us is apt to convey to our friends the one prime motive which sends us again and again to the cliffs and couloirs, overlooking the fact that this is only one of many motives. The relationship between the mountain and the mountaineer is like an elaborate tapestry, of which the warp and the woof are a tangle of threads, some bright, some somber, all significant.

A formal dissertation on Motives would be as dry as Burgess Pass on a hot August day, so I have chosen to trace the result of the impact of the mountains upon the psyche of one person, from "childhood to old age." I have a friend, one with whom I have been on intimate terms for many years, and I have decided that he shall be made the subject of my analysis. I will not name him, for he is still a member of the Club, although no longer active. He is undoubtedly known to many of my readers, and I should not wish to submit him to the slightest embarrassment; so, for the purposes of this essay, he will remain simply "my friend."

I have picked this man as my victim, not because he was a great mountaineer, but because he was a typical mountaineer. He is one of those for whom, as John Cordelier says, "the ascent of a great peak is the only perfect object upon which his energies can be spent." He was a careful climber with a flair for technique and a certain gift for imparting his knowledge to others.

I do not intend to describe my friend's accomplishments; this is not a panegyric or even an "appreciation." I

The impact of mountaineering on the psyche of individual climbers has most often been so profoundly personal as to be indescribable to others. For this reason, climbers have often found it difficult to go much beyond technical description and raw narrative of their own experiences. Even today, few climbers can express the poetry of mountains, a poetry that can be known but not told.

– R WS

simply wish to trace the way in which the loom of the mountains has woven the threads of motive into the tapestry of his climbing career. My almost life-long intimacy with this man will make my task a comparatively easy one, when a more casual acquaintance might find it difficult or impossible.

My friend's first contact with the mountains came in early boyhood. His home was a large, rambling house on the top of a low hill. I have seen pictures of the place, and can describe it in some detail. The flat hilltop was a great lawn, almost a park. Close to the house was a row of fragrant eucalyptus trees, backed by stiff sago palms. Beyond towered stately breadfruit and mango trees. On the edge of the hill, slender coco palms waved their green fronds in the warm breeze from a sea of that almost incredible sapphire we see in high mountain lakes.

The boy's life there seems to have been very normal and very pleasant. He wandered along trails through dense tropical underbrush. He played under the trees in the park with an occasional companion of his own age. He swam in the calm sea or watched the rollers breaking into foam on the coral reefs. It was not until he turned away from the eternal summer light of the ocean to look inland that he experienced any emotions not common to every boy in his early teens. Beyond the house lay a narrow, crescent-shaped valley, and on the far side of this depression rose range above range of densely wooded mountains. To the boy these great dim bulks were not merely *terra incognita*, they were forbidden ground. He might play in the valley and explore it to his heart's content, but to have stepped into the fringe of forest which marked the first slopes of the mountains would have incurred heavy penalties. He watched the sun on the tree tops; he saw the clouds descend and hide the summits; he lay in bed at night and trembled as the fearful tropical thunder echoed amidst the ranges. Gradually the first thread of the tapestry was woven into place — the Mystery of the mountains. One never-to-be-forgotten day his elder brother took him to a newly established coffee plantation in the hills. I can picture the awe with which he ascended the narrow trail under a canopy of tree-ferns, giving place higher up to mighty ebony and cinnamon trees, draped with flaming orchids. He watched the Negroes, with cries of fury, attack and kill a huge snake asleep on a fallen log. He spent a night in a crude shack, his first night in a mountain hut. One would naturally suppose that after this trip, the mountains would have become commonplace to my friend, but this does not seem to have been the case. Rather, the sense of mystery was deepened by what he had

seen, and throughout his life this thread in the tapestry remained unbroken. The next mountain episode in my friend's life came some years later when, as a young man, he was beginning to earn his own living in a great eastern city. Here I knew him and, from henceforth, can speak of his experiences from personal contact. His daily life was spent amid the stamp of two million feet, the rush of traffic, the roar of elevated railways. He had no realization of what we describe as "The Call of the Hills," yet it was not long before he discovered that they were there, waiting for him. A long journey by street car, a ten-mile tramp, and the city was as far removed as though it had never been.

Sunday after Sunday found him in the hills, and I was often a member of the little party. There is no mystery about these gracious, embosomed New England hills. The gentle slopes, the clumps of stately trees, the occasional out-cropping of rock, constitute a happy playground, and we all felt that they were our familiar friends. We wandered over them and talked "big" of all that we intended to do with our lives. And as the summer days passed, the hills added a second thread to the tapestry — the Friendliness of the mountains.

One day my friend took Horace Greeley's advice and "went West." He seems to have retained little but a hazy memory of the cities through which he passed on his way, or of the wide expanse of the great plains, but the journey through Colorado left a deep and permanent impression. He speaks of a great canyon where the railway is supported on steel girders let into the living rock, and he describes his first glimpse of the giants of the Rockies; mighty fourteen thousand-foot peaks, lifting their snowy summits majestically to the heavens. I doubt if the word "mountaineer" would have conveyed anything to him at that time, unless it was a picture of southern feuds and a prototype of Li'l Abner. Those summits were not a place where one might stand; they were a climax of grandeur. So there was added to the tapestry another thread — the Majesty of the peaks.

My friend lived in the West for some years; I think it was either in Idaho or in southern Wyoming. I know that he saw much of the mountains, but his contacts and impressions were of an utterly different nature from anything he had experienced previously. The ranges which border the Snake River have nothing of majesty and little enough of beauty. No one could possibly describe them as friendly. Their essence seems to be complete indifference to Man and all his works.

In the course of his daily life my friend came into contact with these mountains more than once, and without exception these contacts meant hardship, suffering, even hunger. During these years the "Call of the Hills" was completely silent. His attitude was that of his ancestors who hated and feared the mountains. He meant nothing to them, nor they to him. Yet a new thread was woven into the tapestry — the Aloofness of the peaks.

Shortly before the outbreak of the first Great War, my friend came to Canada for the first time. He was often in Edmonton and although, in the intervening years, he has travelled a good deal, our friendship has remained unbroken from that day to this. What induced him to spend his first summer vacation in the mountains it is hard to say. That was when the Grand Trunk Pacific was under construction, and the name of Mount Robson was on everyone's lips. My friend spent ten days camping near the Monarch of the Rockies with two or three companions. I know that this expedition marked a crisis in his life. That first camp seems to have been very crudely managed. None of the party had the slightest experience in woodcraft. They pitched their tents on a gravel flat close to the railway, in a part of the Fraser valley from which the high peaks were completely invisible. They did a bit of scrambling, without the slightest desire to reach the top of anything. Almost on the last day of their holiday they succeeded in crossing the river on an old log jam (there was a bridge a mile down stream!) and managed to reach Kinney Lake. He did not know it at the time, but his first sight of the great face of Mount Robson undoubtedly turned my friend from a mountain lover into a mountaineer. That mighty cliff with its crest of shining ice must have produced an upheaval in his very being, but he seems to have been strangely unconscious of it at the time. To trace the change, I have had to turn to a small book of verses on many subjects which he started to write that year. Many of these poems are rather revealing. Yes, we climbers sometimes do woo the muse — I have been known to scribble doggerel myself, as the Club song book bears witness!

I have been fortunate in being able to borrow a copy of this book, and I find the following sonnet which clearly owes its inspiration to that first camping trip:

"Among the mountains of the Great Divide,
Where flows the mighty Fraser to the sea,
A valley lies, in which I love to be;

Great buttresses rise up on either side
Whereon, by might of rock and root allied,
Courageous fir trees cling and stand erect,
Sweeping from azure sky with cloud-wisps flecked
Down to an earth-bound streamlet, heaven-supplied.
A crystal streamlet from the eternal heights,
Torrents of diamonds, pearls and opals blent,
Flinging a sheaf of rainbow-colored lights,
Rippling through moss with ferns and flowers besprent;
While here and there a sky-reflecting pool
Lies like a perfect sapphire, clear and cool."

Ignoring, on the grounds of poetic license, the fact that Fraser River at Robson Station is many miles from the divide, the verse I have quoted demonstrates one thing very clearly: that my friend had become keenly aware of the beauty of the mountains, not so much in mass as in detail. If there is any one way in which the mountaineer differs from the mountain-lover it is to be found in the climber's intense desire to come into intimate contact with the peaks, to penetrate into their hidden recesses. He is not content to stand afar off and adore. This verse gives unmistakable evidence of the weaving, not of a single thread but of a hundred, into the tapestry of my friend's life, each one a thread of Beauty. Every summer for several years there was a repetition of this first elementary camp, always in the same general location. My friend's camping technique improved. He no longer pitched tents on gravel flats. He ventured higher in his scrambles, reaching the rocks and even the ridges. I find no record of any complete ascent, not because he found the climbing too difficult but because he had not yet become conscious that the summit differed in any way from other parts of the mountains. This knowledge was to be gained later. He speaks, however, of one great amphitheatre which he visited several times. He has recorded the impression it made upon him in a sonnet which he calls "The Rocks."

Above the region of the forest dense,
Where voice of murmuring stream had died away,
By giant hands, in some long bygone day
Was carved an amphitheatre immense.
Nature seems waiting breathless in suspense.

The whistle of a marmot, shrill and clear,
A friendly ptarmigan that flutters near
Serve but to make the silence more intense.
At night the mountain trolls make grim pretense
Of some wild drama on the valley's edge,
Surrounded by a ghostly audience
Crouching on bastion, parapet and ledge;
While yonder shattered gendarme forms a throne
Where Silence — Silence — Silence reigns alone."

It's a bit shivery and fanciful! I've spent a few enforced bivouacs on the cliffs myself, but I have never seen any trolls or similar critters. However, a poet's imagination is apt to run away with him, and in this case my friend has left us his vision of the rocks in one word in the ninth line of the sonnet. This word gives the clue to a thread which wove itself into the tapestry at this time — the Grimness of the mountains.

What caused my friend to join the Alpine Club of Canada is, so far as my own knowledge is concerned, an unsolved mystery. Perhaps my own love of the mountains may have influenced him. Perhaps it was the enthusiasm of other friends who were members of the Club. In any case, he did join and attended his first Camp. I was there, and was a member of the party with which he shared his first expedition. It was not a climb at all; it was just a picnic trip which took us up some easy cliffs to a wide expanse of alpine meadows, gay with flowers. The incident would hardly be worth recording but for the fact that our leader was that prince of alpine guides, Conrad Kain.

No one could watch Conrad climb without experiencing a sense of pleasure at the utter lack of effort which marked his slightest movement. He seemed to flow up the rocks, as though every foot and handhold had been arranged for his convenience beforehand. We, who were privileged to watch and imitate him, could hardly fail to realize that the mastery of technique is one of the climber's keenest delights. I know that my friend learned that from Conrad. Thenceforth he was a devoted student of the climber's craft. He read exhaustively, and nothing came amiss. G. W. Young, Harold Raeburn, Smythe, Conway, the Badminton Book, the older classical writers — he read and re-read them. He graduated to Active membership at that Camp, but it is not his climbs in this or the immedi-

ately succeeding years which were the theme-song of his early mountaineering career. The new thread in the tapestry might be expressed by the word "Difficulty," if we bear in mind that it was not difficulty as such that intrigued him, but rather the art of making the difficult both easy and safe by perfecting his knowledge of technique.

Some years later my friend spent two weeks at Lake O'Hara. He climbed many of the peaks around that incomparable gem, but it was not the ascents which remain as his sweetest memory, but a lovely valley he visited; at least so I judge from the poem he wrote on the subject. Here it is:
"The way above the cataract is won,
Above the turmoil and the roar and rush
Into a little valley filled with hush,
A little hanging valley in the sun.
Meandering rills, like liquid air, which run
Twixt mossy banks, to thirsty lips appeal.
Amid these shadowy vistas man may feel
That Man and God and Nature are at one.
The clustering larch and balsam have to face
A struggle for existence which imparts
A gallant sturdiness and homely grace
That makes them very kin to human hearts;
And one might find among these glades and streams
Adventures in Contentment and dear dreams."

Reading that, I find no difficulty in believing that the loom had woven a new thread into the tapestry — the Sweetness of the hills. The years came and went, bringing in their wake added experience and a better understanding of the mountains. In the mountaineering sense, my friend was approaching maturity, and he began to feel the insistent demand to pit his steadily improving technique against the difficulties of rocks and ice; to apply his gradually increasing knowledge to the solution of problems to be found only on unclimbed peaks. This is not the place to appraise the standard of his original climbs, nor their importance in alpine history. My sole object is to discover whether the necessity of standing upon his own feet, instead of simply following and imitating other leaders, brought any marked change in my friend's attitude towards the peaks in general.

I have already spoken of the fact that in the early days around Mount Robson, my friend was not aware of any special significance in the Summit, as contrasted with any other part of the mountain. Even after making many ascents, he still thought of the top of a mountain simply as the culmination of effort and enjoyment, the spot where the party rested and relaxed, ate a welcome lunch and admired a panorama which it was hopeless to photograph. Perhaps, to some extent his ideas were tinged with the mistaken conception that a mountain is a "worthy opponent," an enemy to be conquered. He had not yet become receptive to the thought of a peak as something which called for cooperation on the part of the climber.

This attitude was changed after he had made one or two original ascents. My friend made what was, to him, an amazing discovery: that the summit of a mountain is the site of certain spiritual experiences not to be found elsewhere. These experiences were not to be explained by any theory, scientific or psychological, but they were nevertheless vividly real.

The intensity of my friend's sensations justifies the supposition that they would be recorded in his book of verses. I can find nothing of the sort except a rather indifferent sonnet of which he does not seem to be particularly proud. I think the explanation of this hiatus is to be discovered in a certain prose passage which he found and learned to appreciate about this time. It was written by one of the world's greatest climbers, a man whose mortal remains rest in the noblest mausoleum on the face of the earth — Mount Everest. This what George Leigh Mallory had to say on the subject:

"Is this the summit, crowning the day? How cool and quiet! We're not exultant; but delighted, joyful; soberly astonished…. Have we vanquished an enemy? None but ourselves. Have we gained success? That word means nothing here. Have we won a kingdom? No… and yes. We have achieved an ultimate satisfaction… fulfilled a destiny…. To struggle and to understand — never this last without the other; such is the law…. We've only been obeying an old law then? Ah! but it's *the* law… and we understand — a little more. So ancient, wise and terrible and yet kind we see them; with steps for children's feet."

No wonder my friend shrank from putting into new words an experience which had already been so perfectly expressed! Nor is it surprising that, after deep heart searching, I have failed to find any word with which to summarize the thread which was then woven into the tapestry of his mountain life, a thread of unspeakable mystery without which the whole picture is futile and pointless. There is more, infinitely more to this vision of the Summit than appears upon the surface. To my friend it was a revelation, a Key to wider and richer experiences. Thread after thread sprang into its appointed place until the picture, blurred and incomplete until now, revealed itself in all its beauty and significance. First, since one does not make the ascent of great peaks alone, there was the thread of Companionship. Next, for the same reason — the fact that one is never alone on a mountain either physically or spiritually — there was the thread of Sharing. Year after year my friend played upon these threads as though they were the strings of a harp. His greatest joy was to pilot a group of beginners to some dearly-loved vantage point, there to enjoy their reactions to the beauties he knew so well. Perhaps it was a panorama of grim peaks, seen with dramatic suddenness from the top of a pass or ridge. Perhaps it was some hidden, unmapped lake, or a tiny valley, gorgeous with flowers.

We cannot forever live upon the austere heights. Contrary to popular opinion, we are not forever engaged in perilous ascents. Any one of us could fill a book with anecdotes of the lighter side of mountaineering. My friend took special delight in the ridiculous incidents which crop up during every climbing expedition, and he loved to record them in a limerick or a jingle. For example, I find a verse which commemorates an occasion when he was engaged in exploratory work for the Parks' authorities.

Some tourists had arrived with an elaborate outfit, and the packers pitched their camp in the vicinity. My friend remarks:

There's a party of dudes in camp nearby,
They dog our footsteps and follow our tracks;
They have breeches and boots like ours,
Like us they have rucksacks on their backs.
They look like us in many respects,
To every purpose and intent;
But they pay twenty dollars a day,
While we are the guests of the Government!

In such, and similar ways, we find the thread of Fun running through the tapestry.

Indeed, in these happy years my friend came into his own. The mountains and all their glories were his, in a very special sense. He found them kind, but he found them cruel too. He knew what it meant to confront the "Bright Face of Danger" — that strange paradox which is so familiar to every serious climber. He learned what it was to stand by the ashes of a camp fire from which friends had started for the heights, full of joyous anticipation, never to return. Standing there, musing sadly, he recalled the lovely words of Hilton Brown:

"The mist drops low on crag and corrie,

The evening settles on scaur and ben,

Homes the late eagle from his foray,

The light goes out of the silent glen;

The night closes, the shadows soften

On granite mountain and heather hill;

And the climbing feet that came so often

Are still, are still,

And they will not come again."

It is the modern custom to belittle the familiar phrase, "The Eternal Hills," as mere poetic imagery. Any geologist can tell you that the mountains are in a constant state of flux. They are heaved up by mighty forces and then worn down again to a dead level of mediocrity by the slow processes of erosion. Nevertheless, as compared with the brief moment of human life, the hills are everlasting, and as such they seem to have a closer bond with the "unchanging stars" than with anything to be found upon earth.

My friend loved nothing better than to lie at night under the sky when, as he says in one of his poems, "the mountains for companionship draw near," and watch the panorama of the stars. He speaks of one memorable bivouac in the heather on a high pass when, unable to sleep, he kept lonely vigil until dawn, and he recorded his impressions in another sonnet — a verse-form for which he seems to have had a predilection. Here he speaks of "The hidden moon, silvering the distant peaks," and tells how he watched through the silent hours "Cygnus and Lyra And all the bright procession of the stars."

My friend is drawing near to the autumn of his life. No more for him the lonely bivouac, the splendor of the dawn on windy heights, the chip of axe on brittle ice, the drowsy hour on sunny summit. Some day the tapestry will be folded up and laid aside, but still the loom of the mountains continues to weave thread after thread. Life holds, as for all men, its disappointments and its sorrows, but the great hills weave the thread of Comfort. In these days of strife and hatred it is easy to sink into an indifferent materialism, but the mountains weave the thread of Worship. The roar of battle echoes across the world, but the mountains weave the thread of Peace.

I have shown this essay to my friend, and have asked him what he thought of it. He replied, with an embarrassed smile: "I think it's a lot of nonsense! " I find it hard, however, to believe that this is a genuine expression of opinion, for, on turning once more to his little book of verse, I read a poem which bears the simple title of "Climbers."

Whither away, Friends

When the grey of the dawn lies cold and still

On snow-clad mountain and spruce-clad hill,

And down in the valley, the purple of night

Still waits for the touch of the sun's first light

To drive it hence?

To the dizzy heights, Friend;

Scaling the rocks to the névé white

And the snow-ridge, corniced on left and right,

And when sunrise comes in its regal state,

You shall hear us shout from yon far arête

On our upward way.

What do you seek, Friends?

Know you not that the valleys hold

Wealth of silver and wealth of gold?

Yes, but the mountains which seem so bare,

Have burden of treasure more rich and rare

Than any you know.

What treasures are these, Friends?

The winds of God are more than wealth,

For they tint the cheek with the glow of health,

And the pulses throbbing in every vein
Give a sense of joy that is almost pain
To the thrilling heart.
But what of the risks, Friends?
Do we not crawl with bated breath,
Where every step is a game with death?
The rotten rock and the sliding snow
Are trials to be overcome in the glow
Of our youth and strength.
What of the goal, Friends?
What of the summit we strive to reach?
Ah! The climber knows, but he cannot teach;
And he never forgets, though he rarely speaks
Of the boundless sea of snow-clad peaks
That is stretched below.
And wot ye well, Friend,
That whose the summit doth once attain
Shall never be quite the same again;
Like the aged Rabbi of Levi's race
Who in the flesh beheld God's face,
As the Talmud saith.
What of the Man, Friends?
The soul of the climber may well be known,
For the Mountains have voices which call to their own,
And he who would climb must be true and tried,
For the lives of the many full oft reside
In the hands of one.
But what of the end, Friends?
Little we reck what the end may be,
But more than the present in life we see;
So give good heed while this truth we tell,
The man who would love the Maker well,
Must love His works.

Freshfield Glacier. Photo: E.R. Gibson. Whyte Museum of the Canadian Rockies

Hilda Peak and A2. Photo: Greg Horne

1942 : EASTERN CLIMBS

JOHN F. BRETT

Contrary to the opinion held by many, the mountainous districts in the eastern half of this continent offer considerable scope for mountaineering. Since the altitude of these eastern ranges is moderate — the summit of Mount Washington, 6,288 feet, in the White Mountains being usually considered the highest known point (although it is quite possible that some of the unknown and uncharted Laurentians in northern Québec may be found higher yet) — rock climbing, of a character somewhat similar to that found in Great Britain, is the principal attraction for the faithful. The slabs and finger cracks of Chapel Pond and Indian Head in the Adirondacks, the ridges and buttresses of Washington in the White Mountains, the magnificent gullies and arêtes of Katahdin, can test our mettle and afford enjoyment to us all. Further, those who look long and carefully have noticed that the Huntington Ravine running above Pinkham's Notch to the Alpine Garden, just under Mount Washington's bald head, is, during the month of May, plastered with a shimmering ribbon of ice over 500 feet high, from which emerge here and there steep bits of jagged cliffs in the best alpine tradition. An ideal spot to set your trusty ice-axe to work. The war has, for the present, put an end to our excursions in that part of the enchanting land of mountains. It remained to look nearer home, to study anew and more closely, the many cliffs dotting the vast domain of the Laurentian country.

One of the best bits yet found is the Condor's Cliffs, near Val David, in the Laurentian district, near Montréal. Above the wooded slopes rising from the Rivière du Nord, a half-moon of cliffs emerges high above the trees. In front of the cliffs an isolated pinnacle crowned by a characteristic block recalling the silhouette of a condor's head, rises some 130 feet above its base. Good climbing can be had both on the half-moon and on the monolith. The latter is fractured vertically at several places, one of the fine chimneys having received the appropriate name of Fat Man's Misery. Another nearby crack, much narrower still, is known as the Gopher's Hole. This, however, is only for very thin people before lunch. By means of the chimneys the steep edge of the Flake can be attained, and by the latter a point some 30 feet below the Condor's bold head can be reached. The steep and smooth slab above seems to call for a spot of engineering, or possibly rope-throwing. Many pitches of various difficulties as well as numerous interesting rappels have been developed in the flanks of the half-moon, other possibilities remain to be explored. During the Thanksgiving week-end, an effort was made to gather all Montréal members and future members together at La Sapinière Hotel at Val David, our climbing rendez-vous. Fifteen alpinists responded nobly and a very good time was had by all. Later, members of the McGill University Outing Club were our climbing companions and it was a delight indeed to watch the tremendous enthusiasm for climbing rocks displayed by the collegians.

Just before the arrival of the snow this fall a new series of cliffs northeast of the Condor was investigated. These cliffs are higher than the Condor's and present several zones where the rocks are fractured horizontally and vertically in the most intriguing fashion. Some splendid finger cracks are assured. However, the climbing there will be part of next year's program.

The mountains of the west have cast a long shadow over climbing in the rest of the country for most of Canada's history, with the fine and abundant rock of Ontario, Québec and the Atlantic provinces left untouched while climbers headed to the Rockies and the west coast. A notable exception can be found in the early exploration of the Swiss expatriate John Brett, founder of the Montréal section and later president of the ACC. This article, which introduced the rest of the country to Québec climbing in celebration of the new section, shows well some of the hesitant pride which has long defined eastern climbers.
– GP

The west face of Mount Alberta. Photo: Greg Horne

1949 : THE SECOND ASCENT OF MOUNT ALBERTA

FRED D. AYERS

Mount Alberta (11,874 feet), one of the major peaks of the Canadian Rockies, lies 48 miles southeast of Jasper. It can be located on a map by starting at a point on the Banff-Jasper highway seven miles north of the Columbia Icefields Chalet and extending a line due west a distance equivalent to about seven miles. The peak itself cannot be seen from the highway.

The first ascent of Mount Alberta was made on July 21, 1925, by a party of six Japanese climbers under the leadership of Mr. Yuko Maki. Their Swiss climbing guides were Heinrich Fuhrer and Hans Kohler, assisted by Jean Weber, a skilled Swiss amateur climber. A detailed and graphic report of this ascent was written by Jean Weber immediately after the climb. Unfortunately, it has never been published, though John Oberlin and the writer were fortunate in securing a copy from Mr. J. A. Weiss of Jasper.

Mr. Maki's party, arriving directly from Japan, traveled from Jasper up the Athabasca valley and turned east, following Habel Creek to a campsite two miles above its junction with the Athabasca. From here a high camp was established on a small plateau at 6,800 feet near the southeast base of the mountain. The climbing party of nine gained the summit ridge by climbing over ledges and cliffs on the southeast side. They reported the climb to be long and, in the upper portions, difficult. A three-man stand was used to surmount one pitch. They reached the top at 7:35 p.m. and were forced by darkness to spend the night on the summit ridge. The entire following day was used in descending. An extra ice-axe, carried up expressly for the purpose, was left on the summit with a cairn erected around it. Shortly after the climb Mr. Maki and his party embarked for Japan, and later the Swiss members returned to Europe. In the succeeding years the axe on the summit became something of a legend and, according to an often repeated rumor, was believed to be made of silver.

Following the original 1925 climb, several attempts were made to reach the summit again, some of the parties turning back almost within sight of the goal only because of adverse weather conditions. The construction of the Banff-Jasper highway which passes within seven miles of Mount Alberta, has provided a convenient approach to the peak from the east, and the more recent attempts have been made by this route, a practicable one for backpacking. The first party so to use this approach was composed of Henry S. Hall, Jr., Rex Gibson and Bradley B. Gilman in 1988.

John Oberlin and the writer became interested in the mountain a few years ago, John being particularly active in accumulating information and photographs. Finally, during the last week in July, 1948, with a choice of

So formidable are the cliffs of Mount Alberta that it took almost 25 years before a second ascent was made in 1948. A remarkable element of the story of this ascent is the description of the Brocken Spectre near its summit. The witnessing of this rare phenomenon is one of the rewards of mountaineering. Some Canadians are still disturbed that Maki's ice-axe from the 1925 expedition was not placed in the hands of the Canadian Alpine Club or a local museum. It is not too late, however, for this oversight to be corrected.

– R WS

two or three climbs available, we decided to make an attempt on Alberta, though it must be admitted we were not very optimistic about our chances of success. For one thing, rainy weather had kept us confined in Jasper for several days and the partially blue sky under which we were setting forth was accepted with reservations.

We checked out with the park warden, Mr. Ed. Brennan, at Poboktan Creek on July 28 and in the early afternoon of the same day, with full packs, forded the branched channels of the Sunwapta River approximately 200 yards north of mile post 57 on the highway. Then, making use of accurate descriptions furnished by Rex Gibson and Henry S. Hall Jr., we crossed to the south side of the tributary creek whose canyon and waterfalls are so prominently visible from the highway. Here we found the well-trodden but very steep game trail which follows along the very brink of the gravelly cliffs south of the tributary stream.

After following this stream for about two miles we climbed through an enormous jumble of moraines coming down from the left and turned northwestward up onto a grassy slope, then continued up beside a series of small waterfalls. Camp was made at 7:00 p.m. above the waterfalls close to a small patch of dwarf trees near the stream. The tent was pitched not far from a large boulder which was overhanging on nearly all sides. It provided partial shelter from the cold rain which, not unexpectedly, was now falling.

The following morning we found ourselves enveloped in fog with a more-or-less steady drizzle falling. There was no apparent advantage in getting up so we remained in bed until hunger finally drove us out. Yielding to the changed wind direction, we moved our fireplace 120 degrees around the boulder and cooked a late breakfast, mostly over hot smoke.

In the afternoon it cleared partially and at 3:30 we moved off to establish a higher camp, continuing along the stream by which we had camped. Above a rise in the valley floor, we gained the glacier of the Woolley-Diadem amphitheatre, and followed a curving course westward over easy ice, finally reaching the rock saddle (9,300 feet) 1.2 miles south and slightly east of Mount Woolley. The scree slope leading up to this saddle is laborious. With a heavy pack, one assumes a pace and posture advantageous for fossil hunting. Numerous specimens of trilobites were observed, though they were usually small.

The weather had become threatening again and a cold wind was blowing through the saddle. Here we had our first view of Alberta. Due west of us, across two miles of glacier, the peak towered up into the clouds like a great black wall. It was a chilly and ominous-looking prospect. We continued down the talus slope west of the saddle and set up camp on a prominent flat bench of black rock, partially snow-covered, about 400 feet below the saddle. Because of the wind we found it difficult to keep the tent down on the smooth rock slabs and were eventually forced to construct a sizable wind-break of rocks on the south side of the tent. An adequate supply of water was available 100 yards south of camp, at the lower end of a large snowfield.

The following morning, July 30, was cold but the sky was generally clear. Originally, John and I, as a result of a study of various photographs, had planned to attempt the peak from the northwest. However, in Jasper a few days before, Rex Gibson had convinced us that the southeastern approach was a much better one. We left camp at 4:40 a.m. and quickly disposed of the two-mile jaunt across the glacier toward the southeast slopes. Then, on a small moraine, we followed along the lower edge of a peninsula of snow which extends southward from the glacier and lies against the lower cliffs of Alberta proper. Just beyond the tip of the peninsula we turned steeply up over broken, scree-covered ledges and passed left of the base of the large buttress directly above. We then made a climbing traverse on talus along the base of the rock wall on our right, the edge of a snowfield gradually converging in from our left as we climbed. We came to a break in the rock wall, turned up it, and then continued, following an eastward course up debris-littered ledges and gullies onto the talus shelf above the first cliff band (as seen from the east), thus completing, on rock, a sort of S-shaped course.

Above us was the second band of cliffs. We worked northward at first, then left and more steeply upward over shattered rock stair-steps, keeping always left (south) of a long couloir. All the while, continuing a practice begun far below, we were building route-marking cairns at intervals, placed for visibility from above. In addition, we frequently encountered existing cairns, usually not visible from below. These encouraged us considerably. They seemed to be built according to two distinct styles of architecture: one a loose heaping of rocks, the other a neat stacking into well-balanced columns. We attempted to construct ours in conformity with the latter principle. The upper portion of the second cliff band was surmounted by climbing up a steep nose between two gullies which converged upward. A sheer, smooth wall was just to the right of us. This brought us to the top of a partially detached spur from which we crossed, over a narrow gap, to the talus bench beyond. This inclined bench is a prominent feature on the southeast slopes of the mountain and lies directly under the tremendous, black upper cliffs.

All morning the view southward had been growing more impressive. In that direction were the great out-post peaks of the Columbia Icefield, among them Mount Columbia and the North Twin, second and third highest peaks in the Canadian Rockies. From below at sunrise we had watched the illumination of the North Twin in rose and golden colors. As we climbed higher, first Mount Columbia, then the South Twin had come into sight. Now from our high vantage point, we had a commanding view of the whole scene in the full light of mid-morning. This array of peaks rising above the headwaters of the Athabasca has been called by some perhaps the mightiest that the Rockies can show.

We turned again to our problem. Earlier in the morning, while crossing the glacier, we had noted on the southern portion of the summit ridge of Alberta, two broad notches and two corresponding south-facing steps. Both of the latter had appeared quite steep and our decision now was to attempt to reach the summit ridge north of the steps if possible. Accordingly we began to work our way northward on the yellow talus bench and at the same time upward. We passed from yellow to black rock and then continued between two icy patches of snow and on past the base of a rounded black buttress. From here we moved upward and northward along the face of the wall, more or less in two-dimensional stair-step fashion, over a series of ledges which were convex outward and fairly widely spaced. Eventually we reached the upper of two very long, parallel, horizontal ledges, one about 20 or 30 feet above the other. Each was about five feet wide, slanted out and down, and was covered with new snow. These two ledges extend, with numerous interruptions, for 500 yards or more along the lower southern portion of the black wall as seen from the east. They are in fact members of the lower part of a system of such ledges breaking the otherwise virtually impregnable defenses of the wall. Without a coating of snow these ledges would be not at all obvious from the saddle south of Mount Woolley.

We advanced along the upper ledge, critically viewing a smooth, shallow, and steeply inclined trough above us. It extended upward toward evil looking black ribs which appeared to loop back and forth high above. I started up this trough on an exploratory skirmish while John looked dubiously. After 20 feet I encountered a cairn, built in the loosely heaped style. To me this appeared an argument for continuing farther. John, however, insisted that we first explore northward along the ledge. I took another look at the trough above me and came down without overly much persuasion. Before long the upper ledge became too narrow for comfort. We cautiously retraced our steps to a point where we could climb down to the lower and slightly more commodious ledge and followed it northward to the south edge of a huge couloir. Here our ledge was cut off completely, though it continued beyond the couloir. John remarked that the portion of the couloir below us looked something like a giant elevator shaft. The drop-off to the glacier was almost unbroken because the broad talus shelves were no longer below us.

With some difficulty we climbed up a 30-foot high spur which rose above us and roped up on the little platform at its top. The wisdom of John's counsel regarding a further search along the ledges was now obvious. From here, as far as we could see upward, the route was considerably easier than the one in my trough. At the top of the spur on which we stood, we discovered to our surprise an old sling rope. It was arranged for roping down into the couloir and not down onto the ledge which we had been following. Also, we observed with some misgivings the fog which was beginning to form next to the cliffs high above.

From where we stood on the platform, a slanting ledge, almost covered by new snow, led upward toward the back of the couloir. We followed this for about 100 feet, then continued up and slightly left over rotten and quite steep rock, to a more broken area where we were able to traverse to our right into a chimney, nearly full of snow, which constituted the back of the couloir.

We followed this narrow, rather straight-walled trough for 300 feet or more. The snow in it was, for the most part, in good condition, probably offering better and more secure climbing than would have the bare rock. At one spot, presumably the habitat of a small waterfall in warmer weather, John, here leading, broke through an icy crust and dropped to his hips into the air space behind. He struggled out, making decisive remarks on the obstinacy of the trap, and we continued.

At the top of the 300-foot pitch the trough expanded and we came onto a sizable snow patch where the angle eased off a few degrees. We crossed to the north wall of the couloir and, feeling for little icy shelves under the snow, here thin, we approached the rock rib bounding the couloir on the north. John reached the crest of the rib via an icy gully, whereas I chose a rock pitch immediately right of the gully. Neither variant was wholly satisfactory as a climbing route.

Initially the rib was very steep but it gradually merged into a broader area where, in the words of Jean Weber, "the grade was quite agreeable to the body's craving to be at intervals at ease in a straight-up human-like position." We here entered the cloud zone and soon after arrived on the crest of the summit ridge just above the northern of the two steps as we had hoped. The time was 4:05 p.m.

All day long we had been waiting for the moment when we could stand up on the ridge and make a quick dash along it to the summit. The view which greeted us was disheartening. As far as we could see through the fog the ridge was dangerously narrow, with precipitous drops on both sides, and consisted of a series of little notches and shattered pinnacles. This was going to require time. As we moved along the crest, traversing, circumventing and straddling the pinnacles, the amount of snow and ice increased. We soon passed a small, square-shaped platform, deep in snow on its east side, the only such refuge on the entire ridge and probably the bivouac spot of the 1925 party. It was becoming windy and cold with occasional whirling flurries of snow. Eventually we passed two successive snow crests, each of which we had hoped would be the summit.

Suddenly we were brought up short by something we had seen from the glacier but had forgotten: a 60-foot-deep gap in the ridge. From below it had appeared insignificant, but from here it assumed new proportions. The near side of the gap was a snow-covered ice slope, very steep and having, in the fog, an indeterminate amount of exposure. The fragile snow-saddle below, with its delicately curving crest, appeared to offer no secure belay whatever for the last man down nor for the first man up on returning. Just beyond and dimly visible was a snow crest which appeared most certainly to be the summit. Rather than turn back here, we decided on a rather desperate procedure. We drove one of our axes all the way into the hard snow a short distance back from the rim of the gap, and, using a 150-foot nylon rappel line over the axe, roped down into the snow saddle. I was delighted to have the security the fixed rope offered because, half way down, the veneer of snow over the ice was only four or five inches thick. We hitched our way across the saddle horse-back fashion, shaving off the beautifully formed crest

of snow ahead of us. The ends of the rappel rope were knotted together and packed securely into the snow. With only one axe between the two of us, we had no desire for our lifeline to be blown out of reach by the wind! For 20 feet, the far side of the gap was steep but not icy. Beyond this the grade lessened and the ridge mercifully became a little broader, though we had to keep well to the left of the crest because of large cornices.

We arrived expectantly on our goal, the little snow summit, only to see another and higher one materialize out of the fog ahead. Then, as we stood, the mist thinned momentarily and revealed, beyond the nearer crest, still more of the white ridge undulating gently up to a second and still higher snow summit. We experienced all the emotions characteristic of such a situation. However, on proceeding, we were relieved to find that the ridge became relatively easy and also that the fog had made the distances appear greater than they actually were.

Without warning, John, who was ahead, let out two unintelligible and piercing yells, which gave me quite a fright since it was my axe which was back at the gap. However it developed that his shouts had only been "The axe! The axe!" I moved up a few steps and saw what was causing his excitement. Not more than 300 feet ahead, projecting out of the snow and dramatically silhouetted was the axe left by the original party 23 years ago. The summit at last! It had taken us two hours to cover the 600 or more yards of ridge behind us.

We reached the axe at 6:15 p.m. It was standing in the top of a cairn which was all but completely buried in snow. The axe, far from being silver, was of standard Swiss manufacture, though weather-beaten by long exposure. On the head, bright against the rusty steel, were the initials "M. T. H." in flashing gold letters. If the axe were new and shining when placed in the cairn, it must almost have looked like polished silver. The record was inside an inverted and very rusty tin can, and was in a remarkably good state of preservation considering the length of time it had been there.

We decided to take both the axe and record down with us in the belief that such historic articles should be preserved in a museum. A notation was made on our own record stating that we were removing both items. They were subsequently given to the museum of the American Alpine Club in New York.

We remained on the summit a total of only 15 minutes, then returned along the ridge, retrieving our rappel line and axe at the gap. While we were still on the ridge the fog cleared almost completely in the south and west, revealing spectacular views that had been hidden from us for so long. First to appear was Mount King Edward in the south, with glimpses of icefields and peaks beyond. Then, so far below us as to seem almost unreal, we saw the channels of the Athabasca River coursing over the wide gravel flats of the valley floor in a chain of a thousand intricately-braided links. The downward sweep on this side of the mountain can only be described as terrific. It amounts to over 7,000 feet in a horizontal distance of two and a half miles.

On the left, the view was still obscured by a great banner of fog which was streaming outward and upward from the ridge. Quite suddenly, almost on the northwestern horizon, the sun broke through the clouds and I saw, projected on the fog banner at the left, the ghostly shadow of myself surrounded by large concentric haloes in colors brilliant as any rainbow. Extending outward from me through the thin mist was a column of shadow which appeared to converge and focus my image. The Spectre of the Brocken! I had seen it before but never like this. I waved and so did the spectre, the shadow band between our arms sweeping through the fog in perfect unison. At the same time John, some 40 feet ahead, was being held spellbound by a similar vision. He, of course, saw only his own image as I was seeing mine.

We continued along the ridge, picking our way carefully. The apparition on my left imitated me, meticulously executing every movement as I did. Then a cloud drifted before the sun and the brilliant figure faded, only to reappear a minute or two later in hues more dazzling than ever. Finally the colors grew dim for the last time, the sun disappeared, and we were left with our race against gathering darkness.

At 7:45 p.m. we turned off the ridge and started down the east wall, following the same route which we had used during the ascent. By 9 p.m., after two rappels and a bit of climbing, we had descended only 300 feet. We halted on a little ledge 4 feet long and 2 feet wide and prepared to spend the night since we could not safely go farther in semi-darkness. Fortunately the sky was clearing rapidly and there seemed no imminent danger of storm. We put on dry socks and heavy mittens, as well as every other item of clothing we had with us. An ample lunch cheered us considerably and we settled down after roping ourselves to the mountain as a precaution against dozing off.

The night was long and there was not much divertissement. At infrequent intervals salutes boomed from the ice cliffs of the North Twin, as they had been doing ever since our arrival in the area. About midnight an arch of pale green light appeared in the northeastern sky and we hopefully waited for a display of the aurora borealis but nothing happened. The moon came up and climbed at its prescribed angle above the frigid landscape, though infinitely slowly. We shivered. Eventually a brilliant yellow sun broke over the horizon, but the light it supplied was the coldest we had seen recently.

Our cramped muscles were too jumpy for climbing. We remained on our perch for another hour until the sun's rays had perceptible warmth. The sky was almost cloudless. In the early morning the rocks were icy. Later, the rapidly melting snow began to send countless rivulets of water down the face of the black wall. The snow itself became mushy and treacherous. We had no intention of climbing down under these conditions and resorted to rappels for almost the entire extent of the upper cliffs. The general thaw was loosening the masonry and we had to be continually on the alert for falling rocks which were coming down from the wall with alarming frequency. Some of them fell from great height with no warning sound except a vicious hum as they went by, which hardly could be regarded as a warning. During the descent we made a total of eleven rappels, six of them 100 feet or more in length. Five were from pitons, the remaining six from sling ropes. No pitons were used during the ascent. On the lower slopes of the mountain, under a balmy sun and free of the danger of falling rocks, we descended the ledges, gullies and talus slopes in sleepy fashion. After a slow, two-mile climb up the glacier we reached our tent at 5:30 p.m. We had left it practically 37 hours ago.

In conclusion the writer wishes to thank Major Gibson for his hard-won but generously-given information regarding the general climbing route. Rex would have been a member of the party had not rainy weather postponed the date of departure beyond his available time. John and I were fortunate in having reasonably good weather while we were actually on the mountain and in finding snow conditions about as good as they are likely to be on Alberta. Our predecessors of recent years were much less favored in this respect.

Mount Columbia from the north. Photo: Byron Harmon. Whyte Museum of the Canadian Rockies

1950 : WHY CLIMB MOUNTAINS?

NOEL E. ODELL

S uch a question put to any mountaineer is clearly a challenging one, and a prompt answer may not always be forthcoming. The challenged one may need time to explain, indeed to justify himself and his pursuit of climbing. A mere pretext, however pertinent or wittily expressed, may seem quite inadequate to him. Nevertheless, that great climber, George Mallory, who lost his life on Mount Everest, when asked why he wanted to attempt the ascent, simply and summarily replied "Because it is there!"

The fascination of mountain climbing is really quite a complex one, and it arises in the first instance from a fundamental love of Nature, and of wild and beautiful landscape. However, mountain climbers are of all types and all callings, and in the practice of the pursuit, some phases appeal to one and others to another. But fundamentally behind these, and common to all, is the love of Nature, in perhaps her wildest and most sublime form.

An eminent Italian mountaineer and writer, Guido Rey, expressed the situation in the following words: "The mountains are so kindly and so great that they reject none of those who turn to them, and they are good to all; to the men of science who study them; to the painters and poets who seek an inspiration in them; to the sturdy climbers who zealously seek violent exercise; and to the weary who flee from the heat and turmoil of the city to refresh themselves at this pure source of physical and moral health."

And surely it can be said that the same true thesis applies to mountains the world over, and to hills of all magnitudes.

From all high places of the earth there is to be derived just that store of refreshment and recreation so yearned for, consciously as well as unconsciously, by the large sections of modern populations, which are pent up under urban and industrial conditions. And it is this class of manhood and womanhood that comprises the bulk of our modern alpine and climbing clubs throughout the world. Exiled during the greater part of the year from the sight of much else than bricks and mortar and entrapped daily within the confines of dismal office and noisy train or street-car, it is they who — unable to resist the inner impulse, that hidden flame perhaps once lit long since when chance or good fortune revealed to them the vision — make headlong for the high hills, there to worship varied fashion, but in no uncertain earnestness, at the shrine of pure Nature so remotely removed from our modern cities.

Earlier mystical philosophers undoubtedly were drawn to the mountains, fully conscious of the spiritual benefit to be obtained by sojourn and solitude amongst these supreme works of Nature. But these were necessarily men of predominantly contemplative habit, dreamers or sentimentalists mainly from the Orient, in whom was no desire

The spiritual qualities associated with the high places of mountains have been the subject of countless essays and articles in alpine journals all over the world. The ineffable, however, is elusive and few writers have been successful in communicating anything close to the full dimensions of how mountains affect the aesthetics of those who climb them. Himalayan mountaineer Noel Odell, however, comes as close as anyone in expressing the inexpressible.

– RWS

to test their strength and nerve on rocky peak and ice slope. The few in Europe who, earlier than the eighteenth century, ventured to pit their skill against the difficulties of the mountains were in truth "rarae aves", who would, on account of the claimed "insanity" or "useless folly" of their ambition, be subject to an even larger amount of incredulity and ridicule than has often in more recent times been accorded to advanced followers of the pursuit.

Such of the former group were men like Petrarch, Gesner, and Professor Josias Simler of Zurich, the latter figure being of considerable historical interest to mountaineers, since his writings give us first mention of the rudiments of the art of snowcraft as early as the year 1574. Conrad Gesner was a remarkable Swiss physician and naturalist who in the sixteenth century wrote to a friend "On the Admiration of Mountains." He said, "I have resolved to climb at least one mountain every year. What a pleasure it is to behold their hugeness, and to stand on a height far above the clouds! It awes the soul to be surrounded with the snow cathedral built by the World Architect in a single day! How empty and lowly is the life of those who crawl about on the level in order to earn their keep, and live for the passing day — who know not the earthly paradise of the mountains!" — and this, mark you in the sixteenth century, when the Alps were considered by many to be the haunt of evil spirits or monsters, and glaciers to be dragons descending the mountain valleys!

But we will have to wait until the mid-nineteenth century to see the arrival on the scene of a community of virile men ready to hold strenuous converse with high mountains, its spirit of romance and adventure restive under the conventions and restrictions of growing cities, yet imbued with a more practical philosophy than that of the earlier mystics. These laid siege to the Alps in particular, a region geographically accessible to the large centres of commerce and industry; and as the years went by and devotees increased, the greater summits were one by one attained. It was the invariable custom for these travellers to be accompanied by local peasants, often mountain hunters of chamois, who as time went on, became recognized as professionals with expert knowledge of the peculiarities of the ascents, and with whom it was deemed inadvisable, if not impossible, to dispense.

Later on, however, under the initiative of such skilled English climbers as the brothers Pilkington, and Gardiner, Hudson and Mummery, the practice of guideless climbing became increasingly adopted, to be given a greatly expanded vogue after the First Great War, when many alpine climbers found themselves unable to afford the considerable fees necessary for guides. Moreover, this band of expert leaders had frequently served its novitiate in rock climbing on British crags where it is possible to attain the highest proficiency in this specialized phase of mountain craft, apart from a modicum of ice and snow work under winter conditions. Rock climbing in Great Britain, apart from on the Continent, and more recently in the United States, has now reached a very high degree of skill and specialization, some might say over-specialization or artificiality.

In general, however, it may be claimed that the specialization of rock climbing is only the result of natural development, or evolution of the sporting aspect of the pursuit. For as Mr. Arnold Lunn, the ski mountaineer, has said with much truth and succinctness apropos of the broad issue of mountaineering specialization: "Mountaineering in its ultimate essence is not merely mountain travel. It is a duel between inanimate nature and the spirit of man, and the first duty of the mountaineer is to preserve the reality of this contest. A virgin peak is a problem, but once the peak has been proved climbable, new conditions must be introduced in order that the struggle which would lose all significance if its outcome were certain may be renewed with redoubled zest. Guideless climbing, the forcing of virgin ridges on peaks which are no longer virgin, winter mountaineering, and ski mountaineering are all modes of the same mental attitude. Difficulties, artificial difficulties if you will, are invented in order that the game may continue, for a game in which one side is assured of a walk-over will soon cease to find players."

Now, mountaineering can mean different things to different people, and while specialized rock climbing for its own sake can satisfy the most exacting demands of the gymnast or acrobat, the circumstances and surroundings under which it is conducted are likely to make a definite appeal to those of healthy philosophic proclivity. For our smaller hills are no mean hills, and in season can have most of the attributes, and perhaps all of the proportions, of real mountains, where mountain-lore in its many varied and fascinating phases can be indulged by pilgrim student or sportsman.

It will not be generally known, perhaps, that after the disastrous first ascent of the Matterhorn in 1865, when Lord Francis Douglas and three others lost their lives, Queen Victoria urged that a ban be placed upon mountaineering.

But it was not to be: mountaineering had already caught the imagination of a considerable number of prominent Englishmen, for it was they who were largely responsible for teaching the Swiss to climb their own Alpine peaks, and who inaugurated the pursuit as a sport with the foundation of the Alpine Club (London) in 1857, the original of all alpine clubs.

In these remarks I have been referring to mountaineering as alpine calling or alpine pursuit, rather than alpine mere sport. Actually to many mountaineers it is much more than alpine pursuit: it is alpine philosophy, and indeed of the nature of alpine religion. Few have expressed this aspect of our calling in more elegant terms than that international statesman, philosopher, and mountaineer, General Smuts. On the summit of his own Table Mountain, above Cape Town, when unveiling the memorial to members of the Mountain Club of South Africa, who had died in the first Great War, twenty-six years ago, General Smuts delivered an oration which was quoted throughout the world and was referred to as having been worthy of Pericles. After referring to the supreme sacrifice of these climbers, to whom Table Mountain had been the cathedral of their religion of the mountains, the General said: "Here for alpine thousand years their memory shall blend with these great rock masses and humanize them. The men and women of the coming centuries, who will in ever increasing numbers seek health and inspiration on this great mountain summit, will find here not only the spirit of Nature, but also the spirit of man blending with it, the spirit of joy in Nature deepened and intensified by the memory of the great sacrifice here recorded." He continued — "And so it has come about finally in man all moral and spiritual values are expressed in terms of altitude. The low expresses degradation both physical and moral. If we wish to express great intellectual or moral or spiritual attainments, we use the language of altitudes. We speak of men who have risen, of aims and ideals that are lofty, we place the seat of our highest religious ideals in high Heaven, and we consign all that is morally base to nethermost hell. Thus the metaphors embedded in language reflect but the realities of the progress of terrestrial life.

"The mountain is not merely something externally sublime. It has alpine great historic and spiritual meaning for us. It stands for us as the ladder of life. Nay more, it is the ladder of the soul, and in alpine curious way the source of religion. From it came the Law, from it came the Gospel in the Sermon on the Mount. We may truly say that the highest religion is the Religion of the Mountain. What is that religion? When we reach the mountain summits we leave behind us all the things that weigh heavily down below on our body and spirit. We leave behind all sense of weakness and depression; we feel alpine new freedom, alpine great exhilaration, and exaltation of the body no less than the spirit. We feel alpine great joy. The Religion of the Mountain is in reality the religion of joy, of the release of the soul from the things that weigh it down and fill it with alpine sense of weariness, sorrow and defeat.

"The religion of joy realizes the freedom of the soul, the soul's kinship to the great creative spirit, and its dominance over all the things of sense. The mountains behold us and the stars beckon to us. The mountains of our lovely land will make alpine constant appeal to us to live the higher life of joy and freedom."

On one occasion, on my way home from India during the Second War, I had the good fortune at Cape Town to make the ascent of Table Mountain with alpine climbing friend of General Smuts, and to visit Maclear's Beacon where this historic oration was delivered. That pioneer climber, A. F. Mummery, in the last chapter of his classic book, My *Climbs in the Alps and Caucasus*, describes the true mountaineer as alpine wanderer, in the sense of one who loves to be where no human being has ever been before, who attempts new ascents, and who equally, whether he succeeds or fails, delights in the fun and jollity of the struggle. This aspect of mountaineering should ever make alpine wide appeal in all countries fortunate enough to have mountains awaiting exploration. Canada is in this category, with alpine vast terrain yet to explore in the northern Rockies, as some of us found in 1947 during our expedition to the Lloyd George Mountains.

But of the more accessible ranges it can truly be said that "the mountains are good to all;" and the languid and the robust, the specialist and the more catholically minded, are each entitled to ask whatever they require of them in proportion, for their inspiration, and restoration, as well as active operation, whether in quiet contemplation, less strenuous roving, or more vigorous climbing. In the mountains at any rate they will be enabled as Mummery said, to rise above "the foul miasmas that cling to the bottoms of reeking valleys." Indeed, one's spirit must aspire ever upward, metaphorically and in actuality, raising higher and higher one's lethargic body. Or, to express it, as Robert Browning does, in another way, "*alpine* man's reach must exceed his grasp, else what's heaven for?"

The north face of Mount Rogers, B.C. Photo: Roger Laurilla

1956 : VITH GRADE CLIMBING

HANS GMOSER

I t surprised me to find that most climbers in this country don't sympathize with artificial climbing. They also don't seem to practice a classification of climbs according to their difficulties. Most of the famous alpine routes are looked upon as "suicide climbs" and some of the climbers go even as far as saying that climbs of the VIth Grade, which is the limit of the human ability, have nothing to do any more with true mountaineering. A lot could be said against that, but too much has been said already about this subject. I think there would be a much better understanding if each party knew as much about the other side as it does about its own. So I have chosen to tell you about one of those "crazy Grade VI climbs," to give you an idea of what we see and find in it. The name of the route doesn't matter here.

It was still pretty chilly as we walked along the lakeshore; a light fog kept the peaks above us hidden. Turning off the road we followed a path through the forest for a while and then found ourselves above the mist. Right in front of us rose a steep and forbidding buttress which was our goal. Looking past it, we saw all the "Goiserer Berge" and the "Dachstein Massive" with its glaciers. We didn't look too long. We were nervous, maybe a little bit scared, but there was also an eagerness in us to get there and to begin the game on the rocks. A short scramble over some grassy ledges brought us right to the beginning of the climb. The sun was still in the fog and the surroundings looked very unfriendly just then. Our eagerness seemed to have reached a record low and our gang of four was as quiet as if we were in church. Karl K. was my companion, and Franz was with Karl M.

The end of the Second World War brought a radical change in attitudes toward climbing. More traditional aspects of the mountaineering ethic were challenged by energetic, highly skilled young mountaineers. Foremost among these was a young Austrian named Hans Gmoser, who with a small but select group of friends, dramatically upgraded the standard of climbing in Canada. Gmoser went on to become a successful mountain guide and later founded Canadian Mountain Holidays, a heli-skiing empire centred in Banff.

– R W S

Above us there was overhanging rock, so smooth that there wasn't even a crack for a piton. With one foot we were standing on a 50 degree slab and the other foot we had in a horizontal crack between the wall and the slab. After about eight feet the slab broke off and below it we saw nothing but fog. We took as much time as possible to prepare for the climb. Then we were ready, still too soon to have overcome our nervousness. As I was first out on the slab, I was supposed to be the first over the overhang. In a crack too small for me, but too big for pitons, I inched myself upwards.

Every now and then I looked down to see my three pals, one foot in the crack and one foot on the slab, just as if they were keeping the overhang from falling completely. There wasn't much to hang on to, and my feet had to be satisfied with the poorest of friction holds. Finally I found a little nose, just big enough to hang a stirrup on. (How far this was against the "rules," I don't know.) This was a lot of help. But my knees were trembling so much that I was afraid it might shake the stirrup off the nose. My other foot, resting on a tiny knob, looked more like part of a sewing machine than a human leg. I was now most of the way up on this first pitch, but things got worse the higher I went. Then, almost at the goal, I was at the end of my wisdom, as well as at the end of my strength. No more holds on this cold, gray bulge and the depth below me was pulling like mad on my fingertips — and on my nerves too. It was high time for me to get down to the slab again. Karl M. had the next try, while I had a chance to observe this maneuver from a comparatively safe spot. But he didn't get any farther. After he was down again, our spirits were very low. Nevertheless I decided to have another final try. Meanwhile, the sun had come out and even patches of the lake below were visible. From up there it looked as if it was just one straight drop down into the water.

This time I made it. Don't ask me how. At one point I had wedged myself horizontally between two holds, and when I made a frantic dash upwards, I got a terrific hand-hold which was the key to the whole affair. From then on the climbing was a little easier. A few pitons which were already placed gave us a lot of comfort, even though we could look down to the lakeshore between our feet. The satisfaction of having mastered the overhang, and the beautiful weather, gave me terrific moral support, so I was able to get the next couple of rope lengths fast and clean behind me.

As we were all four on the ropes for this first half on the climb, I always had a long rest while the last two moved up. The trees seemed far below us and I could already see a few houses of the town, which had been hidden behind a hump. It was peaceful and quiet, and an occasional short rope command was the only sound. Soon I had reached a little platform which was the end of the first and most difficult step on this buttress. A few patches of grass and some alpenroses made me almost forget the difficulties of our climb.

After I had belayed Karl K. up, I stretched out on our little nose and literally let the sun shine on my stomach. It was warm and wonderful. Deep blue sky above us and down below on the lake we could see the little motorboat making its first trip over to the other side. Those gentle green hills over there made a very soothing contrast to our immediate surroundings. Before long I was sound asleep, and it wasn't until I could hear church bells from the village, that I woke up again. Holy smoke! 12 o'clock already. Where are my friends? I looked around and saw them several feet below me, trying to free the rope from a crack. They had been there for two hours, but now the rope came loose and it was high time for us to proceed.

We changed the lead and Franz went ahead. He had to get across a three foot crack onto a vertical and smooth slab. He just let himself fall over, got his rope and a stirrup into a snaplink and there he was on the slab, like a fly on the windowpane. He made his way along a hardly-visible diagonal crack to the right and soon disappeared around the edge. Only by the rope could we follow his progress.

After a few minutes he told Karl M. to follow. I went right on Karl's heels. The steepness and exposure were at their utmost, but the rock was very firm and so were the pitons which led up to a tiny ledge on which Franz was waiting for us. We called this little spot "Fliegenband" (Flyledge). Above it were two respectable overhangs, while below it there was only space, except for the lake 2000 feet farther down. Karl M. went up to the ledge and from there started to work on the first overhang. I took place beside Franz and snapped my safety loop into our piton. Above us, poor Karl M. found himself confronted with quite a problem. Piton after piton went into the rock, and he sounded like an old steam engine. When he was up on top, he could not pull the ropes in. They were crossed so many times between the pitons, that they just looked like a spider web. Now Franz had to climb up there, depending completely on himself. He dug his fingers into the rock. He labored from one piton to the other, finally having undone the whole "rope salad." This was the end of the major difficulties, and over much easier terrain we arrived on the big plateau just below the main summit.

The peak itself didn't interest us at all. It was one of those really fashionable ones, where you can find everything from two-week-old babies to cats, dogs, and ladies with painted fingernails and high-heeled shoes, which all get up there over well-prepared Alpen-vereinsteige (Alpine Club trails). We cut across some meadows and scree to one of the mountain huts. There we sat down in the grass, and while we untangled our ropes and ate our schmalz-brote (lard sandwiches), we looked at all the mountain peaks around us. The caretaker of the hut brought us some lemonade which was a real treat after a day in the hot sun. We would have liked to stay longer and enjoy the warm sun and the beautiful view upon all those familiar mountains. Unfortunately, there was still a long way ahead of us. Very easy, but still long. We went down the trail and after a few hours we walked on a real road again. At the first inn we stopped, and looking back we saw the mountain and on it the forbidding rock-faces, on which we had found an adventurous but romantic way.

Well, what is there more to say. We sat down and celebrated the occasion with a glass of beer each, and our thoughts wandered off to new mountains, new climbs. Everybody sat quietly by himself. Only in our eyes could one see the happiness and satisfaction which we brought down from the mountain.

Climbers ascending King's Trench icefall, Mount Logan. Photo: Pat Morrow

Crescent and Snowpatch Spires, Bugaboos. Photo: Pierre Lemire

1960: FIVE DAYS ON SNOWPATCH

FRED BECKEY

I t was July 26, 1959, but we did not count that day. We only spent about two hours on the face, and about half of that time was spent in climbing a rock overhang below the level of the Snowpatch bergschrund. As the day began to fade, I left in my two ropes and upper pitons.

There was really no route: we just picked a likely series of cracks that binoculars showed ran through the overhangs on the first 800 feet of the east face of Snowpatch Spire. The remainder of the 2,050 foot wall was a barrier of high angle slabs broken by an occasional shallow gully and crack system.

Rising directly above Boulder Camp, the east face is the most spectacular wall in the Bugaboos; it appears in full view from the trail along Bugaboo Creek and en route to virtually every climb in the area. Among climbers there had been a great deal of speculation as to when — and if — anyone would care to challenge its defences. If it were in the Alps this wall would rank with the greatest rock walls, the ones now famed in alpine history. In some not-too-distant day the Bugaboos will become internationally famous as Canada's most attractive rock and piton playground. But it is still the day of pioneering — the time when the big faces are being climbed.

The east face interested me, and it had an equal fascination for Hank Mather. We had done some climbing together in the springtime, near Vancouver, and with the good spell of weather at hand, it seemed logical that we join forces to make an attempt. We studied the face and concluded there were two classic possibilities on it: a direct route from the glacier to the summit, keeping well north of the snowpatch; and a right-traversing route that eventually led back to the north summit. We chose the former, after many hours of discussion. With the glass, we picked out each lead, each belay point, and each overhang. Of these, there were three major ones: we named them the Moss overhang, the White overhang (actually an inverted column), and the great Black overhanging band. Working through these, we knew, would be largely direct aid. Our hope was that we could force a piton route through, leaving fixed ropes, and then climb through in several continuous days. The upper portion of the wall had many questionable sections, but we knew that it veered back just enough to give hope of offering a possible route. We knew that we would have to live on the face a number of days. We had to be prepared for a sudden storm.

After establishing a well-stocked mountain tent on a moraine near the foot of the wall, we systematically set about the climb. July 28 was largely my day to lead. I double-roped above the bergschrund, and had to dig moss out of nearly every crack. On the overhang it was exhausting work while dangling in slings. Because of the moss and the problem of finding usable cracks, this lead took seven continuous hours and about 40 pitons; due to the fact I had to descend into the

Scanning the Canadian and American alpine journals of the 1960s and 70s, one of the most common names encountered will be Fred Beckey's. The list of his first ascents around the continent evinces a stunning combination of talent and vision, and Beckey stories are often at the heart of tales from the period. Sadly, many of his own tales of climbs have been lost through his tendency to simply give route descriptions in his accounts. This story of the ascent of the first Grade VI in the Bugaboos is a happy exception, with Mr. Beckey's joy on the route a tangible pulse throughout.

— GP

bergschrund it was about 160 feet high. The belay ledge, just one foot wide, over-hung the first half of the lead. A free rope just dangled to hit the edge of the bergschrund. I pulled up rucksack loads of ropes, pitons, food, clothing, and water; then Hank came up to take the pitons out. He continued up the next lead, find-ing it possible to climb fifth class for about fifty feet. Then, on to the next belay, the climbing again became largely sixth. He found a pedestal roomy enough for one hip, anchored in, and rappelled down. The bottom rappel turned out to be mostly free, as we had expected. So near the glacier, there was no need to spend a night sitting on the wall.

On the following two visits to the wall we spent about half the time prus-siking and pulling loads to old positions. I had lead three, which gained through a sometimes-poor, sometimes-good, moss filled crack section. There was one short overhang. We belayed from the top of an arch; there was room to sit. Hank had the fourth lead, which curved awkwardly left. Again, there was much moss to remove, and some of the pitons were very difficult to place. He used two bolts on this pitch, and during trips back to the glacier firmed up lower belays with two other bolts. The fourth lead took all day; in fact, we had to leave it unfinished and rappel off just at dark.

Now we had to plan the final push We rested several days, made a new route on the west face of the mountain, and stirred into action as August 5 dawned well. When we reached the high point Hank completed the awkward lead with some giant angles and wood wedges for wide cracks. He established himself in a hanging belay and I came past to work up a dangerously loose chimney. A wide stem, several untrustworthy pitons, a bolt, and some difficult free climbing put me on a ledge that was to become bivouac number one. We pulled our duffle-bags and rucksacks to this ledge and spent the remainder of the afternoon climb-ing pitch five and part of six. Pitch five was an inside corner leading toward the Black overhang. There was no belay spot on the lead so I set up a hanging belay with two stirrups. Hank climbed up a vertical wall with pitons for aid and lateral tension as he worked up onto a slab on the left. This brought him to the Black overhang, where it was necessary to place our largest wooden wedge. Even so, he could not get over the overhang's lip with the equipment he had, so he finally had to drill two bolt holes and place our smallest type of bolts (3/16 inch), then more blocks and giant angle pitons. It was an exhausting place, and once over, he

swung down the rope for the night. We had hoped to find a bivouac ledge higher, but we did not want to chance the uncertainty of completing the pitch in time.

We roped ourselves in on the ledge below as best we could. We were tied to pitons, and sat up all night inside our zeltsack. Sleep was rather impossible under the conditions, but we did drowse and get some needed rest. In the morning we were shivering with cold, and had to prussik up a fixed rope that was frozen solid from running water for the first thirty feet. Fingers became so cold that they burned with pain. Hank tensioned up the overhang and spent about two hours completing the remainder of a crack he was using to direct-aid to a sloping plat-form. Here he put in a bolt for protection and pulled up the loads. Some of the rucksacks became stuck on the overhang; it became necessary for me to take them up when I prussiked up the pitch. All this added to the confusion of ropes and equipment, and greatly delayed us as well. The first half of this day was undoubt-edly the low point of our luck, progress, and morale.

At about four o'clock we were organized enough to continue onward. The character of the climb now changed drastically — or so it seemed. There were no more overhangs, and we could even glimpse the top, about 1,000 feet above us. To our left was the famous snowpatch, at about our height. Technically, we knew the worst was over; with care, luck, and good weather we felt confident that we would climb through. To lighten our loads we threw about a dozen small bundles of equipment off the wall; many of them fell clear, and all were picked up on the glacier below by Elfrida Pigou. Feeling more optimistic we progressed with renewed vigor, and completed four leads before dark. These were largely fifth class, with an occasional piton for aid. Two or three times the climbing was extreme — it was never easy. We stopped at a pre-selected ledge. We were thank-ful that there was a tiny patch of snow here, for our water and canned fruit were almost gone. We tied in again and spent another uncomfortable night — this time on a small patch of granite sand on a 30° ledge. Occasionally a light would flicker from the camp below. In the morning a signal confirmed our concern over scud clouds floating by: the barometer was falling.

Except for the second lead that morning, the final push was all fifth class. We were concerned over the prospect of a storm, so climbed with anxiety. The last two leads turned out the easiest, thankfully, and shortly past noon we stood happily on the summit.

The Bugaboos around us seemed more beautiful than ever. It was the first chance we had to admire the vista and get our perspective back. We saw Elfrida climbing over the Bugaboo col. The thought of hot tea on the Warren got us into action. The rappel descent of the west face route went quickly, as we had left in our slings from the climb of a week before. We drilled a bolt anchor on the slab just after the short summit rappel, as piton cracks were poor and there was not any natural anchor. Future parties on any Snowpatch climb would do well to use our descent route to the Warren. Now that the east face had been conquered there was only one more chore: that was to prussik back up the ropes on the first three leads on the wall. We had left them in just in the event a storm overtook us and we had to make a sudden retreat.

The Vowell Spires. Photo: Roger Laurilla

The Whitemantle Range, Coast Mountains. Photo: Baiba Morrow

1962: THE FACE OF THE SQUAMISH CHIEF

ED COOPER

The Squamish Chief is probably familiar to most of those who have driven from Vancouver to Squamish. One can hardly miss it, as the Chief dominates the view several miles either side of the highway. It has a beautiful setting at the head of Howe Sound, above the town of Squamish with Mt. Garibaldi visible in the background. The first time I gazed at the Chief, in 1958, it was with awe, and without a thought of attempting it. One's technique and ambition grow, and in the fall of 1960 while rock climbing in the area with Jim Baldwin of Prince Rupert, B.C., we looked at the 1700-foot face of the Squamish Chief and decided it didn't look so bad. In fact we would have started up at once except it was late in the year (November) and the monsoons had come. Instead we planned a spring assault. One rainy day early in May we arrived at the base of the Chief and went at the brush with machetes and axes until several hours later we found ourselves at a small clearing at the bottom of the face, staring up at an absolutely incredible view. Staring too long, I got dizzy and nearly fell over backwards. It later took less than fifteen minutes over the trail to the bottom of the face. The excellent trail is still there, blazed right from the highway. At this time our base camp was located up an old dirt road near the Chief in an abandoned dynamite shack.

We returned several days later in a moderately heavy rain, and set up an equipment tent, stocking it with ropes and pitons. Enthusiasm being at a high pitch we decided to go up a way, and wound up climbing the first pitch. The rain-soaked rock, lichen, and moss forced us to climb it all artificially. The piton cracks on this pitch were the best for the next 1500 feet. At the end of the pitch was a nice ledge (in fact, the nicest for the next 900 feet with a large tree to which we anchored our first fixed rope.

The next day we again returned, spent much time in organizing equipment, and for good measure climbed the second pitch, the flake chimney. Although water was everywhere dripping, this was climbed entirely non aid (+IV), and was one of the two non-artificial pitches on the entire climb. From here our work would begin — we would have to step out on the "apron," part of the smooth flawless wall.

Any further progress could now only be made with the use of bolts, as there simply were no piton cracks. While many climbers consider the use of bolts unethical, it would have been absolutely impossible to do the climb without them, and over 130 were used. Neither Jim nor I had ever seen a rock formation anywhere else with as noticeable a lack of piton cracks. My ascent last year of the East Face of Bugaboo Spire had used only twelve bolts,

The late '50s and '60s were the years of the iron-men of the Canadian climbing scene. Technique, equipment and guts timely intertwined, producing a wealth of new routes, alpine and rock, several of which would go unrepeated for years. The first ascent of the Grand Wall on the Squamish Chief by Seattle climber Ed Cooper (whose photos would become well known to readers of the Journal in subsequent years) and Canadian Jim Baldwin is a good example of the no-holds-barred ethic of the day: the ascent stretched over a month, attracted a great deal of attention, and got its share of criticism in the climbing community. Whatever one might say about about the siege ethic and the 136 bolts on the route, the ascent started the Squamish climbing scene on a roll that has lasted into the present day.

— GP

the most I had used on any other climb. For the remaining distance up the apron and the beginning of the Grand Wall to the bottom of the Split Pillar many bolts were used, occasional knife blade and other odd pitons coming in handy, always behind flakes of one type or another, and never in cracks on the face proper.

Low on the apron we were spotted, and the word quickly spread about the climbers on the Chief. Soon small crowds would gather every night both on the highway and at the very foot of the wall to watch us descend. These small crowds grew to large crowds until one weekend the highway was jammed with 12,000 cars all attempting to get a look. Before we realized what happened, the residents of Squamish, not without some interest in the tourist business, sponsored us everything we needed, including 1500 feet of nylon rope. Quite novel and enjoyable at first, all this attention that we received turned from a boon almost to a bane. We were not left alone for a moment. One afternoon a newspaperman had the gall to shout up at us to come down immediately so he could get some pictures. About this time all the publicity drew several other climbers, who planned an assault on the face very near ours. Fortunately this did not happen. All this was not without effect on our climbing; we no longer felt that we were doing the climb because *we* wanted to do it.

To return to the climb, the ascent of the Split Pillar was accomplished mostly with pitons. The upper extension of the Split Pillar, above the only sitting ledge in 750 feet, was especially trying. It ominously split even further from the wall when pitons were being driven behind it, and in one instance the lower piton popped out while the upper piton was being driven, the climber (Jim) not falling because of our precaution of snapping into upper pitons as soon as we started to drive them. The single feature that bothered us the most was the Sword of Damocles, a giant 200-foot flake that extended out from the upper portion of the Split Pillar and vibrated like a giant gong when bolts or pitons were being driven in or behind it. It was possible to look up under the Sword of Damocles, at its start, until the view disappeared in a black abyss.

Altogether some two weeks were spent climbing and fix-roping the first 850 feet to the top of the Grand Wall. Here the route would go on long traverses and it was impractical to fix ropes any more. We prepared carefully for the final assault. With all the rope we had acquired we had enough rope to lower some food and two gallons of water to a prominent ledge with trees on it, some 650 feet

below the top, and 400 feet below the last of the severe difficulties. Our plan was to reach this ledge at the end of the first day or the beginning of the second day on the face, *before* the sun would reach us (the Squamish Chief faces directly west, and receives the afternoon sun about 1 p.m.).

Waiting a week until we were assured of several days of settled weather, we set out with a small quantity of food and two quarts of water apiece early one June morning. We had more difficulty than anticipated in clearing the upper section of the Grand Wall of hardware, and Jim was caught by the sun working hard on this section. He was quite spent upon reaching my position at the top of the Grand Wall, and rather than stopping there for the night I made the mistake of pushing on to the next lead. Although I made it in a rather desperate fashion as darkness was closing in, the extra height gained did not offset the added effect of exhaustion produced by the effort in the oven-like heat. (Temperatures down in Squamish reached into the high 90s we later found out.) All our water was finished that evening, and we could only hope that we would reach the large tree ledge before the sun hit us the next day. We spent the night a rope's length apart, Jim sitting at "rat's rest" (for an unexplained rat that bothered him during the night) and I at "sleepy hollow," a small cave in the rock in which it was possible to lie, but not sit. The night remained hot and still, with clouds of mosquitoes.

The next day promised to be even hotter. One p.m. found Jim still struggling up the lower part of the slightly overhanging last pitch to the tree ledge, the detached flake pitch; another large flake that vibrated ominously. By the time I had removed the hardware and reached him we both felt at the end of our strength and could only lie exhausted the rest of the day. We drank a gallon of our two gallons of water, that had been lowered to the tree ledge, on the spot. It was impossible to eat any food. Greatly weakened, but feeling somewhat better, we climbed slowly above the tree ledge until the sun reached us, and then descended to an excellent ledge (the best on the entire climb, being a level five feet by seven feet) where we spent the rest of the day in the shade of a small tree. The large tree ledge, though many times larger than this ledge, had all been disappointingly sloping at 30°.

The next morning we were again out of water, and moving slowly and irrationally, it was here we made some mistakes in our choice of route which caused us to spend even another day on the wall. Even very little things now became difficult, but by early that afternoon we had reached the entrance to the Roman Chimney (for the giant sweeping pillars which flank it on its right side). There is here an amazing chockstone wedged in the very bottom of the chimney. The next day, with Jim belaying from this chockstone, I started up towards the large overhang which completely blocked the view of the last pitch, a vertical *dièdre*, which we knew was above.

Working entirely on pitons I reached the lip of the overhang where it was necessary to place a bolt on top of a small ledge. This was by its very nature a hazardous position, and I had prussiks attached to the rope, ready for immediate use in case of a fall which could leave me hanging. While placing the bolt, I was twice conscious of the piton I was standing on shifting its position. Once placed, a large crack fanned out from the bolt, and another bolt, in a more difficult position, had to be placed. In all my mountaineering experience, this was the most spectacular place I had ever been. Jim followed and removed the hardware, and continued on the last lead, the fifty foot *dièdre*. We had only four pitons that fitted the crack, so that it was necessary, as on several other places during the climb, to take the lower ones out and replace them higher as we moved up, not a practice that is recommended for common use. The very last piton came out as Jim grabbed a bush overhanging the *dièdre*. Less than a half an hour later, late in the afternoon of the fifth day, we reached the cool water of the stream running beside the trail up the back side of the Chief, and drank our fill of that sweet nectar of life.

Arriving back in town that evening, we did not even get a full night's sleep before being awakened by reporters and photographers. I must add our indebtedness to those people of Squamish, especially the Mackenzies and Pat Brennan, who were kind, and understanding of our privacy, and without whose help and assistance the climb would have been even more difficult than it was. Regarding the time it took for the initial ascent, it must be remembered that many, in fact most, of the days were only part days, and much of that time was spent in prussiking up, untangling snarls from the previous day, and rappeling down. Even on the final assault we climbed only one full day (the first) and half of that day was spent in gaining our previous high point and removing hardware from previous days. We would have spent nights on the face in the initial phase of the assault, except that there was no ledge, until about the 1000-foot level, that was really suitable for spending nights and storing supplies. We did spend one night on top of the Split Pillar, at the 600-foot level, but this proved uncomfortable enough (one can fall off it not only in the front, but also in the back, where it is split away from the main wall by a foot and a half) that we did not spend another night there. Further, due to the slow progress one makes with bolts, it is impossible to spend much time in any single day putting them in before it becomes necessary to stop for the day. Slow progress makes one psychologically discouraged, which makes for even slower progress.

With all the bolts in place, and some of the pitons, no doubt the next party will climb it in its entirety in as little as two days, and will not be able to understand the long time spent on the first ascent, and bolts or pitons placed in seemingly ridiculous or superfluous positions (much of this due to the effects of heat on the final assault). But no one who climbs the face of the Squamish Chief will fail to appreciate the fact that he has done a difficult climb.

117

Mount Temple, North Face. Photo: George Noble. Whyte Museum of the Canadian Rockies

1967 : MOUNT TEMPLE, NORTH FACE

CHARLES LOCKE

"We had lost contact with the ground. It was as if we were completely and seemingly forever part of an environment of vertical rock, ice and cloud."

— John Harlin

E ven before I began climbing, the reputation of Mount Temple's north face reached my ears. Her sneer of cold command and the icy shadow of her cold gray walls invested in my heart a feeling of tinyness and helplessness; and yet within my body the secret coals of desire flared up whenever I heard people talking about it or whenever I studied it while riding up the Whitehorn sedan lift across the Bow River valley not far from Lake Louise. I wanted desperately to be one of the party to make the first ascent.

As each day of the summer of 1966 passed, I kicked myself for procrastinating and worried constantly that someone would attempt it while I labored away the sunny summer days. While in the Bugaboos during the first weekend in August, Brian Greenwood approached me and asked me to accompany him and Heinz Kahl on an attempt on this north face. I needed no persuasion, and gave up my job.

The 5000-foot high north face could be broken down into three rough sections. A large and conspicuous ice couloir, named the Dolphin, dominates the lower half of the face. Above this icy section the face immediately steepens into a seemingly vertical rockwall which Brian, in his article in the *American Alpine Journal*, calls the depression. This depression is capped for over half its length by a hanging glacier through which the possibility of exit remains uncertain. The upper section consists of a glacier which flows down from the summit and hangs even further down to the left of the depression.

On the evening of August 2 we met in Banff to formulate plans. Brian and Heinz had differing views as to which route we should follow. Heinz swore that the only route up the face was to climb the rocks to the right of the Dolphin until the lower edge of the depression. From there he proposed to traverse across to the hanging glacier along one of the ice ledges which cross the face. He then proposed we climb through the glacier and from there work our way up the easy snow slopes to the summit. Brian remained adamant in his belief that we should climb up the right-hand side of the depression and traverse leftwards across the depression then push our way through the glacier on what appeared to be a ramp. I had no preferences myself. We decided to postpone our start until Thursday August 4 in order to give us more time for preparation.

Wednesday afternoon we walked into Lake Annette to reconnoiter the face. Soon after we arrived thunderstorms poured rain upon us and lightning raked the ridges. It rained more or less continuously throughout the night but by 4 a.m. the clouds appeared to be breaking and we started. We realized we had to move swiftly so as to avoid the rockfall on the lower face.

The huge north faces of the larger mountains in the Rockies were becoming increasingly attractive to the big wall climbers of the 1960's. Prone to rock and ice falls, these steep walls challenged endurance, skill and luck. Brian Greenwood and Charlie Locke were pioneers on these big routes. An interesting footnote to this article is that Mr. Locke later became owner of Lake Louise ski area, which he might have looked down upon through much of this historic first ascent.
– RWS

This we did as we headed toward the right-hand and smaller of the two prominent couloirs that sweep down from the Dolphin. Brian and I rapidly ascended the firm snow and then traversed onto the rocks to the left; Heinz followed somewhat more slowly. On stopping to wait for Heinz, Brian and I recalled that he had not been feeling well the previous day. Upon reaching us Heinz told us of his discomfort and decided to descend. It must have taken great courage to do this and I admired him for it; I am certain he wanted this climb as badly as anyone.

The sun had now begun to wake up the mountain. Serenaded by the hum and clatter of almost continuous rockfall, we climbed swiftly up these rocks. On a small ridge, perhaps halfway up the face and a little below the top of the Dolphin, we roped up. I'm afraid I cannot remember each pitch but a few remain vividly in my mind. Brian started up. We "leapfrogged" for four pitches until the ridge was blocked by a seemingly vertical buttress. The only feasible thing to do was to traverse left on a ledge or at least what appeared to be a ledge. Soft snow on 45-degree smooth ice didn't give us a great deal of confidence in the ledges which the face seemed to offer. Brian was able, by carefully packing down the snow, to form steps that held his weight. But often these precarious steps would not be adequate and he was forced to chip out steps in the underlying ice. Following the upper rim of the ledge, he continued his traverse, his hands on the rock and his feet on the ice. The idea of continuing this slow procedure all the way across the face seemed ludicrous, so at the first opportunity Brian left the ledge and ascended diagonally upward for a short distance. I joined him, retrieving the occasional piton he was able to insert into the loose rock to retard a swing should either of us fall. Lucky thing he did, as I slid a few feet while working my way up to the top of the ledge.

I led up one rope length then Brian joined me and traversed a few feet to the edge of the depression. On returning he seemed heart-broken. We had that sudden realization that we could not do the direct route. The snow ledges we had looked upon for years proved to be more formidable-looking than the ones we had just crossed. The chimneys we viewed from the bottom were waterworn corners, the rock appeared devoid of cracks, the ramp through the ice was non-existent. We were not about to turn back although small cirrus clouds foretold the coming of a low-pressure area.

We climbed up a not-too-prominent buttress, occasionally venturing into the depression. The quality of the rock made the grade 5 climbing quite pleasant and helped shield our disappointment. We used a few pitons — some for protection, others for aid — as we slowly worked our way upwards. Toward mid-afternoon a small plane flew by the face four times. We realized that someone was looking for us and I began to doubt the fact that I was in the Rockies and visualized myself struggling up the north face of the Eiger. The next day we learned that it was Bill Smythe, from the Moraine Lake Lodge, and Heinz checking on our progress. Just as we reached the small ledge where we spent the night, an ominous roar deafened us and a large amount of snow and ice parted company with the glacier, swept the depression, shattered on a small ledge we had just traversed, and crashed into the depths below. We were thankful that we had veered from our intended route and succumbed to the safety the buttress offered. It began to rain as we cooked soup and made ourselves as comfortable as we could. The rain later turned to snow but as we were huddled under an overhang we kept relatively dry.

Dawn came and we found ourselves enveloped in a sea of mist. Wet snow was falling as Brian prepared to lead the first pitch. Above, the climbing seemed difficult but not excessively so. Whereas on the previous day Brian and I alternated leads, today Brian led all but two short pitches of the final 500 feet. The continuous tension of the never-ending grade 5 pitches, unrelieved by easier climbing, was beginning to have its psychological effect on me and I was only too glad to let him lead.

A final steep section, requiring aid for a short distance, ended with a strenuous pull over an overhanging bulge. We were now nearly on top of the face and after two short ascending traverses over rock and snow were standing on top of the wall. Unroping, we continued to the summit.

During the previous day and a half we encountered some difficult climbing but at no point did we go to our limit. We used about 35 pitons (not including those used for anchors). Most were used for protection with the exception of the one short stretch where we resorted to direct aid. Brian grades this climb as NCCS III, F7. Even though we veered from our proposed route, we felt a great sense of achievement. The centre of the face, continually swept by rock and icefall and capped by a glacier, through which the possibility of exit appears uncertain, remains unclimbed. Perhaps some day its lure will attract some climbers who will push the perfect route up the north face.

Fairy Meadows, Sir Sandford. Photo: Ray Kodama

West face of the Howser Towers. Photo: Dave Stark.

1972 : THE WEST FACE OF NORTH HOWSER TOWER

CHRIS JONES

W
hen do climbs begin? Not when we rope up at the start surely, but when the idea of the climb first begins to intrigue us. Maybe we have read about the route in a journal, or have seen a peak in the distance that excited us. Then, often over several years, some of these shadowy ideas begin really to take hold to become climbs that we simply have to do — we are obsessed by them.

It must have been sometime in 1966 that I first read Chouinard's Yosemite exposé, with its call to arms to attempt the great alpine walls. "The future of Yosemite climbing lies not in Yosemite, but in using the new techniques in the great granite ranges of the world… The western faces of the Howser Spires are from 3,000 to 5,000 feet high… Who will make the first ascents of these breathtaking rock faces?" (*American Alpine Journal*, 1963)

In 1967 I was in the Bugaboos for the first time. That year I went 300 yards beyond Boulder Camp before breaking my leg bouldering, (or perhaps failing to boulder), an activity I have subsequently shied away from. A bad omen, I should have sold all my gear and taken up bird watching. Shortly after my crash three Chicago climbers arrived in camp having just climbed the west face of North Howser. Chouinard, who was with us on this ill-fated trip, questioned them closely on their climb and afterwards said that he was certain their route was near the existing Beckey-Greenwood route, and not on the big face. (Beckey has since said their route should be called the Northwest Face.) Around 1969, thinking Canada once more, I read both Zven-Growski's account and Beckey's, where he states "it is the highest precipice in the range and, until Brian Greenwood and I climbed it on August 5, perhaps its outstanding unclimbed challenge," but from all I could tell the real prize was still waiting.

At this time the idea of the Howser face was just one of many. I made a point of talking to Beckey, however and received the usual vague reply, and from Chouinard heard about the violent storms that sweep into the Howsers from the west — "You wouldn't be able to move in one of those mothers." By early 1970 Canada was again luring me, and I began to comb old journals for new clues. The description of the first climb on the back side of the Howsers — the West Buttress of South Howser by Beckey and Chouinard — was intriguing enough, "an overwhelming panorama of granite buttresses and couloirs…. Our immediate reaction was: Patagonia, the Howsers looking like FitzRoy and Cerro Torre and their satellites all grouped together." But I had yet to see a single photo of the face. By all accounts the wall was larger than El Capitan with a reputation for bad storms. Obviously this was not a climb that would appeal to everyone — I was far from certain that it appealed to me. One evening in Galen Rowell's "war room" he showed pictures of what he had seen of the Howsers from

While a few Canadians were struggling at the leading edge of what was being done in technical climbing, professional mountaineers from abroad were targeting first ascent routes on big walls in Canada. If Chris Jones's article sounds like a lot of name dropping, it is because he was included in a circle of the most accomplished climbers of the day. Adventurous Canadians, modelling themselves after these big names, were becoming increasingly outbound in their thinking. Their attempts on famous routes in places like Yosemite taught them much.
– RWS

Pigeon. "What about that pillar on South Howser?" said he. "Yes, could be… or maybe the big face, it sort of appeals more," said I. Whatever, we were going to get a close look at the beast. Sometime later Brian Greenwood suggested that we join a Calgary group who were having supplies helicoptered into the Howsers, and, when Galen was finally unable to come, we established ourselves under a boulder beneath these Patagonian walls.

Several days of snow and liar dice later the weather cleared and we had our first real look. Or was it real? Vast granite walls bore down on us, enclosed us, demoralized us. Camp was on a spur beneath Central Howser and, way below our spur, the almost unbelievable wall on North Howser began to pass us and continue some 2000 feet more to the summit. Bigger than the west face of the Dru, it was far more oppressive than I had supposed: too large to comprehend, too large for us. Luckily there were alternatives. From the glacier above us a ledge led onto the southwest face of North Howser and connected with a prominent crack system. While this was not the big daddy, it promised to be an excellent climb, and one we would come to grips with. After the climb, in order to photograph the face, I went as far as I could down the spur between Central and North Howser. I made a schematic of the face with the possible routes marked down. Though not at all certain that I wanted to return, I knew one thing — the problem of the west face had not been solved.

During the winter, knowing I do not have to put plans into practice for some months yet, I usually become bolder. Sitting round a good fire with a jug of ale, snow swirling outside, I wonder why I did not attempt such and such last year. Getting too old, too cautious? After all, it was not that bad! By insidious means such as these the formerly impossible becomes possible, even attractive.

The following spring Galen and I studied pictures of the wall, thought about it and decided to give it a whirl. It seemed to us that the climb would take three to four days, combining the scale of El Cap with the objective problems of a remote alpine expedition.

Certain climbs become landmarks for us, before we attempt them we know that we are deliberately reaching out, and, when they are behind us they provide a basis, a reference point. Perhaps the most significant climb for me in this respect was the Walker Spur of the Grandes Jorasses. It turned out that I could do, even enjoy these legendary climbs — it was all pretty exciting. Four years later under

Chouinard's watchful eye, we were attempting what appeared to me to be an awesome new route — the north face of Assiniboine. Once more this enabled me to expand my horizons and now we were up against it again on the west face. No American party, as far as we knew, had yet climbed such a large Yosemite type wall in a remote alpine setting — was this what Chouinard had been talking about?

In the spring of 1971 all sorts of rumours popped up: a Calgary contingent were going to helicopter into the Howsers to siege the climb if necessary; then Chouinard was supposed to be going in. In the end a poor spell of weather washed out the Calgary team and it looked as if Galen and I would be hoofing it alone.

A week before Galen was in Canada, I was in the Bugs with Tony Qamar and sold him on the west face, sight unseen. This was good for morale all round, a three-man party being stronger than two. We ferried loads into the Howsers and saw my old adversary in a new light — this time we were after it. Back down the dusty Bugaboo road and in again I met Hans Gmoser loping down. "Where are you headed?" "Oh, to the back side of the Howsers." "Ah-ha, unfinished business," said Hans with a knowing smile.

Originally we had planned to use bat tents, but as only Galen had one, we ditched that idea in favor of lighter gear, the old compromise between speed and safety. There was snow visible on some ledges so I hoped to avoid having to haul water. The discussion was resolved when I stumbled and threw our water bottles to the depths below. With four days food, ice axes, bivouac food and so on, our haul bags would be heavy enough anyway. After another excellent meal on the supplies we left last year, labeled "ragoût de boeuf" on the can, but known to you and I as stew, I was woken by both the alarm and snow drifting onto my face. "Hell, we're screwed, its snowing." "Damn right, I'm getting wet, move over."

Later that day it cleared, and we took the chance to make a topo of our proposed route and the variations. The harder we peered at the climb, the better it looked. The following morning, as I was about to enter the descent couloir, we noticed my day pack was coming apart. Already looking like a patchwork quilt, I fixed it again — we were not about to stop now for lack of equipment.

After a hard first pitch Galen called down that the climbing eased above him. This lower part of the wall has only one weakness, and from the spur we had never been able to see what it was really like. The overall difficulty of the route would depend greatly on this section, and it was turning out easier than we had anticipated. In a gully for the most part, the climbing was mostly moderate fifth, sack hauling evolving into horrendous bouts of sack carrying. Delicate face climbing eventually took us onto a ledge leading to the spur we had to reach.

After one day we were where we had expected to be after two, the weather was perfect, and ahead the climbing looked superb. I was both pleased and disappointed, for we had built ourselves up to a major effort. It would be good to see if we were up to it.

The next day we had all the difficulty we wanted, the climbing being consistently at 5.7 or above. With a lighter haul sack and the increased steepness of the face we began to cover ground rapidly. The second man would jumar up the rope and immediately begin the next pitch while the third man would remove the pitons. Our Yosemite experience paid off as we seemed to devour each succeeding pitch with cold-blooded efficiency. It was hard climbing, some dozen pitches being 5.8 or higher, but all free save for 30 feet we kept right on storming up. As we neared the summit our topo was a decisive factor in enabling us to choose from a number of possibilities. After a region of poor rock, the first on the climb, we broke out onto the summit ridge. Racing the clock our 34th lead brought us on top just before sunset, to be greeted by the shouts of a party on Bugaboo Spire.

Back at camp the next day we went over the climb. True, it had not been as demanding as we had expected, yet it was probably the first Grade VI in the Interior Ranges on what is most likely the greatest granite face in the Interior. Although we had not made a personal breakthrough to a new alpinism we had made an exceptional climb that stood as its own justification. The fact that we had been prepared to go beyond what was familiar, to try something new, was also most significant to us, for the decision to attempt a major climb, to crack the aura that surrounds it, is often as hard as the climb itself.

Chivalrous aid climbing. Photo: Georgia Engelhard. Whyte Museum of the Canadian Rockies

The summit of Good Neighbour Peak, with the north face of Mount Logan in the distance. Photo: Barry Blanchard.

1972: YOSEMITE: EL CAP, SPRING '71

HUGH BURTON

Half a year of planning, psyching up, getting in shape and scraping together money. Finally it's cruising time. A $150 grant from the Alpine Club of Canada buys more iron and ropes in Seattle. Another huge semi floats past a heap of soaked equipment and shivering bodies. Two days of miserable hitching, but finally we're swept into the valley down a corridor of blue skies and 85° breezes.

After gazing at pictures for months, it's finally there in front of you; tangible and twice as massive as you expected. A vertical desert, shimmering like a mirage in the heat waves pouring off the valley floor. You shake your head and look again, but it's still there. An exquisite flow, continuous from the ground right through the glass-smooth, immense, final headwall. We wonder why it hasn't long since been climbed but don't argue about it much and fix two leads instead. El Cap at sunset: a scarlet temple two weeks high. What an incredible trip it's going to be.

At 3 o'clock we wake abruptly to the sound of bursting water bottles. A typical valley bear is scrounging around in our haulbag for food. We're short some water but go on anyway. The haulbag just barely budges on the low angle slabs but the nailing's cake and we make good time.

Steve gets into some thin stuff and ends up ripping five pins. The fall gives us confidence and we start to settle down. On the second try he gets it. A few bolts then a steep pendulum from a wild corner. We're working in twilight now and still no ledges. We string our hammocks and cram ourselves into the corner. It seems strange hammocking so uncomfortably so close to the ground but it feels good to be up.

The morning brings rain and low spirits. Steve does a long lead ending in some loose stuff to a tiny stance. We decide to pass up a hammocks-in-th- rain scene while we still have the choice. We just barely make the ground with our four ropes. After getting together some more food and water we jumar back up in the morning.

Finally we're off! Over a small overhang, then some more borderline nailing to a new crack that heads skyward. A blank section that we were worried about takes six bolts horizontally right out of the top of the crack. The sun slowly creeps around the Nose and soon we're bathed in its golden glow. The sweet scents of pines and baytrees waft across the wall promising another warm spring day. Steve places two more bolts before I lower him to attempt a pendulum. Numerous unsuccessful cliff-hanger catches and God knows what else pass before he gets his pin up under some loose flake by hitting it in on the run. Gale force winds spring up and whip our dangling

The inclusion of this ramble through Yosemite big wall climbing in the 1970s might block an opportunity to detail some of the world-class wall climbing being done at home by the Squamish hard core — Hugh and John Burton, Steve Sutton, Paul Piro, Gordie Smaill and several others — but illustrating Burton's stature amongst the Yosemite climbers is probably the best way to show how the Canadian abilities on rock were skyrocketing. Burton and Sutton were responsible for a number of major wall routes in the mecca of Yosemite, and like much Canadian talent, eventually melted into the States. Happily, however, not before they had created many of the Squamish classics.

– GP

127

ropes horizontally across the wall. It's really wild! Deep solution buckets unlike anything I've ever seen before go mostly free to face-climbing in a corner. Darkness rapidly sweeps the wall. Hammocks again. No ledges yet except the 4th Class jugs in our backs. We re super uncomfortable so instead of sleeping we eat popcorn and gaze down the wall all night. Drops of rain alternate with an unbelievable array of stars.

Dawn comes. Two long leads on strangely contoured rock leave us on the phenomenal Mammoth Terraces. We decide to pack it in for the day. Immediately we break into our bivy equipment specially carried for such dire circumstances We explore our split-level bivy ledge, our first haven from the vertical in three days. The sunset rises to a crescendo of scarlet then leaves us breathless in a sea of brilliant stars. There's some saying about red skies at night so we aren't terrified by some harmless-looking fleecy efforts collecting to the southwest. One minute you're gazing into infinite depths of space; an hour later you wake up in a blizzard. Quickly we pile our gear which is neatly distributed all over the ledge and haul out the rain tarp. Maybe Jimmie sabotaged our haulbag or something, but our 9 by 12-foot tarp is only 3 by 8 feet. It's worse than useless. Snow blasts in from all sides and the howling winds tear at us. We polish off our emergency bivy stash and try to stay warm. Light comes agonizingly slowly but with it comes a lull in the storm. Everything is totally soaked and our iron and ropes are buried.

After coming so far it's hard to admit defeat. We're screwed so bad it's almost funny. Getting down will be a problem in itself. We cram our unneeded down equipment and food into the haulbag and give it the boot. Enviously we watch it float effortlessly to the ground unharmed. If only we had parachutes! We aren't sure if there's a rap route down from Heart Ledge so we decide to retreat down the Salathe. That was a bad mistake! We shoulder the 40-pound packs and start rapping, Immediately it starts to hail furiously. The wind gusts to 50 and waves of hail sweep down the wall and over us. We have to place bolts hanging at the end of several rappels that end up in the middle of nowhere. Ropes jam and freeze up, jumars slip, and we freeze solid. Fingers seem like elbows when you're trying to get the brake bar setup on. Eventually we get close enough to reach the ground with our four ropes. Actually we're short by 30 feet. Steve strings all the etriers and slings together and we drop down the last bit off jumars on the end of the rope. We're so wrecked we can barely walk.

Hot showers are unreal. We return to El Cap to watch the progress of my brother John and Paul Piro descending from two days up on the N.A. Wall. They're totalled too, physically and mentally. We returned next morning to retrieve our jumars but some beautiful turdish creep relieved us of them overnight. So we split.

Mounts Victoria and Lefroy. Photo: Greg Horne

O, Le Tabernac. Mount Wilson, Alberta. Photo: Jeff Lakes

BUGS MCKEITH

I ce climbing in the Canadian Rockies in winter is a very recent development. Only in the last two years has it become popular and then only with a handful of local climbers from Calgary and Banff.

There are basic differences between ice climbing here and in Scotland, the traditional hot-bed of the sport. Most significant is the quality of the ice: green and plastic at its best in Scotland, typically hard blue or grey and extremely brittle in Canada. Here after the first freeze in late October or November the ice rarely gets a chance to thaw and refreeze (as it does frequently in Scotland) until late on in the spring. During the average winter the temperature may easily drop to -50°F (-45°C) on one or two occasions. Snow has no chance to consolidate except in avalanche gullies. In fact the powder snow avalanche constitutes the greatest single objective danger. Many of the best climbs emerge not on a ridge or plateau as they might in Scotland but at the base of huge avalanche bowls which after heavy snowfall can become veritable death traps. The often virtually bottomless snow poses yet another problem — the approach. People will argue till Doomsday about the relative merits of snowshoes, alpine skis with skins and climbing boots, and the much lighter cross-country skis and boots in conjunction with climbing ski waxes. I personally favour the latter and have found that even in deep soft snow where virtually helpless on foot, one may move more quickly and with less effort than over the same distance on foot when the ground is clear of snow. After initial frustrations with technique and waxes, most eventually come to the same conclusion.

The Canadian Alpine Journal *recorded many important pioneering advances into winter mountaineering, but perhaps none as significant as the rapid evolution and popularization of ice climbing. Two climbers at the extreme edge of this very exacting and demanding sport were Bugs McKeith and John Lauchlan. Both advanced both the tools and the technique of ice climbing. Unfortunately, both died at the peaks of their careers in climbing accidents.*
– R W S

The late development of winter ice climbing in Canada was primarily dictated by the extremely hard and brittle nature of the ice, which virtually precluded the traditional process of step cutting. Apart from the loomingly obvious Cascade Icefall above the traffic circle on the Trans-Canada highway near Banff (almost climbed by Lloyd McKay and a friend from Vancouver in 1965) and a few other isolated ventures, nothing was done until the full potential of modern ice climbing equipment was realized and the Terrordactyl stood out as the tool best suited to the purpose.

In the winter of 1972–73, seeds were planted to blossom into one of the most exciting things to happen in the Rockies since the big peaks were first climbed. Cascade Icefall became a deservedly popular route, for a while looking as though it had become the only ice climb to do in the Rockies. About this time the Scottish winter grading system was adopted and the climb was considered the textbook Grade 3. But it didn't take much imagination to realize that there was more to do — a lot more! In March, 1973, three new ice climbs were done: the straightforward but equally enjoyable Rogan's Gully (Grade 2); the short but impressive Bow Icefall (Grade 3, 300 feet high,

100 feet across) drooped over the centre of a horseshoe of black crags in a dramatically remote mountain setting, and on which the usual tactic of hauling skis and overnight gear was adopted; and Bourgeau Righthand (Grade 5) — the real breakthrough. From an idyllic cave found near the foot, Tim Auger, Brian Greenwood, George Homer and Rob Wood climbed the 1200-foot ribbon of ice in two days.

More than anything this made us realize that perhaps the real plums were not so improbable after all. With the first freeze in early November and the first burst of activity on the 60-foot, 60° frozen spillways of the Glenmore and Exshaw dams, interest began to centre on the Weeping Wall, a 600-foot high, 300-foot wide sheet of high angle ice standing only minutes from the road. The previous winter Rob Wood and Gerry Rogan had managed to get about halfway up the right side, but afternoon sun had brought down a deluge of icicles and loose snow and forced retreat. In late November Gerry Rogan, George Homer, Jim Elzinga and I found a gully up the left side, by any standards a good climb, including several hundred feet of water ice from 60° to 90° (Snivelling Gully, 600 feet, Grade 4). The Weeping Wall itself remained inviolate.

About a month later, Rob and I returned for a supposedly more determined attempt. On Christmas Day, after three noonday starts and 10 hours climbing, we were up. The hardest part had been getting Rob out of his pit every morning. It was on this climb that we first used in earnest a technique unwittingly evolved through my own lack of boldness. On two previous occasions, faced by pillars of brittle vertical ice and lacking the guts to frontpoint up them, I had attached aid slings to the shafts of both Terrordactyls and had found that even on vertical ice I could relax and spend as much time as I wished, clearing rotten ice and placing each axe alternately to my complete satisfaction. On the Weeping Wall (600 feet, Grade 5), where we frequently encountered as much as three feet of loose powder snow overlying rotten 70°, 80°, and 90° ice, the technique proved invaluable, and was to become the key to the harder climbs which were to follow.

A week later, on New Year's Day, 1974, Tim Auger, George Homer and Rob Wood climbed Bourgeau Lefthand, an elegant 600-foot pillar of ice, in three days from a bivouac at its base. The climb rises in two 300-foot tiers — thin, poorly protected 80° ice on a smooth open wall in its lower half rearing up to finish with 60 feet of fluted vertical ice running with water. When they completed the climb they were all soaked to the skin. With the air temperature at -28°C, their clothes immediately took on the texture of suits of armour — and they were still faced with the long descent. No joke! Unlike the Weeping Wall, Bourgeau Lefthand had taken three long days of climbing which included establishing satisfactory belays on high-angle ice. Could this be the first controversial Grade 6? Certainly compared with the two existing Grade 5 routes it seemed justified both for logistical and technical reasons.

Now the focus centred on Takakkaw Falls. The panic reaction, when the later-confirmed rumour of two Colorado climbers in the area with Takakkaw Falls as their objective, was typical. For a while it seemed we had really lost our prize marrow. Exactly who they were, how far they got, or if they even attempted the climb never came to light. Anyway it was still there! Here, however, was a comparatively unknown quantity. It was eight miles from the road and various summer photographs of a huge volume of water spewing out over a thousand foot crag conjured up various images of an improbable freestanding column of vertical ice; so when Rob and I skied in a few days later, with Lucy the Alaskan Malamute carrying a couple of 150-foot ropes in her backpacks, we were pleasantly surprised to find a perfectly feasible ribbon of ice in the back of a gigantic gully. It might well have been a typical Scottish gully but for its scale and the huge quantity of ice anywhere from 50 to nearly 200 feet wide rising in a series of 80° and 90° steps for over 1000 feet.

Within less than a week we were back, this time with Doug Lemond's dog team and considerably more gear and food than we could possibly have carried between us. John Lauchlan, who abandoned troublesome skis near the road and walked in, joined us later. That night in the picnic shelter below the Falls the temperature dropped to -45°C.

Two days later, with a pillar of rotten, overhanging ice mushrooms that looked like the hardest part of the climb below us, we were barely halfway up the Falls. Prepared for all the nuances of cold and technical difficulty, the last thing we expected in the Rockies in January was a thaw. Sure enough it came, but only after three days of the heaviest dump of the winter. Rob and I had a close encounter with an avalanche whilst digging out some gear near the base of the Falls. Then John, immobilized without skis, was taken out by helicopter while we staggered out to the road with the rest of the band-waggoneers, Tim Auger, Jack

Firth and Steve Sutton — the climb and the gear abandoned.

When things returned to normal and the big freeze set in again, John, Rob, Jack and I were back, and this time despite continuous light snow and constant battering by spindrift avalanches we made the top in two days from a snow cave a third of the way up the Falls. But our problems were by no means over. Takakkaw Falls (1000 feet, Grade 6) like several other ice climbs in the Rockies is one of those routes which must also be descended!

With the three big plums out of the way, interest diversified and some surprisingly good routes turned up in unexpected places, such as Professor's Gully (1000 feet, Grade 4) low down on the north face of Mount Rundle by Jack Firth, John Lauchlan, Peter Zwengrowski, Murray Toft and Lorraine Drewes; and Louise Falls (400 feet, Grade 5) near Lake Louise by Jack Firth, Eckhart Grassman, Tony Mould and Peter Zwengrowski.

Earlier in the winter several impressive icefalls directly above the Trans-Canada highway near Field, British Columbia, had been visited but the ice had been found to be of hopelessly poor quality. By March, however, the ice had consolidated and three outstandingly good routes were done, including The Carlsberg Column (700 feet, Grade 5). This last done by Jack Firth, Eckhart Grassman, Peter Zwengrowski and John Lauchlan in one day has a very impressive first pitch, a freestanding 160-foot column of vertical ice. Meanwhile I had turned my attention to a 600-feet vertical waterfall draining the glacier on the north face of Mount Stanley. Here it was only too obvious that we would really have to stick our necks out.

The ice was more-or-less continuously vertical throughout, very thin and brittle, and overhung by several enormous icicles which threatened the lower part of the route. From an excellent bivouac in a large rock cave near the base of the climb, John Lauchlan and I had a first look at this tenuous curtain of ice. I felt fully extended on the first 80 feet, a honeycombed two inch vertical sheet in places detached from the rock behind by as much as three feet, and with minimal protection questioned my own judgement in continuing at all. But by the time I had rigged a bolt belay where the ice momentarily eased to 80°, I was convinced that with time, perseverance, and ingenuity the climb would go. A few weekends later, this time with Rob Wood, two more vertical pitches were added on somewhat thicker ice over two days, and the halfway point, a narrow ledge at 30 feet, was reached. The next section looked separate, with giant icicles hanging out far beyond the ledge. But it was a few more weeks before I finally cornered Dick Howe for what we hoped would be a final push. I was mistaken.

Leaving the comparative security of the halfway ledge, I snaked up through a long, slightly-overhanging section into a zone where rotten ice, often overlying several feet of loose snow, alternated with awkward ice roofs formed by broken icicles, some as much as three feet wide. I finally smashed my way between two icicles into a small cave five hours later, only a hundred feet higher, soaked with perspiration and utterly exhausted. The following weekend I was back again, this time alone, and several hours hard work only added another 50-foot vertical section with one two-foot roof to the climb. Then at long last, the sixth day on the climb, Dick and I returned and finished off with a magnificent 150-foot vertical pitch, an incredible open sheet of blue ice with a clear 600-foot drop to the snow. Nemesis (600 feet, Grade 6) seemed an appropriate name. Certainly for two months of the winter it had been the bane of my life and although my tactics might seem questionable to some, I for one had enjoyed every minute of it, from the red wine and dope nights in the cave to the neckiest moments on the climb, even though I still had a toe on the ground, so to speak.

Sunset on Mount Waddington. Photo: Pat Morrow

1977: TIEDEMANN TIDINGS

JOHN WITTMAYER & DON SERL

The summer was slipping by and the number of times I'd been climbing could be counted on one hand. I was feeling unproductive, indeed uninspired, as I sat in the pub listening to amazing tales of glory and triumph from the lips of the conquering heroes as they recounted their latest mountain exploits. One night, while politely listening to these lies, I heard rumours that a foursome was planning to visit the Waddington Range to put up some new routes. That sounded interesting.

I telephoned Don Serl, the Chief Yahoo of the group, and asked if he would consider making it a fivesome. "Well, not really," he drawled, "but there's always a chance that either Greg or Neil won't get it together." As it turned out neither Greg nor Neil did, which left a threesome, Don, Doug Herchmer, and myself. Doug is a successful professional fairly high up in the Forest Service echelon. Consequently, he is a person of gracious diplomacy and good taste. His major weakness is skiing, and he turns into a real animal at the mention of the word 'piste.' Don, on the other hand, is a dope desperado of the worst sort, leading young, innocent climbers to their utter destruction. This desultory character is, of course, a fanatical climber, which in no way put me any more at ease....

Ragged holes of milky blue sky opened before us as our Beaver bee-lined its way from the tourist town of Campbell River to the snows of Waddington. I had only been in a small plane once before and started out a little nervous on the flight in, but soon the views became completely absorbing and I forgot all about the crashes recently reported in the papers. Rushing past below were emerald green grey inlets and rocky coves scattered with charming islets. Suddenly, there was the huge hallucination of the Coast Range spread out before us. Mysterious peaks appeared and disappeared in white swirling cloud as we winged our way up the Homathko valley.

"Well, there it is. Over there, see?" the pilot said, pointing to the grey tooth of stone hooded with snow and ice which rose above the clouds.

"Wow!" We were semi-speechless. Don and Doug commenced a mad scramble for their cameras and began snapping away like a couple of piranhas. Doug was drooling all over his borrowed camera and Don was shouting something at me over the roar of the plane. I finally figured out that he wanted me to duck my head so that he could get a particular shot.

Waddington was awesome in its enormity, absolutely dominating everything else around it. East of Waddington reared Combatant, Tiedemann, and Asperity, and the jagged Serra Peaks. It was all very impressive.

Our pilot began the descent, circling to the north of Mount Jeffery (damn close I thought, gripping the edge of my seat) and floating down, down, down to the cold grey water of Tellot Lake. Soon we were on our own. On the way up the glacier we stopped to consolidate our air drop. Everything was accounted for and in fine shape except for the two dozen eggs we had included. That was an experiment.

In last ten years, the voice of Vancouver climber Don Serl has floated through volume after volume of the CAJ, telling stories of explorations from the Chehalis to the Yukon to the Himalaya with a wry sense of humor, gentle jibes at himself and his partners, and a capacity for unusually literate reflection on our game. These two stories capture his spirit well.
– GP

We established base camp far up the Tiedemann Glacier. It was a fine camp, with a lovely panorama. Looking down the glacier I was amused by how our tracks weaved back and forth to miss the heavily crevassed areas. To the south lay Waddington, with its tangible air of mystery, defeat, and glory. North was Tiedemann, aloof, almost scornful, unexplored. The classic snow ridge followed by the earlier ascents lay on the far side of the mountain, but this side, the 5000-foot south face, was unclimbed. "It's cold and steep and wild," I thought to myself as I poked my head out of the tent to gaze at it for the tenth time. The stubby blue hanging glaciers on Waddington caught the last rays of the setting sun.

Inside the tent we passed the glowing pipe around again and made up our minds, somewhat soporifically, to climb Tiedemann first and try Waddington if there was time and decent weather. Through the night the avalanches crashed down on either side of us.

Mount Tiedemann, about 12,700 feet, has a 3000 foot snow and ice couloir rearing up its south face. The couloir is headed by a light-coloured, broken rock band, perhaps 500 feet high, which cuts across the face. A rib of snow and rock bounds the rock band on the left, while above lies a snowfield, starting off soft and gently sloped, becoming harder and steeper, parabolically. The final part of the peak is composed of numerous ice-choked gullies between buttresses and towers fronting the summit snow dome.

We gained height slowly but the scenery wasn't half bad, and we were getting there. Late in the afternoon we stopped at a passable bivouac site in a shallow bergschrund. As we dug our platform, ugly clouds which had been piling up all day moved in like uninvited guests, hostile and belligerent. We ate a rather insipid meal and after a few hilarious moments, the three of us wedged into a two-person bivy sack. Poking and jabbing each other for the best position, we drifted off to sleep as the storm drifted in.

We woke covered in spindrift. The morning, although far from perfect, was not bad. We stashed our overnight gear. tied into our frozen rope, and set off up the couloir once again. The angle steepened to 45 degrees plus. At midday we arrived beneath the rock band. It looked tortuous and intimidating.

"Why don't you take this lead Don," I humbly said, with Doug looking at me like a grateful lamb saved from the sacrifice. Don mumbled something unintelligible to us as he did the first few slabby moves. Then he disappeared up and around an obscure corner, leaving us to wait our turns in silence below. Despite the fact that the rock was loose and plastered with snow and ice we had decided to move together, using running belays for protection. I couldn't suppress the thought that if one of us fell there was a chance we would all go, accelerating through space, bouncing off the snow here, the rock there, but always down and down....

By the time we reached the top of the rock band the weather had deteriorated further but we were getting close now and we strained on up the snow patch. I put thoughts of an open bivy up here out of my mind. Okay, we could certainly continue up in this weather, but then there was getting down too. In a storm, and perhaps after dark, that would present problems. We kept moving up. The howling wind lashed at us, the snow crystals stung our faces.

As if in a dream we huddled in the icy gully we hoped would lead us to the summit. Driving snow made it nearly impossible to see where we were going. I didn't want to go up. I was too tired, Goddamn it... the wind was blowing so hard I could barely think... just wanted to rest... stop... shut my eyes. Don and then Doug disappeared higher up into the unfriendly gully. My hands were very cold... didn't want to hold the rock. Suddenly a shout. The roaring wind selfishly carried the words away but I knew it meant they were on the top. I pulled myself up the icy rock... just a little more... my legs really tired now. And then I was moving out of the gully, walking the last few steps to the summit. Don and Doug were grinning at me and taking pictures. bracing themselves against the blizzard. I was grinning too as I stood at the top. "Hell, that wasn't too hard."

We spent a chilly five minutes on top before starting down. The gully was difficult in driving snow but on the snowfield we sailed past what had taken ages to climb. We reached the top of the rock band as the daylight began to wane. Down-climbing proved impossible so we made a series of frigid rappels off nightmarish anchors. Don toppled out of a stance part way down while fumbling with ropes, harness, and communications, but luckily landed on some blocks a few feet lower and stopped. By the time we reached the top of the couloir it was positively dark. We were too tired and numbed to stop to put on crampons, so just kept on descending. Part way down Doug hit an icy patch and shot off down the slope. Don had him on a poor boot-axe belay and was torn violently from his stance. Fully expecting an enormous jerk on the rope, I rammed myself into a self arrest.

The slack whipped out, but nothing further happened. Axe-less, squirrely Don had managed to stop himself with desperate mitts and boots, and Doug had arrested into a patch of soft snow which had collected in the couloir.

We collected our wits and plunged on down, soon reaching the vicinity of our previously dug snow cave. In the darkness and not sure of its exact location, we stumbled around in the storm trying to find it. I was the one who literally fell across it, as I plunged through the roof of the hidden 'schrund. Snow had buried everything, spilling into our cave and completely filling it.

The thought of food and sleep soon supplanted the drive for shelter as we painstakingly redug the cave to tolerably comfortable proportions. We cooked and brewed, chatting sparingly, and then, still wet and cold, managed a few hours of sleep, interrupted by bouts of alternately pushing, digging, and cursing at encroaching masses of spindrift. The storm which had dogged us for most of the preceding day blew itself out overnight.

Our poor base camp was in ruins when we dragged ourselves in the next afternoon. The tent had collapsed, wetting most of our gear. It was disheartening. We re-erected the tent, dug out our supplies, and then ate huge quantities of goodies. The following several hours were spent drying gear and putting camp back in some semblance of order.

Finally we relaxed into the sound sleep of comfort, warmth and security. We talked little about the climb during the following few days; what was there to say? The others shared my feelings. The desire to climb Waddington seemed to have redirected itself. We abandoned the Tiedemann Glacier for the Plummer hut and spent a couple of sunny, relaxing days on Claw Peak and the upper Tellot Glacier. We basked in warmth and satisfaction, and then, regretfully, shouldered our packs and set off to face civilization once again.

1981 : SLESSE: WINTER MEMORIES

DON SERL

There's this great system of runnels and couloirs left of Lowe and Kiesel's rib on the north face of Slesse that cries to be climbed. We had the good fortune to do just that on a memorable January weekend. It was one of those rare combinations of perfect companions, faultless weather, an awe-inspiring venue, and superb climbing. I'd love to repeat the route but I'm afraid to — so much of it is not reproducible and my remembrances are so precious and irreplaceable that I fear to alter them with a new reality. Perhaps it's best just to concentrate, for the present, on the other apparently equally fine routes on the Slesse-Crossover wall. Perhaps. Not that one is likely to be disturbed by strangers way back in there, seven hours and more from the road, even given the infrequency of the stable winter weather necessary for the climb. Nor, given the necessary weather, does one need to worry much about hazards above — the dangers, such as they are, are susceptible to control. Although admittedly few belays or decent runners can be found and occasionally the snow and ice thin over rock bands to the point where crampons meet rock, 45 and 90 m beyond one's companions who are also intently plugging up their respective pitches, mindful always of the consequences of carelessness. Nor even, I suspect, would the quality of the climbing change much — it would differ, true, but I'd reckon it'd never be much easier or a lot harder and one would always have to surmount the crest of the rib where it closes the top of the couloir 20 rope-lengths up and then one would still have to get up that last 30 m of the main gully, up snow so steep and unconsolidated that progress could only be made by hacking out a groove and back-and-footing up it. But even if as before, the great curl of the cornice proved to be insurmountable and the side walls remained unclimbable and the only realistic alternative was to carve a tunnel 25 feet, four body lengths, out into the fierce horizontal cold — even then unless one was supremely favoured the full moon would not serenely shine down as one bubbled out a chuckled whoop of amazement and pleasure and finality before settling in to bring the others up out of the gully, up through the tunnel, to be reunited in the moon-whitened notch.

No, it could never be recreated, nor should I try. Perhaps some day I'll repeat the climb, perhaps not. For now, the memory will suffice.

The summit of Mount Logan. Photo: Pat Morrow

1979 : CHOIR HITS LOGAN

JOHN LAUCHLAN

I guess we shoulda gotten a map, eh?" "I thought you turkeys had been up here before…." "Don't look at me, Rockland's drivin!" So the first CMC Junior Boy's Choir expedition finds itself lost… and not even out of Alberta yet. A quick detour around Lesser Slave Lake and we end up more-or-less back on the unbelievably dusty trail to Kluane Park and the southwest buttress of Mount Logan. After collecting Elzinga in Whitehorse, and an interesting time trying to keep Robby from drowning himself (first in Chivas Regal and, shortly thereafter, in the river just outside town), we head off for Haines Junction. Rush… rush… weather looks good… head for the bar to find Richard… maps spread all over the place… fork over the traveller's cheques and we're off for Kluane… looks good, looks good… maybe we'll fly in tomorrow!? Hmmm… weather doesn't look so red hot up in this direction… two weeks later… *two weeks later!!*… we're still sitting in the rain at Kluane airstrip. Read all the books, ate and drank away all our money, racked up a truly remarkable radio-phone bill phoning our various ladies… and all we've got to do is play soccer in the mud with the rodent people. But… next thing you know…

"Well, what d'ya think, Slimey?" "Looks just like the picture, doesn't it?" We hop out of the Helio-Courier, put down a cache and wait for Richard to pick us up in the chopper to take us to the bottom of the route where he's dropped Jim and Robby. In a flash we're at the bottom, dragging our bags out of the Jet Ranger. Richard is staring up at the seracs above. He won't turn down the engines or get out. He doesn't like it here. Phil and I are not staring up at the seracs above. We have to get out. We don't like it here either. Jim and Rob have already buggered off to find a semi-safe place for base camp… leaving us to drag the loads up there… nice. Base camp is a joke. Poised precariously under a rock spur, like a zit under a wino's double chin, we listen to the thunder pour down all around us. Only room on the platform for one tent — Hein and I grab it… the others take the bivy sac. Night falls. It cools off, calms down. Jimmy and I roll the first 1200 feet of rope into our packs and head off up the first couloir. Really straightforward, we fix the lot and get back to camp just as Phil and Robby head up to fix some more. In three nights we have the ropes pushed up to the top of the couloir and move camp up there to acclimatize a bit, and so the other two get a decent sleep.

While the big bruisers head down to carry some more loads Robby and I head up towards the Renshaw chimney — the section that had taken a day and a half for Dick and Urs to get over on last year's attempt. I have been fingered for this lead since we first started talking about this route — and secretly I'm looking forward to trying to flash it — but I complain about it anyway… wouldn't want these guys to think I was keen or anything.

As approaches to climbing become more extreme, it becomes more and more difficult to encompass the mountain experience in traditional literary forms. This tell-it-like-it-really-is article not only illuminates the hazards of climbing on big mountains, it offers candid insight into the way climbers really talk and think. Few articles published in the Canadian Alpine Journal *so fully articulate the pleasure and the pain of being totally committed to climbing as a way of life.*
– R W S

It looks shorter and shorter the closer we get. I grab the rack and start up the lower section of the chimneys… run out of rope. Rob comes up. We look up at the dripping ice-choked corner above us where Renshaw had gone. We look at the sun-drenched series of flakes 15 feet to the right. We speculate on the quality of Renshaw's eyesight and I start laybacking up the flakes. It goes quickly. Rob jumars and dances up the loose pitch above and we break out onto the ridge section. We run out of rope and head down, raving about the rock, the views. The next couple of days see all the bags and fixed rope brought up from below and the section above fixed to last year's high point. Spirits are really high, we've been going well and its not nearly the horror show we were psyched for.

Rob's still not sleeping well though so next day I give him a couple of codeines and do a few short carries by myself while Phil and Jim go up to lead the serac. I return to Camp 1 and Rob is awake and wants to go up to do another carry. I protest that he's still a bit doped but he insists, so we go back up to do some more bag dragging up the ridge.

Weather is hot — really hot. Eventually clouds roll in and it starts to snow like crazy. We can hear the others coming down from above so we cache the loads and head down the ropes. Rob seems OK so I bomb off ahead to get a brew going. As I rap down towards our camp I can't absorb what I'm seeing. The configuration of colours in the tents is not right. The bivy tent we draped over them to deflect spindrift is hanging in tatters below. Suddenly it begins to make sense… I notice the deep gouge in the couloir running from the rocks above camp, through what used to be Rob's and Jim's tent and on down the couloir. Good thing I didn't give Robby more codeine….

I arrive at Dresden and begin to try putting the mess together. The boulder has gone right through the tent. The poles are like pretzels. Gear all over. Robby arrives… freaks. Jimmy raps out of the sky as we are cramming the remains into the one good tent. He takes it in before he says anything… his eyes bugging out… but we've played this game before, Jimmy and I. He looks up at the sky, pelting whited-out slushball that it is, and says, "Nice day up on the ridge today." "Ya really, we had some great views of the Hummingbird," I reply as I drag the tattered remains of the tent off the platform, all the while staring up at the rocks above in anticipation of a repeat performance. "How'd the ice climb go?" "Really well, Phil made a great lead. Ran out of rope before the lip though." We pile into the tent,

still carrying on this inane conversation… it snows harder. Looks just like the one that pinned us down for four days on Mount Vancouver last year. Four of us crammed into one tent… snowing like a bastard… trying to brew up… tent starts collapsing under the weight of the cement falling from the sky and down the couloir… nice. We pile out to shovel off the tent before the poles buckle… discuss the situation. "We've got to get out of here." "Where can we go though? There's no place to stop on that ridge up there." "We'll be able to bivy below that pinnacle and then check out the area on top of the serac." "OK but we'll have to fix the tent quick. We won't have much left after a few days of this kind of storm in those bivy sacs." Out comes the needle and thread as I scrunch up in the brightest corner and try to sew up the other tent. The others are trying to straighten the poles. No room, so Rob pulls out a bivy sac and crashes out on the platform. Sometime during the night Phil's innerboot gets kicked down the couloir. Rob's duvet is gone, too.

Morning sees the storm let up a bit so we pack up and bolt up the fixed ropes. Rob, still a little doped up and sleepless, collapses. Phil stays behind with him as Jimmy and I head up to look for a camp site. We drop the bags at the pinnacle, jumar up the serac and continue to the top to see what's there. I sigh some kind of thanks as I pull over the top and find the first small flat section on the route so far. Can't make it here with the gear tonight but tomorrow we'll be OK. Rap back down to the pinnacle to meet the others. They've got the bags and tents up. The storm hits hard again as we hack out the bivy site. I'm burned… we're all up-tight, bitching… "Just shut up and go to sleep."

Next day things suddenly take a turn for the better. We get all the loads up to the flat area, dig a fantastic snow cave and, miraculously, the weather clears. Dry out day. Finally we can sit around without being tied in… first time on the route. A chance to take stock, examine our position, our motivations. We're burned out but regaining strength quickly. We haven't got the big tents up with us… but do we need them? We figure we're only five days from the summit in a continuous push. We've got 20 days food and gas. In spite of the near disaster below, our position is damn good… getting keen again. Still I wouldn't mind getting this bloody exercise over with. The two weeks wait at Kluane has really put the screws to all our plans. Jimmy's wife has had to move all their stuff out east by herself, Phil and Robby are late for their jobs which may or may not still be there… and me… this expedition had all the earmarks of being the last straw for my relationship with Judith. Torn between mountains and women. I haven't enough time for either… wasting potential with every schizoid turn of mind and motivation. Every big route, every engrossing keenness a slap in her face. The questioning bivies, a longing to be home… and yet every clear spell I stare past my texts to the mountains and kick myself. The guilt turns in my stomach like a knife… but I'm here, where I think I want to be. There is no answer Reinhold, all you can do is what motivates you, regardless of how confused that may be. But still, there are the consequences of my actions to face… brood, brood, brood.

"I can't sleep, let's go." Elzinga, who's been brooding too, has his boots on before the others can crack their lids. We pile out of the snow cave. Phil leads a gross pitch of steep almost-ice, while Jim and I stand in the driving snow. We decide to leave our helmets off today so we can wear more to keep our heads warm… bad move. We follow up the ridge flutings until we get funnelled into a rock step below an easy angled section… put in a pseudo belay… grab the rack. Just 40 feet of steep corn flakes and we'll be cruisin' for the rest of the day. I'm going well. It's hard and steep and icy and loose but I'm feeling really confident. Absorbed… crampons biting into the crud, mittened hands curled over icy nubbins… this is what it's all about, this is what I'm here for…. Suddenly the world explodes in my face. A block the size of a coffee table comes out in my arms. In my panic I try to hold it… no way… I lob off trying to push it out of the way, like a scene from a nightmare, I come onto the rope and spin around just in time to see the full weight of the block land on Elzinga's unprotected head and shoulders. He recoils like the slow motion of the Kennedy assassination, and slumps onto the belay…. Terror… blood… Jimmy comes to… slips out again… Phil and Robby start setting up a lower… I try to talk to Jimmy, try to push my nose back together… *down*… lowers in the driving snow, to knife-edge ridge… bundle into the snow cave, dive for the radio. Three days of storm and avalanches before a helicopter can get in… we sling out, forced to abandon all our gear.

Judith meets me at Haines Junction… we split up. I phone Calgary… Bugs has been killed on Assiniboine. When it rains it pours. And so the first Junior Boys Choir expedition came to an end. A trip of extremes and intensities that had left us all changed in major ways, physically, emotionally, and financially. Meanwhile there's a lot of expensive equipment halfway up the south-southwest buttress of Logan. When I get back up there this coming year the first thing I'll be looking for is that one special little piece of cord… the one I use to hold my shit together.

The east face of Snowdome, with Slipstream near the centre of the photo. Photo: Greg Horne

1982 : AGGRESSIVE TREATMENT

JOHN LAUCHLAN

"How can you break both front posts with one kick?" "I don't know, but I just did. I'll send them a letter, maybe they can explain it." "Do you want to bag it?" "Naw, I'll just lash 'em on and keep going." Dwayne and I soloed on while James fiddled with his crampons. It seemed a bit presumptuous, carrying on. We were attempting a new route in winter on the east face of Snowdome. We were on the next gully system left of Slipstream, but the character of the two lines couldn't have been more different. While the ice of Slipstream shone blue and inviting to our right; the smear above us was malnourished and anemic. In fact, a lot of the ice above us was rock. Oh well, we're supposed to know what we're doing… I read it on an Everest poster.

Picking our way through the rolling water ice steps of the lower benches, we finally broke out onto the alpine ice that leads to the bottom of the "real" climbing. James catches us just as we arrive at the base of the first pillar. We don't pay a lot of attention to it. It's quite steep but only about 30 feet high before it kicks back. We've all spent the winter teaching ice climbing and have gotten pretty cocky about soloing around on the steep stuff. "Want a rope for this?" "Why don't you drag one up for me… just to see how my crampon stays on." I grab the end on the rope and clip it onto the back of my harness. I mean, it's not like I could actually fall off something like this… I'm not so used to having this hulking great pack on my back, but then… it's only 30 feet. I start off. James fiddles with his crampons, Dwayne stares out at the valley as he feeds out the rope on automatic pilot. No problem here… up a short fan, around onto the steep stuff, up alongside a little rock corner, tools over the top and we're… AAAAaaahhh!!! I drop about half a metre as both tools and both feet cut through the ice simultaneously. As I fall I dart my foot out to the right and catch myself in a precarious bridging position. "*This is vertical snow!!!*" Having broken through the surface of the ice my left foot and hand tool are pushed through into the rotten depth hoar behind. I am just able to hold myself in position… every time I move slightly, the skin of ice that supports me breaks off. Below there is frantic activity. James hurriedly buries his ice axe while Dwayne tries to decide whether to belay me or untie and watch. "If he comes off, really let him run a long ways before you try to stop him dead." "If he falls that far he probably will be, but better him than all of us."

In the canon of pioneering ice climbs, this first ascent on the east face of Snowdome in the Columbia Icefield is a classic. Ostensibly, Lauchlan and his companions James Blench and Dwayne Congdon are in training for a major Air Canada sponsored expedition to Everest. Though one of the finest climbers in the country at the time, Lauchlan never made it to the Himalayas. His death on a solo ice climb in 1982 presaged some of the difficult circumstances his companions would face in the Himalaya.
– RWS

Battling off panic, I try to calm down. I've got to find a way to take the weight off one of my arms so that I can move up. I lean slightly onto my left hand tool. I'm slipping through!! I regain my bridging position just in time. My pack is pulling me over… sapping my strength… better do something. I slowly lean the other way. The rock is slightly overhung and devoid of man sized holds but if I can press my forearm against it the prickly rock might give me just enough friction… I lean. It holds… a little. Very, very carefully I pull out my Chakal and grope for a shaft placement. I manage to fiddle the axe in sideways behind the skin of ice and, after a series of swimming and bridging manoeuvres, pull over the bulge. "Had a little problem down there guys." "We hadn't noticed." My heart still racing, I climb up to the base of the next steep section and bang in three ice screws. No more foolin' around. The others, clued into the technique, make short work of the pillar. Much to my disappointment neither of them falls off. The pitch above looks like the real thing, finally… beautiful blue pillar, nice and steep, the better part of a pitch high. "I'd like to do this one." "Thought you were worried about your crampons." "They seemed just fine on that last bit. Besides,

I've never had a chance to lead something steep like this with a big pack on." Dwayne and I look at each other. "OK, James but we've got to make a pact. No more fiascos… right?"

We all agree so James takes the rack and sets off. Thirty feet off the belay, just into the steep part, he stops to set his second ice screw. "Look at this guy. Just because I told him that I had to rest on my tools on Slipstream he's gotta do without." "Well I just thought I'd try… it's not that bad actually." After struggling to get the screw in before his pack gets him, James yells "I'm in," and proceeds upwards. After making about two moves he drives his Terrors deep into the ice and hangs back on his umbilical cords. "I'm totalled." "Good" we say, thankful not to have to follow his ethical lead.

Fifteen feet higher James stops suddenly and bangs in a snarg. "Guess what… more vertical snow." He explains that just above him the ice changes suddenly. With no rock corner to bridge to, there is no way to continue up safely. Leaving his pack at the snarg, he traverses right into a small groove in the rock. The ice is only an inch or so thick there, but at least he might be able to protect it with rock pegs. Half rock climbing, half ice climbing, and extremely slowly James pieces together the groove as we watch expectantly from below. He disappears over the top. "Got it," he finally yells down. A good thing too, the sun's going down. Manhandling the packs up the pitch we soon find ourselves searching the ledge system for suitable accommodation. Failing to find a berth, we fight for a seat in "coach." Good thing we're all little folk, or the three of us never would have kept our buns on that glorified foothold, let alone got the tent up on it.

Anyway the next morning is cloudy, as winter mornings tend to be on faces that catch the early morning sun. I run out the rope from the tent to get a look at the continuation of our gully system. In the hurry of impending blackness the night before I hadn't gotten a look at it. It doesn't look too appetizing. The breakfast menu consists of a choice between vertical porridge on the left, or thin ice on the rocks to the right. Now it is rumoured that unreasonably thin ice has been climbed by comic book heroes and the criminally insane… but even Albi can't put a belay in verglas. We opt for the ugly looking rock corner on the left.

The climbing turns out to be surprisingly good… for a couple of pitches. Dwayne and I swap leads up thin ice runnels tucked into a corner. Very reminiscent of the north face of Les Droites. Of course this can't last forever… this is the Rockies we're talkin' about here.

"My turn!" James forwards as we look up at a grotty corner of rock. "Well OK, but I get next try," I say, thankful he's been aware of his place in the rotation. James does his fingernails-on-the-blackboard imitation for the better part of an hour while we make jokes about the belay. He's forced out to the right of the corner and soon yells down a cheery, "No belay. No cracks." Fortunately we have carried our courage in my rucksack so I send him the "Bold" kit on the haul line.

Actually it wasn't James's fault about the bolt. The kit was kind of buggered up and he'd only used it once before… and Rockies rock being what it is… I'm sure none of us could have put it in any better. It is unfortunate that it had to break though, the handle I mean… before he could try a second one. I follow slowly up the awkward rock, crampons flailing, to arrive at James's island of insecurity. This belay is even funnier than the last one… except this time it's my turn. We decide to leave Dwayne down below. If I come off maybe one of these belays will hold! The next pitch was extremely frightening and I'd rather not talk about it. I will hint however, that it goes straight sideways, features a thin crust over crud rock, two tied-off blades, and three terrified climbers. It ends, finally, with a buried axe belay. James and Dwayne whimper across the traverse and we crawl neurotically up towards the final fiasco… the serac. We hadn't actually formed a plan for getting through this thing. Yesterday we were brilliant alpinists, you remember — capable, competent, all that stuff. Now we just want to go home.

Arriving at the end of the ice section of the serac, we put in all our remaining ice screws to hang back and look at the 12 metres of overhanging snow that loom over us. I gather together all the ice tools in anticipation of aiding over the stupid thing on axe shafts. "Jeeze, this is going to take all bloody night." Have you ever noticed what amazing things fear can do for creativity? Since it turns out to be my lead, I look frantically for an easy way out. To our right a crevasse cuts into the serac — maybe I can bridge up that thing! I crawl onto the wind roll below the overhang and pick my way over to it. No way… the thing's just as overhung as anywhere else… but what about… I chimney back into the crevasse, five, eight, ten metres… *alright!* A pale blue light shines through the snow above me… we can burrow our way out! An hour later, in the pitch dark, three soaked and shivering figures pop out of the Snowdome Glacier and bumble off home. Like hypothermia, swollen heads respond only to aggressive treatment.

Mount Augusta, from Mount Logan. Photo: Pat Morrow

Sir Sandford in evening light. Photo: Roger Laurilla

1983 : FIRST NEWFOUNDLAND ASCENT OF CAUBVICK

R. J. ROGERSON

Since this year the boys from upalong was climbing Everest, we Newfs decided we should do our bit. You see we has this mountain down the Labrador right on the border with Quebec which few of us has seen and none from here had climbed. Some of our neighbours impolitely called her "d'Iberville," after this French pirate as burned our houses. That was some time back I'll grant but we is not into Imperial France and we was glad when a right gentlemanly cuffer out of Ottawa said she should be "L1" until we makes up our minds. Well we made our minds up and now it is official. We calls her "Caubvick" after this native woman who went to London with Cartwright and some other Inuit. I believes she was the only one in the group to survive the smallpox. Anyways she's immortal now and stands up there, the highest in the Torngat, a tall cone of rock at the meeting of three ridges, two of which we shares with Quebec. The third is ours alone.

The first Newfoundland ascent of Caubvick, and only the fifth recorded ascent, was not a fancy affair but we all had a real good time. One native son called Hazen Russell and two come-from-awayers Bob Rogerson and Tim Keliher (though add up the years the last two has been here and it's almost the same as Hazen's age), we climbed her on 27 July 1982 along the Minaret Ridge. Fine old view from there and though we hears that some has soloed it, we used a rope for the last three pitches. Nice feeling of security, like a handy sheet in the rigging when you's up for barrelman. We didn't have a fancy Air Canada flag so we just hoisted the Provincial flag and the flag of Labrador up there.

The CAJ, like climbing itself, has had a long, albeit sometimes unintentional, history of humour. This piece, by the otherwise unheard-from Mr. Rogerson, details the ascent of the elusive Mount Caubvick in the majestic Torngats of northern Québec, in that unique voice of our strange brother to the far east.
– GP

Now we wasn't really out for just the climbing; we also has our own Newfoundland glaciers — and I don't mean the bergs that comes right down home in the spring — but real glaciers in the mountains. I mark we is the only province east of Alberta as has them in this whole Dominion. We looks right careful at them since one at least has moved for'ard a couple of metres since last year, pushing his way down the valley right stroppy like. We drilled holes in them like you'd think they'd spring a leak but for the fact we bungs 'em up with aluminium poles. We dug snow pits just like clearing the wheelbarrow path in winter, except it was swimsuit weather most the time. And we measures all kinds of fancy things; if we was tailors we could fit them with a suit of clothes by now.

Anyway the boys got right keen on this climbing thing and Hazen and Tim downs their tools just two days later to up and climb Mount Caubvick by another ridge; the one we shares with no one. We hears she's called the North Ridge but to us she's the Newfoundland Ridge and always will be. She's a longish climb on loose rocks with the crux a single pitch at the bottom, just above the col. She'd be a real exciting climb if you stayed right on the crest but would take more time. As it was we was ten hours from the camp at the terminus of Minaret Glacier. We reckons that's a new route anyways. Seeing as how one of us at least will be back next summer and many years after that it looks like we might finally make it as a bunch of climbers at home instead of going upalong. It's pretty country in the Torngat and we be right proud of it.

Bow Summit cornice. Photo: Craig Richards

1987 : EVEREST... THE LIGHT WAY

SHARON WOOD

I t was only a few days after Dwayne Congdon and I had stumbled off the summit of Mount Everest when Barry Blanchard roused me from my semi-conscious void within the sanctuary of my sleeping bag. "Hey, Woody! I have this climb I'd like to do with you on the Rupal Face of Nanga Parbat. The biggest vertical face in the world: no sponsors, small team, alpine style, unclimbed line, 8000 metres..." I responded with a groan and a few words of protest. "But it's a small 8000er." I didn't know there were any small 8000-metre peaks. I was operating on a much different frequency at the time. I had been dreaming of learning how to rock climb again. I mean really rock climb with a sleeveless tee-shirt and a pair of gaudy lycra tights. To enter a rock-climbing season sun-tanned and minus the atrophied appearance I am so accustomed to after high-altitude adventures that are exclusively mind-and-lung expanding. "Bubba, ask me later."

Barry's source of energy and enthusiasm had always been an admirable enigma to most of us mortals. He and Albi Sole had been the victims of my biggest regret of the Everest Light experience, which still looms very large in my mind. They had been slotted for the second summit team, due to begin their bid once Dwayne and I were safely down. In spite of being healthy, strong, and chafing at the bit, they were called down off the mountain. Circumstances had denied them the opportunity they deserved. Dwayne and I hadn't helped their chances by cutting it close to the line. Of course all eleven of us came on this trip aiming for the top. We came with the awareness that our odds were slim on an expedition-style ascent on a very big brand-name mountain.

The last piece by a woman included in this book represents likely the finest achievement by a female climber in the country's climbing history. Sharon Wood's ascent of a new route on Everest's West Rib and North Face clarifies the potential for all women in the game, is a clear testimony to the power of good teamwork, and well tells the story of what is arguably Canada's most significant achievement in the Himalaya.
– GP

Back on the 19th of March we were the first expedition to arrive. We selected the choice location for our Base Camp at the foot of the Rongbuk Glacier at 16,800 feet. The Americans who closely paralleled our schedule, route, and style, arrived a day later with a permit to climb the Great Couloir. The Spanish arrived approximately a week later with permission to attempt the North Ridge. Base Camp offered colorful and diverse entertainment. The price of luxury is quickly paid when you drive to 17,000 feet. Donning nearly every layer of clothing we owned, and under the influence of a condition close to the worst hangover I've ever experienced, we attempted to create order out of our six tons of supplies. Within hours, amidst total chaos, Jane Fearing, our cook, had succeeded in turning out a fine meal, a demonstration of only one small quality that remained consistent throughout our sojourn. It is an illusion to believe that climbing is the feature attraction on a project of this nature.

One day James Blench defined the role of an expedition member rather succinctly: "You go with a group of people you believe in, you give it all you have, you throw it all into one pot, and with the direction of a good leader you see what you come up with." I'm sure at times we may have all looked like good little Socialists. However, in reality, every one of us was a strong-willed, single-minded individual, who was not accustomed to aligning his or her purpose with more than one or two people at best. The one thing we did share in common was a recognition of the need to channel the diversity in this situation in order to accomplish our objective. Jim Elzinga was unanimously accepted as the leader. The cooperation and compliance that ensued was a source of constant wonderment.

Camp II at 19,500 feet was established at the base of the spur by the end of March. Camp III was established halfway up the spur, and reclaimed several times before it was successfully occupied by mid April. Due to the blessing of some good weather and relatively straightforward climbing and fixing, Camp IV at 24,000 feet was ready for occupation by the third week in April. Old abandoned caches and carcasses of box tents were grim reminders of the wrath of this mountain. I recalled reading an account of a team loaded with big guns who were defeated by the next section because of the winds and the sustained work load above 24,000 feet. We too were beginning to wear. All but Albi Sole and I had been stricken by a virus which attacked the respiratory tract that crippled our force and pace. Interestingly enough, all but Annie Whitehouse on the American team had been afflicted by the same virus.

We spent days building our camps, spurred on by the sight of the tattered remains of efforts before us and of past horror stories of expeditions losing up to fifteen tents to the winds. I will never forget that dramatic photograph from Tom Hornbein's book of climbers leaning 45° into the wind attempting to salvage the remains of their Camp IV. We also spent many extra days laying down and maintaining fixed ropes on easy ground to ensure we remained intact when the winds picked up. As the season advanced, our fears materialized. I remember one day watching Jim Elzinga, who weighs 200 pounds or better, get lifted off his feet and hurtled back down to the next anchor. By April 20, Camp V was installed through the tenacious efforts of Barry Blanchard and Dwayne Congdon.

By this time it felt as if we were beginning to spin our wheels. There is a paradox that exists in an expedition-style ascent. The multitude of incremental steps that promote a slow but strong and consistent progress tend to block the attainment of the ultimate objective. In securing the platforms from which to extend, long exposure to altitude burns you out by the time you're in position to make a summit bid. Our work force above 24,000 feet was down to half. We had to change our objective of climbing the West Ridge Direct to traversing out onto the North Face and climbing the Hornbein Couloir. To some, this appeared the only viable alternative. To others, it was a hard blow, a compromise. They would have rather failed on the hard way than succeed by a less technical route.

After reading Tom Hornbein's account and given the mountain we were on, I was not confident we had anything in the bag. A week later on the 6th of May, another crucial decision was made. The summit teams were selected. This painful process was made easier by the mountain having already pared us down to four. Dwayne Congdon and I were to be the first assault team and Barry Blanchard and Albi Sole the second. The strategy from here would go as follows: Two teams of two would fix from Camp V across the north face to the bottom of the couloir in four days. Meanwhile, whoever was capable would ferry the remainder of supplies necessary for Camp VI to Camp V. Within the week, following a rest, Dwayne and I would commence our summit bid. Being the first summit team we would install Camp VI at 27,000 feet and go for the summit the next day. If we failed to reach the summit, we would at least fix as much of the technical sections as possible with 6 mm Kevlar rope for the second team to move through on.

With a concrete plan now in place, the hulking expedition machine began making steps forward. Everyone put out to his maximum capacity even when his cards were played out. Jim had contracted a bad viral infection which permanently bound him to Camp II and below. From there he continued to maintain a relentless grip on the orchestration of the strategy. Over the next week we succeeded in carrying out the initial stages of our plan.

On May 15, on parting from Camp I to begin our summit bid, Todd Bibler, a member of our American neighbors, shouted out some parting words of wisdom, "Glory or Death!" Coleen, Dwayne's long-time mate, failed to grasp the nature of Todd's humor. Later that day, Jim Elzinga took us aside for a little pep talk. He said that no matter what, make sure you treat this climb just like any other mountain: don't die for it.

Barry and Kevin Doyle joined Dwayne and me. They would carry in support through to Camp VI. At Camp II, we waited out two days of storms before we started up, in spite of unsettled weather. On this day, halfway up our 5000-foot carry, when the conditions were especially compromising, I tried this little tidbit of Jim Elzinga philosophy out on Kevin. It didn't wash. If the truth be known, one's bearing on reality and the margin one leaves for longevity is altered significantly in a place like this. On May 19, at Camp V, we strapped on the oxygen for the first time. Our circulation improved almost immediately. However, with two oxygen bottles on top of all the supplies for Camp VI and above, our packs were pushing 70 pounds.

The pace was discouragingly slow and painful. I didn't dare take my pack off for fear of dropping it or losing energy needed to up it back on. As the four of us crept across the face, every now and then someone was toppled over by the wind. An ominous lenticular cloud capped the summit. Late in the afternoon we left the ropes and entered the couloir. It was constantly being flushed by surface avalanches from thousands of feet above. Periodically, rocks dislodged by the raging winds ricocheted down off the walls of the couloir. Near misses were stripping away our resolve. At 8 p.m., I saw Barry step out of the couloir into an alcove. This would be our Camp VI, at approximately 26,800 feet. Barry and Kevin remained with us and did everything they could to help us get settled. It was painful to watch them turn their backs to return to Camp V. This day had been a far more demanding test of their commitment than of ours, as we had the sweet incentive of the summit luring us on the next day. We remained outside preparing our equipment and securing our tent until after midnight, reducing ourselves to a devastating level of exhaustion.

On May 20, at 5 a.m., we arose covered in spindrift that had been driven through the walls of the tent during our few hours of respite. We made the first and one of the only radio calls of the day. The boys indicated that the lenticular cloud was holding its ground and obscuring the summit from 28,000 feet and above. Their words were barely audible over the screaming wind. We stepped out of the tent at 9 a.m., eight hours behind schedule, and loaded up our packs with one oxygen bottle, 600 feet of 6 mm Kevlar rope, and a few pitons. I tucked a portable radio on full volume deep inside my jackets. Our oxygen would last ten hours on a low flow rate of two liters per minute. All was not in our favour as we plodded up the icy couloir where trailings of old ropes hauntingly dangled on the walls. In the initial stages of the day, Dwayne's sense of conviction was considerably stronger than mine. As the day wore on, when his energy waned, mine would surge. We played off one another's fluctuating strengths throughout the day. To save time, we elected to climb unroped.

When we reached the rock pitches at the Yellow Band, we began to string the rope out. A few hundred feet later we came together, having both assumed a much different mode of operation. The climbing had consumed our disappointment and pessimism. A very intense level of concentration and commitment prevailed. Every now and then I'd get a boost from the voices that crackled over the radio inside my jacket from our anxious onlookers 10,000 feet below. By five o'clock in the afternoon we had covered half the elevation to the summit. With no verbal communication necessary, we continued on. We seemed to be operating in perfect synchronism, matched in thought, determination, and decision. The voices that wafted up from the depths of my jacket had a marked change in tone. Now I was hearing the odd broken phrase with the words, bivouac, or benighted, and speculations of where we would spend the night. We were unquestionably on our way to the top, and we certainly didn't have any intentions of spending the night out. The wind had died to a low roar confining us to the protection of the face on the summit pyramid. One final step of fifth-class climbing and we gained the endless ridge.

We stepped onto the summit at sunset, 9 p.m. We wrestled with flags and cameras for twenty minutes, then turned our attention to the descent. Unfortunately the conditions would not allow us to sit on our backsides and surrender to a quick slide back home and live to see our friends' smiles the next day. Darkness intercepted us at about 28,500 feet on the traverse back into the couloir. We were separated about halfway down where we reached our fixed ropes. We both continued alone under the assumption that everything was under control but not particularly fun. We were slipping deeper and deeper into a very efficient state of function, that of survival. Meanwhile downstairs, the team helplessly watched as our head lamps grew further and further apart. I was too preoccupied to realize the radio had ceased working before the summit.

I arrived at Camp VI ninety minutes before Dwayne. During the wait, my mind had its first chance to register anything beyond putting one foot below the other. I thought of the implications of having separated from Dwayne; my thoughts raced randomly, entertaining everything from the best to the worst of scenarios. One of the most pleasant memories I recall was the sound of Dwayne's footsteps outside the tent at 3:30 a.m. During the interim before dawn we managed to create a few more exciting moments for ourselves when a mishandled stove blew up, leaving us quite cold and thirsty, and me with little facial hair. At dawn, we reassembled the radio, and pushed the button to re-establish contact with the rest of the team. There was no question as to whether it was a team success. Dwayne and I were lucky enough to climb off their shoulders to reach the pinnacle of everyone's efforts.

James Blench on The Wild Thing, Mount Chephren, Alberta. Photo: Kevin Doyle.

1988 : MOUNT FAY, EAST FACE

BARRY BLANCHARD

Typical Cheesmond logistics. Karl and Dave drive from Calgary after work on Friday. Pick me up in Canmore and arrive at the roadhead at midnight. Ski four hours through the dark to reach the Moraine Lake cook shelter. Sleep 'til 8 a.m., then ski up to the East Face of Mount Fay. Climb the face in two days and ski out on the third day. Should all fit into a long weekend. So it is that I've bought into another winter adventure with Dave. This will be my first climb with Karl and I'm looking forward to it. We all share the same spirit. There is something enchanting about moving through the cold yet being warm. As I ski, frost forms on my eyebrows and tongue, but my skin is engorged with blood and is warm. I think of all the cold belays when movement is an unattainable luxury. It's good to be warm now. I appreciate it. There isn't much of a moon out. The road rolls on through the trees as a grey strip. I feel like I'm driving with the lights off. The East Face of Mount Fay is 3500 feet high. Rockbands and snowfields alternate to form the first half of the face. Incredibly, a waterfall ice system has etched a line through the rockbands. It's like a stream of liquid silver flowing over concrete steps. This ice is our key to the lower face. The upper half of the face is formed by a vertical pillar of rock rising from the last snowfield directly to the summit. If we can climb the pillar the route will be wild!

At 10 a.m. the next day we have to sit 1000 feet away from the face. It's too hot. The sun is hitting the top of the face, causing wet snow avalanches. The avalanches auger deep runnels into the snowfields. At 11 a.m. the sun leaves the face and the snow gradually stops sliding. At noon we start climbing. At the top of the first snow ramp we cross a short traverse with 100 feet of air underfoot. We're unroped so I concentrate on my technique. Like an inverted dinner candle, thin at the bottom and thick at the top, a vertical pillar of blue ice forms the first pitch. Halfway up the pillar I'm pumped, I'm breathing at my limit, unable to advance or retreat. Equilibrium. I hang off my tool, place an ice screw, and clip into it to rest. Dave and Karl shout up encouragement. The pillar is the only way to make it up this rockband. A downhill skier once told me that there are two lines out there. One is the in-control and the other is the out-of-control line. A little to the right of that line is another line. Only this line is finer, fainter, more like a strand. On one side of the strand is genius, on the other side is madness. The interesting point being that both genius and madness are *out of control!* I finish the pillar on the line. My arms are flamed and I'm breathing like a locomotive. Finding no rock or ice to anchor to, I hammer my axes, like snowpickets, into firm snow. I dig a trench and sit myself in it as a backup.

"Son, on alpine routes, your anchors have to be bomber," says Jim Elzinga. Dave and Karl jug up in the dark.

Barry Blanchard is part of a community of extreme climbers whose interests lie not so much in summiteering as in challenging the most difficult and vertical routes alpine style. Blanchard is also one of the finest mountain writers in the country. Blanchard's brief but brilliant discourse on the fine line separating madness and genius could be seen as an epigram for his climbing life.

– R W S

Bivy time. We start to hack out a ledge. I'm working away with the shovel when my leg punches through. Dave is automatically excited. He burrows down and discovers a natural snow cave that's big enough for the three of us. As usual the day ends late and we'll start tomorrow early but this is alpinism and feeling ragged is part of it. In the night I wake up cold. My bivy sack has slipped down. My shoulder has pressed my down bag against the snow. The bag is wet. I'll pay for this mistake. The next day we follow the line of ice from snowledge to snowledge. At midday, Karl is leading a Grade 3 ice pitch. Dave is belaying from beneath a rock island on a large snow ledge. I am climbing up to re-establish our belay.

There is an explosion. Loud like artillery. The sky is full of large chunks of snow. A cornice has cut loose! I scream to Karl and Dave and lunge my weight down over my tools to drive them into the snow. My breath is knocked out of me, I see stars and feel pain in my right shoulder. I curse and bear down on my tools flexing my body harder. There's a deep rumble like a freight train passing by, then spindrift, then silence. It's over. I look up. Karl is still on the pitch and he's white with snow. Dave looks at me and then at the mountain. He looks like a person who just got shot is supposed to look; wide eyes, white all around the iris and a boneless, slack face with his mouth slightly open. When your heart is in your throat, you have to release it. We shout to each other. We curse. We make decisions. It's good to SHOUT. The raw taste of terror slips from my throat with every word. We decide to continue. My shoulder is bruised and stiff. Dave and Karl weren't hit. We agree that I won't lead anymore. Dave takes the next hard pitch. A half rope length of thin window panes of ice alternated with patches of air like a checkerboard hung vertically with ice on the black squares only. The pitch ends on a small snow ledge where Dave gets an anchor. While Karl and Dave fix two pitches up a mixed chimney, I dig a snow cave. During the night I fight to stay warm. My sleeping bag is dead. Water has spread through it, turning the down into lumps.

"On the 5th day we held up our bags and they looked like sacks of potatoes" — Urs Kallen, relating his great Deltaform epic to me. History repeats itself and I become another climber soldier in the battle against hypothermia.

In the morning, it's snowing. It's been storming for the past 30 hours. We decide to abandon our attempt at the summit pillar and get off the face as fast as we can. We jug to our highpoint and enter into no-man's-land. Steep walls of snow-covered limestone with no systems to follow. We have to traverse right and gain the "escape" ledge. My shoulder is feeling better, so I take the traverse. The climbing is delicate. My front points hook on small edges with my heels hanging over air. I scrape snow off finger holds then press hard through gloved hands getting my tips to cling. Strange. Slow moves keep me just in balance. This is alpine climbing. Complicated work and never feeling solid. There are too many variables. Too many things that could go wrong. The alpine architect I've aspired to be doesn't exist. You can't control it all, it's too big; it's the earth. You dance along the line, ease from move to move, hope you don't come off but know you wouldn't be surprised if you did. When the pro gets scarce it gets serious. A wolf loping through the forest, stalking. It takes in the earth around it and reacts intuitively. An alive animal. That's the mind space I'm in as I slowly push myself from hold to hold. Time passes in the world outside, but inside I enter the realm of timelessness. I move slowly and strangely maintaining that delicate degree of balance. New information comes in, and the cassette of personal climbing history IS carry in my head goes into quadraphonic. I'm grooving. Then comes the new world. A move I can't do. The past doesn't cover this future. The present shrinks to my decision. There is no logic or reason here. No time for A+B=C. I'm past my flat-land-cruisin- around-the-city image of what I want to be. It's just me here and I have to go with how it feels! If I'm truly ready for this door I'll open it. From the end of the traverse we rap off a knob onto the big "escape" ledge. Karl does an incredible job of kicking steps across several rope lengths. Above is more hard climbing. We won't make it off today. We dig out our third snow cave in the dark while it snows. I spend the night fighting for warmth. Warmth is my brother; cold and hypothermia want to kill me.

But! Won't let you get me, you son of a bitch. My teeth are chattering but that's as far as you'll get right now. No fuckin' way! C'mon muscles, I'm monitoring some more. C'mon muscles, tense up. I can control the shivers. You won't get my core. I can feel you there. You want it, you're a damp whoring mist that wants my core, forget I can move, motion is my domain. You're not going to win.

Karl kicks open the door of the snow cave and reveals more snow to start our fourth day on the face. At noon I pull over the summit ridge into a sandblasting wind. Dave's there, having just led the pitch. We huddle together and plan our descent as we wait for Karl. Once again, Dave is late for work. Another weekend climb in the Rockies. This team is hungry: no breakfast, and a box of Smarties split three ways (that's 17 each, I counted them) for dinner last night. We're ready to go home. Dave took a good picture of me on the second morning of the climb. I'm jugging up the rope. Spindrift has coated everything. The sky is obscured. I'm exerting, but I'm smiling. Looking at that shot, I'm reminded of a little gem that Karl gave me and I've carried ever since: "It don't have to be fun to be fun."

Satialla. Photo by John Clarke

Mount Jacobsen, Monarch Icefield, Coast Mountains. Photo: Ray Kodama

1988: COAST MOUNTAIN EXPLORATION

JOHN CLARKE

"You come here on your holidays?!"
— Logger at Kingcome Inlet, July, 1985

On the western limits of Canada's mainland, the Coast Mountains stand white and beautiful. The trees and the glaciers reach far into each other's zones and ocean, forest and snow come together so that the salt air of the tidal inlets, the soft green light of the forests and the hard glare of the icefields seem to overlap. Glacier follows glacier. Range follows range, and however many climbing parties come and go the remoteness seems unaffected. The Coast Mountains are twenty thousand square miles of prime wolverine habitat where your passing will make no difference.

Why do something that has no relevance to day-to-day life, makes no sense to your friends and takes you to places you have no reason to be, with money you don't have? Let's face it, explorers are addicts! We have fits of terror when confined to the city during weeks of precious summer weather, and on winter evenings we dare not go near the maps if there's anything else to be done around the house. When we finally do get to them, they are spread on the floor and our eyes glaze over as a new area is identified and we just know we're going there. My fascination with the remoter parts of the range started with visits to the homes of Phyl Munday and Neal Carter. Out would come old albums bulging with black and white photos of bush camps, river crossings and fairy tale snowfields. I remember being impressed with their

No less an explorer than Peter Croft once profiled John Clarke as "one of the best, not just in Canada, but in the world" at solitary mountain exploration. Readers of the Journal *have for years been entertained by the tales of John's wilderness forays — often with others, but often alone for months at a time. John may be the clearest reminder we have of a more mystical approach to the high peaks, with a solemn reverence and faithful love for the wild. This brief introduction to his life and loves gives only a touch of his Coast Mountain exploration.*
– GP

fondness for the glaciers and forests as well as the peaks. For them, long valley marches were never considered a purgatory to be endured to get to the good part, but a chance to experience the complete climb. They were both anxious to see the rest of the Coast Mountains explored by British Columbians. Phyl encouraged me to go to the Whitemantle Range and Neal always spoke of the rugged peaks around Headwall Creek in the Toba country. I couldn't resist the new wonders around every corner, waiting in the sprawling ranges they described.

Long high traverses from one inlet to another work best for covering large high areas. These traverses start in forest-cloaked valleys where unknown waterfalls pound down boilerplate granite walls. At the heads of valleys, vast masses of ice flow down to meet the trees. Once on the glaciers we stay as high as possible throughout the traverse; each pass we cross revealing irresistible side trips to individual summits. After about ten days out, time takes on a dream-like quality and the outside world recedes. We become soaked in the scenery and fully involved in the cat and mouse game of weather, topography and food supply. Never knowing how a long traverse will turn out is a big part of its appeal; indeed the best memories seem to be of the trips with the most anxiety. The same madness hits every spring: we want to escape — not the frenzy of the city but the frightening predictability of it. And no amount of exploring is ever enough. We walk through the door after a punishing trip and march directly to the nearest maps. There's always another obscure range out there somewhere, with its own unique challenges and adventures.

Ski touring in the Tombstone Mountains, Yukon Territory. Photo: Pat Morrow

1988 : GRIZZLY

Graeme Pole

Sometimes you get where you're going, and sometimes you don't. One summer day in 1985 my destination had been the summit of Mount Coleman. Grizzly and I met on the trail of Sunset Pass and my destination quickly became the car, which I then drove north to Big Bend with an eye to other summits above the Saskatchewan Glacier.

The bear had left indications of its presence along the trail — two scrapes and a scat. But it didn't look like bear scat. And the scrapes? — well, probably a porcupine. So I chose to continue. Now, two years later, I'm bashing through the boulders and willows in and along Noyes Creek; heading for the pass at its head, and a look at some new country. A couple of kilometres in, I start to get a weird feeling — like I'm not alone here, and I really don't want to be doing this today. I've seen a few deer tracks and the odd boot print, and at first am inclined to take them as the probable cause of this freshly broken tree branch lying at my feet. This branch which because of its placement could only have been stepped on by a dedicated bushwacker, or a heavy animal able to clear the low coverage above. Not by a deer. Reluctantly now, I am less inclined to think of anything but grizzly. The low angle of the early morning sun blinds me to the willow slopes ahead. I have been making lots of noise but the creek makes lots of noise too, and would probably mask my presence until it's too late… The weird feeling becomes much stronger.

Paranoia? I search the ground for evidence of that which I know to be true. And nearby on a mud flat where the creek makes a small lagoon, there it is… two fresh grizzly prints, one over the top of a boot print. I have turned for home before even beginning to rationalize why. Sure it's a big valley. And grizzly could have made this track yesterday and be long gone by now. But he is travelling in the same direction as I, and although browse doesn't look to be too abundant, it is late August and this is perfect denning terrain, perhaps worthy of a couple of days of grizzly's time in exploration of a winter home. But rationalization is unnecessary in face of the reality: this is grizzly's place. I am the one intruding. He has made his presence known. To see fresh grizzly sign on the trail being travelled is much like seeing rockfall down the couloir one is contemplating climbing, or fracture lines on slopes of the same aspect as that which one is about to ski. Warnings. What one chooses to do in light of such warnings largely determines one's longevity in the mountains. So, with a wisdom not possessed two years earlier, I leave grizzly to his valley. I do not reach the head of Noyes Creek this day, but after driving south to Bow Pass, hike to the summit of Observation Peak instead. Sometimes you get where you're going, and sometimes you don't. And sometimes when you don't, the view is much more of a complete thing.

I bring to this meeting
My belief that I will not encounter you;
That I am immune to the threat of your presence.
After all, it's been three years now
And we are yet to meet.
Thus in ignorance I walk onto your ground
Without even the courtesy of making noise
To let you know that I am here.
You bring to this meeting
The knowledge that perhaps within a few decades
Your kind will no longer dwell here
Driven from these valleys and meadows
By those whose fear demands blood,
To the only solitude remaining — eternity.
I see your shoulder come through the trees
Fur and muscle rippling in the sun
A beauty so primal
And I see in your eyes
The dismay of all your kind
And of all the others of the land, air, and water
Who have vanished before you.
I am aware that you could take my life in an instant.
But I wonder at this moment
Who of us is really the most afraid
For I also see the reality of that which each of us is defending
Though fear of meeting you is my greatest concern in these
    mountains
I do not curse you, grizzly.
Nor wish that you live any other place
Nor travel any other trails
Than those do I.

The Giant Steps. Photo: Craig Richards

1991 : IN PRAISE OF SOLITUDE

STEVEN HORVATH

I've been sick for a few days with the flu. It felt remarkably like being at altitude again — take 5 steps and then rest to catch my breath. So I sleep a lot, try to catch up with my reading and avoid unexpected sprints to the privy. But what views of glaciers and dark, water-stained granite walls open up when I finally do make it to our one luxury — a real toilet seat propped up between two boulders. Finally, a reasonably good night and a morning that is too perfect to just watch from the sleeping bag, so I pack up and leave for Mount Laag. (Paul has assured me that it will be just what I need; a nice, long, airy ridge, a fun scramble in E.B.'s.) Walking slowly up a small pocket glacier I gradually become aware of... well, of something. Something different. Then I realize what it is — I am alone, by myself, as I used to be in the mountains years ago when the world was still young, years before ambition led to the need for partners, for someone to share the responsibilities and the hauling of hardware.

I stop to think, catch my breath and look around at the things that one can see when there's no need to "crank the boogie meter to the max" to get to the climb before your competition or bad weather. A white moth lies on the snow, lacelike pattern of frost on its unfolded wings. Lichens form delicately tough abstract patterns on granite boulders that look like rejects from Henry Moore's workshop. A long cascade is hanging frozen in space from the escarpment to my right. I get up and continue walking. My pack feels just right. Another almost-forgotten bonus of going light and alone: no hardware, no ropes and slings; only the ice axe, camera and some goodies. I finally make it to the ridge proper, sit down on a grassy spot, look around and then slowly change into my old E.B.'s. The air is still, with a strong blue presence. Too fast a move and it might ring with a clear high note of a crystal bell, the sound of Xmas past. I carefully store my books under some rocks, remembering my many not-too-pleasant experiences with summit-dwelling rodents.

Despite what might appear to be intense competition among today's climbers, mountains still work their inevitable magic on the souls of even those with the most precisely calibrated "boogiemeters."
—R WS

Like that airy bivi on Mount Remillard when the little devils chewed right through the shoulder straps of my old Joe Brown even as I was sleeping in it, trying to use it as a bivi bag. Paul was right, the ridge is a delight; narrow, quite exposed and not too steep. Then an overhanging section, but I bypass it on a steep and loose face to the right. Too steep for my present condition and too loose for my fatigue, but then, as I stop to catch my breath I realize that I am in the middle of a hanging garden. Moss campion in gloriously purple bloom, a banzailike miniature pine softly green against the white and grey granite, blades of grass, yellow arnicas, mountain asters, and occasional hummingbirds dive bombing and inspecting my red pack. I finally arrive below the summit block. Some 50 feet of pleasantly exposed low Class 5 and then it's time for a summit lunch and a siesta. I sleep for an hour or so, completely secure and relaxed, comfortably stretched out on a narrow grassy ledge on the leeside of the summit and then sit up, and enjoy my pipe and watch the clouds slowly move across the summer sky. A "nothing" day? No hard rock, no F.A., not even a hope of an epic, no adrenaline rush, no expletives deleted and certainly no boogie meter cranked to the max. Just a lazy summer day with no one for company but myself. Cruel but fair.

North face of Mount Alberta. Photo: Greg Horne

1993 : AN ALBERTA SUMMER

JOE JOSEPHSON

I had been on Baffin Island and, for a number of bizarre and unimaginable reasons, no climbing was to be had. Rather than play tourist and trek past all those great peaks to Summit Lake, I was compelled to retreat home to the great peaks of the Rockies. Baffin has nothing on the Rockies — except perhaps raw seal meat. For what was left of that summer, most of my time was spent watching the rain and working far too much. But, when the weather cleared, I began my courtship with the jewel of the Rockies — Mount Alberta.

Trevor and I swung five days off each. Our options were an unclimbed peak that Trevor knew about, or the North Face of Alberta. Many climbers would consider an untrodden summit the most desirable of all mountain experiences, yet we were drawn to that huge face lurking just over Woolley Shoulder. We were not to be the first nor the last. Mountains such as this have a draw to them like that old music tape that you've heard a thousand of times; you just can't resist its moving melodies one more time.

But what is it that draws people to this area? Is it the write up in the over-read 50 Classic Climbs? The publishing of a new guidebook? The history of great names and efforts? Or just the sheer wildness and beauty of it all? Perhaps all of these. You can research the stories and the note-worthy ascents through the books and journals, but they don't fully portray the adventure found on Mount Alberta. Aside from a personal experience, the greatest feeling of spirit can be found, strangely enough, in the Alberta Hut near the base of the East Face. Some people may question the need and aesthetics of a hut near Mount Alberta, and having used the hut, I can hardly criticize it's existence, but if anything is to explain the draw of the mountain, it would be the Log Book. More than an entry of names and routes, it is a journal of human history. The short, long, terse, arcane, epic, hilarious, banal, serious, awed, famous, unknown and the ridiculous are all chronicled there.

You can read about the people and adventures that don't get written up in the magazines. Sensationalism and drama are not needed, for on Mount Alberta they come naturally. You can read about Masamitsu (51 years old) and Yokoyama — they traveled here in honor no less than four times only to be repulsed each time by the magnitude and weather. With frightening regularity, there are tales of rare "ball lightning" jumping across the ridges. Found are the images from 35-pitch sieges, to bold solos. From his words, you can almost see the infamous 'Grande Frommage,' Dave Cheesmond, on his many trips and hard routes "over Woolley Shoulder". Passing time in a storm, you can be inspired by ascents of the North Face and amazed by gripping retreats. While you recover from the difficult slog up the scree you can catch up on the adventures of people you may know or perhaps have only heard of.

There are those living nostalgically back in the golden days of mountaineering, when the peaks were new and the valleys unknown, who claim that the climbers of today have lost their sense of place. This remarkable article argues eloquently that climbers are still in touch with the mythology of the peaks, and that mountains continue to inspire awe in direct proportion to the commitment climbers make to their ascent.

– RWS

The log book sets the scene from August 1984 onwards. Pre-hut history is left to the journals, articles, word-of-mouth and the ever expanding mythology of Mount Alberta. The summer of 1992 found the log book with a new chapter. Not a finer chapter, and by no means better written than previous years, but with its fill of refreshing and amazing tales. By the time Trevor and I saw the peak in early August a number an unprecedented number of folks had already traveled before us.

After a long but stellar alpine season in Alaska and the Rockies, Andy and Julie topped off their tour with the sixth ascent of the North Face. They did a fine job in good weather and were impressed by the length and difficulty, appalled by the grossness of the yellow band, and ready to clip bolts in California by the time they were done. Zippy and Glenn gave a typically modest and light-hearted account of an attempt on the remote and still unclimbed West Face. My good friend Bruce had been in with Murray and cruised the Japanese Route. Back in the city he was aching that I was up to do the North Face and he didn't have the time to come along. No matter how good a trip goes it seems the grass is always greener on the other side.

Drinking tea and napping the afternoon away at the hut I thought of our friend Frank, who was at the moment somewhere on the Japanese Route. What kind of experience was he having? We left, then slowly picked our way to the base of the North-East ridge, tired but anxious about the upcoming days. Then — Wow! — a person's first sight of the North Face is truely an unforgettable moment. Any one who finds their home and spirit in the mountains will be transfixed upon what is (at least in my relatively untravelled opinion), one of the most aesthetic of all mountain faces.

Descending a snow rib while looking for the descent point that takes us to the base of the face I stopped.

"Hey Trevor, look at this. It can't be!"

"You're right. Holy shit, I can't believe it!"

We had found fresh grizzly tracks in the sun-baked snow. He or she had pounded up from the depths of Habel Creek and across crevasse fields in search of food, perhaps trying to escape the thickness of the Athabasca Valley just as we try to escape the urban jungle. Almost certainly we were being watched as we traversed from the hut. As a climber I find the face to be utterly compelling; I could only imagine what a griz' feels to be in such a place. I did know that I was glad I hadn't been there 30 minutes earlier. After coming all that way up from the "Black Hole" only to find himself rimrocked with no where to go but the way he came he must have been pissed!

Leaving the hut and grizzlies behind, we descended to the base of the face, just as many aspiring parties had before us. The evening went beautifully with fresh water to drink, fine sand to stretch upon and soft light to behold. I kept telling myself it can't be any harder than Mount Chephren, a route I did in the spring. I felt capable, but overwhelmed with a sense of privilege to be venturing onto such a scene. We slept with dreams of big bears and big climbs.

The hardest part of any alpine route is getting your ass in gear and getting committed. We woke without hesitation and efficiently brewed and packed up. It is joyous to be climbing when you and your partner are both fit, keen and working together. In the pre-dawn ink we headed towards the wall.

We made good time up the ice pitches and onto the Yellow Band. There we slowed dramatically. At one of the belays I had lots of time to contemplate our tied off knifeblades, the pain in my bunions, how much I hated my boots, Trevor and the speed at which he's moving, the world and the vileness of the rock. This section of the wall is undoubtably the most sinister and perhaps the most famous. It is here, in 1980, that they believe Tobin ripped his belay and plunged to his demise in a tragic end to one of history's most inspired climbers. He was attempting the route in a style even farther ahead of it's time than George and Jock's first ascent of the face may have been. I gazed across the expanse to my left as the face curved out to meet the North-East Ridge. Some people are calling this the "Wilford Variation," named after Mark traversed the band last year while retreating from a solo attempt of the North Face. I thought of my friend Sean who did the same traverse and also of the Coloradoans who did it long before Mark ever saw the face. I could imagine the fortitude and drive it took for Mark to continue up the difficult North-East Ridge after surely scaring himself silly.

At this point, our story of ascent becomes nothing out of the ordinary. Pitch-by-pitch accounts become trite with the same old drill of hard climbing, long belays, wet rock, wild moves and setting suns. It does, however have one good quality of a fine climbing tale — an epic retreat. Few experiences in my life have matched the desperation of dicking around for an A3 rappel station under a raging water spout, then having to stand for an hour while Trevor cleaned our fixed rope and reversed the traverse below the crux overhang. Andy and Julie mentioned a dry face; we had no such luck; snow on all the ledges and a night of thundershowers had us feeling like we were getting a body enema. The next stop down, I found a decaying horn of rock with a faded sling looped around it. Blazed upon the ratted nylon were the intials C.D.

I've heard how people call the rusted tin cans and scattered junk along the Chilkoot Trail in the Yukon 'antiques' and say they are part of history, for they tell of the people who travelled there in search of gold. This piece of tat, coated in limestone grime, looking like trash among this dark and beautiful obelisk, parallels those relics left behind during the gold rush. It sparks the images of Carl and his partner and their multi-day Homeric descent in the midst of Class 3 avalanches and trundling microwaves of rock. Their words are found in the log book, but it is that piece of webbing that really means something to me. Nervously using it to rappel, it touched me and now became part of our story.

That is what this article is all about: the stories, images and human history spawned by not only this great peak, but from all of climbing and the characters that make it come alive. The more I climb, the less I want to hear of grades and the more I want to hear and know the wild routes, in wild times, by wild spirits. Leave the grades for the guidebook. They are important only to give an aspiring party some idea of what to expect. In a place like the Columbia Icefields, technical letter grades don't mean squat compared to the "psyche grade". The rumors of hard men, forced bivouacs, rockfall and early winter storms build into a mythology that transcends the objectivity of it all. Years ago I can remember being at parties, and while half looped I would bravely mention a route to a climbing buddy or two and they would respond incredously: "We can't go up there, that's a Greenwood route!", or "James backed off that one; no way man."

Last August on Mount Alberta I found myself a victim of that mythology. We (or at least I) felt that we should be moving either up or moving down. It hadn't occured to me to sit still and wait at the bivi to see if it cleared. So, for whatever reason, we bailed off the headwall, spent hours looking for safe pin placements in the black tile and then lurched ourselves down into the gauntlet of the iceface. Looking up at the wall, it truely seemed alive. A moving, breathing and malevolent creature that cast an image I may never forget. Not only was I a victim

but I didn't realize at the time that we were becoming a part of the myth.

It happened so fast I barely recognized what was happening. I heard the crack and looked at Trev, who had just come down the rappel and reached my station. He seemed okay at first but then suddenly flopped over and spiraled across the ice. Many, many, many rocks were wizzing by constantly, with some of the smaller ones dinging off our helmets. I'm unsure of what exactly hit Trevor but the entire frontal lobe of his UIAA-certified Edelrid helmet disappeared, and a thick wool cap and balaclava underneath ripped. Miraculously, by the time the rock got through all of that and his mangy haircut, he had only a slight cut. Once he regained composure and clipped the station, I collected some shards of orange plastic from the ice as a mute token for Trevor. It was done. We were alive, and neither of us needed to say any more about the high probability of a second round, so we continued our almost robotic procedure of escape.

Fortunately the rest of the retreat went very smoothly and soon we were drying out in the sun near the base, sucking on a spot of tea. By the time we got back to the hut we were baked; utterly exhuasted, hopelessly dehydrated, and quickly falling asleep as an Indian sun set far off into British Columbia.

The next morning we woke no earlier than 10 o'clock and humbly went about rehydrating, drying the ropes (no way did I want to carry such overweighted pigs back to the road), and pounding nails into the creaking outhouse. Soon I spied a familiar gait across the glacier. I hadn't seen it for months since he went off to Italy with Sly. Bubba was back, and alone. Manically driven, he was in for "What else — the North Face." After catching up on the history since we last spoke, much bullshitting, and lending him my rock shoes to add to an already-monstrous pack, we set off in opposite directions. Trev and I were off to the east and the car, our adventure was over and we were faced with nothing more than several hours of tiring pain-in-the-ass kind of hiking. He was off to the west. It was a sight I'll long remember: Bubba soloing across the glacier, hopping crevasses toward the North Face, an animated figurine almost stick-like. I thought of the places he's been, the drive and vision barely contained within, and looking forward to climbing with him more often, perhaps in a place such as this.

After arriving at Woolley Shoulder ten minutes before Trevor, I had some time to feel the cold wind and contemplate our experience. It is always difficult to back off such a route. They require so much thought, time, energy and emotional commitment that I believe it's one of the hardest quandaries I face as a climber. It is particularly hard when the route and skies clear off just after you've bailed. Thoughts pass rapidly back and forth between "Why couldn't I be more a hard man and just go for it" and "Good judgement man, paying our dues". I'm still young enough and passionately driven enough that I feel the urge to justify my actions. An emotion I struggle to accept more calmly.

Despite the wreckage of the attempt I could gaze across Alberta and North Twin and feel at home. The past two years have been filled with uncertainty and doubts about my job, whether I want to immigrate to Canada or return to my home state of Montana that I love so much, and generally which way my life is headed. Sitting upon one of the world's greatest vistas the connection I felt with the Rockies and with the spirits of the truly great friends I've found within were overwhelming. It was hard to turn my back and head down the scree towards the car and the uncertainties of the city.

Soon we ran into Tim and P.A. We were warned of their presence by Bubba and were looking forward to telling them our tale. They had been planning this trip all summer and were fit, keen and overqualified. Trevor proudly showed his helmet. Tim thought the bucket was on his pack when it got hit and you could see the concern in his face as he wondered why Trevor wasn't wearing it. Tim has been involved with many rescues and recoveries of fallen climbers and could not believe that such damage could be inflicted with the owner of the head underneath escaping alive. The myth grows.

This leads to the final, and to me the most amazing, tale of the 1992 Alberta summer. This is not of epic retreats, bad weather or near death experiences. It is to give some overdue credit to Tim and P.A., two of the most unheralded alpinists in North America. Their ability, longevity, and record of ascents around the world anyone would find inspiring. They had been planning on the North Face for six months, plotting every piece of gear and counting every ounce. Their timing with the weather was perfect. This is the most crucial of all elements in success at Mount Alberta. As Choc says, "It's all timing and hormones."

They bivied, not at the safe, soft, sandy ledge near the rappel point, but bravely on the traverse ledge two pitches up the face. No one else has approached the face this way. Combining this early start to the ice face with their abilities, they cruised up to the Yellow Band, up the initial headwall pitches, past our rap-

pel station and bivi ledge, over the crux overhang and polished off several pitches of hard free climbing before darkness halted their advance. They had even gotten off-route lower down while trying to force a direct line: often times a mistake that can stop a party dead in its tracks.

The pair had no stove, so were in dire need of some fluid. By now it was pitch black and the wall was swept clean of excess moisture by the rain, winds and sun, yet they could hear some water trickling down somewhere to the right. Drawing on his big wall experience from years back, Tim lowered down the plumb vertical headwall, and with 1000 m of air beneath him began a Yosemite-style King Swing. The sight this must have been boggles my mind. How often is something like that done in the Rockies? But it paid off: Tim managed to reach the rivulet and fill two liters of water.

The guidebook mentions several excellent bivi ledges high on the route. This pair found only small ledges where they had to sleep on different levels and Tim had to suspend his feet in his pack out over the abyss. The next morning came casually; there is a strange amount of security found in biving this high on a great face. The crux is below you, the anxiety is done and you are virtually guaranteed to tick the route. This cannot be said for the unknown party they spied at first light. Far below, they were heading up the ice face. It is a wild year when a face like this, mired in such history, difficulty and remoteness, sees so many attempts. Some years it goes totally unseen.

After hooting to each other, the upper party rolled back to sleep knowing they had nothing more than moderate, fun climbing to the summit. Having been there, I know what the lower party was thinking: apprehensive of the hard climbing above and scared shitless of the objective danger on the iceface. And by the time Tim and P.A. got moving they could see the other party retreating across the glacier. Who knows what happened, but they must have been simultaneously glad and disappointed to be out of the grips of the face. They had their own reasons to work through and understand just as I did. But for whatever purpose they backed off, perhaps it was intuition, they were lucky.

It started with a roar and erupted into a massive black cloud that charged down the face and darkened the glacier below. Tim and P.A. were witnessing house-sized blocks spontaneously ripping themselves from the flesh somewhere in the Yellow Band. Their previous bivi on the traverse ledge and the route the unkown party just travelled were all but obliterated. After they hiked the route, perhaps this was a signal by the God of Alberta for the pair to take heed and remember that no matter how good you and your timing are, the peaks always hold the trump card.

Comparing stories with Tim later that fall, he told me that the route was a culmination of more than 20 years of climbing. I'm sure it won't be the last great route for this "mild-mannered, ineffectual little fellow." Mount Alberta reminded me of the fullness climbing adds to life and deepened some of the reasons I climb: the challenge, the wildness, and most importantly the relationships with those around you. It spawned the ambition and dreams I have of high and hard places.

The rather remarkable Alberta Summer of 1992 came to a close in late August with the onslaught of the Rockies' infamous late season snows. I'd like to think of these stories as the compliment to the article called "The Many Moods of Alberta," a photo essay by Glen Boles in the 1983 *Canadian Alpine Journal*. His photos chronicle the scenes you may see as you make your pilgrimmage to the peak. Here and in the hut book you'll catch a glimpse of the moods of the people who similarly travel.

> *"…the annual volume is not, as you slightingly called it, "a booklet relating to mountain climbing and club activities", although these of course receive attention.* The Canadian Alpine Journal *is a well-edited, well-illustrated record of important work, scientific and otherwise, done in the mountains of Canada, and is one of the very best advertisements for Canada… the* Canadian Alpine Journal, *will in actual cash more than repay the annual grant, and the indirect benefit to Canada cannot be estimated."*
>
> — Club member J.M. Macoun in a letter to the *Ottawa Citizen*, regarding a federal grant of $1000 to the ACC, May 21, 1923

The Homathko Icefield, Coast Mountains. Photo: Baiba Morrow

1993 : PAWING THE VOID

TUKCHE SIMPSON

CHAPTER 21 — THE CREVASSE

Like my namesake, I've discovered that even if I play all my cards wrong, I can can still suck fame out of the most despairing of epics. Unlike my namesake, however, if I took a dive and broke a leg, at least I'd have another three to hobble away on. I'm actually a little ashamed to be named after him — Joe Simpson dragged himself around Siula Grande with an ineptitude only humans can find heroic; we dogs demand a little more of ourselves. My recent trip to the ever-terrifying Columbia Icefields was a shining example of dogged courage in the face of tremendous adversity.

In the worst weather, a dog will curl up in front of the fireplace and wait for a woman with nails to scratch his belly. When a ferocious blizzard hit Canmore on the first Friday in April, I hoped that my so-called master would look for a woman to scratch both our bellies and give up his ill-fated plans for a ski. In retrospect, of course, believing he would give up climbing plans was even more absurd than expecting him to be able to find a woman. No, instead, he's on the phone on Friday night making plans for a 5:30 a.m. departure, and I overhear him asking the other stupid bugger if it's okay to bring me along. He says I'd be really upset if I was left behind; climbing partners seem to be able to lie to each other with the greatest of ease. I groan, wishing I could find one of his ski boots to eat the sole off of, and he gets off the phone, minces over to me and starts with some crap about, "Are you excited to be going skiing, Tucky…?" Of course I'm excited, you stupid arse, I've seen you in a white-out, and we're all going to die…

So we go anyways, and it turns out that the other bugger is an Alpine Clubber, so I'll probably end up being led around Banff by some turkey in lederhosen. And, the guy's name is Shackleton, so we'll probably end up spending the whole winter on the Icefields, only to die, just like his namesake. Typically, the Icefields are whited-out from stem to stern, and they have to take their first compass bearing off the bumper of the car. All the way up the tongue that day, they try to laugh about the ridiculous situation they're about to drag me into, as if they really enjoyed the prospect of our collective deaths. Stopping to huff and puff by the beginning of the headwall, they first introduce the idea of a retreat, and to offer my support, I grab the string of the compass and try to help us all by throwing it into a crevasse. For this, for God's sake, I get hit! Me, who can save their lives, hit! I trot ahead because I can smell a rather tasty present left behind by the previous party…

As we start up the headwall, the master decides that he now wants me tied to him so I "don't get lost." This is ridiculous, because I'll have to go his pace, which is 30 m between stops while he "navigates." "Navigating" is a

Along with stories of suffering and triumph, the Canadian Alpine Journal *has also recorded the wit, charm and humour that is as much a part of the makeup of mountaineers as their upward mobility. Stand back all you brave climbers! Here comes the fearless Tucky Simpson!*
– R WS

fat bastard's word for catching his breath, I've noticed. We'll never catch up to the advance party if we go this slow, and I can smell that they've got real food, not the freeze-dried crap these buggers are carrying, "to test for the Himalaya" — again, an excuse for being too weak to carry real food. So, I'm tied in, but every time I pull on the rope to get the buggers moving, the two of them kick and swear, and they finally stop to have a talk about untying me. Right in the middle of the Athabasca Glacier, where thousands of people probably die in crevasses every year. They talk about what a "pain" I'm being, and they decide that I should be untied right there, abandoned like poor old Joe, hanging over the edge of the serac, waiting for Simon to cut the rope.

Cut loose, I wander not two feet before he shouts to me, "Tukche — stay close by! There are crevasses around!" Of course I'm going to stay close by, you bone-head (and I don't mean bone in the scrumptious sense of the word!) — I have to follow if I want any dinner at all. And sure enough, ten feet later, the big dive! Right through one of the bridges that these bastards had just said were "hard as a rock this time of the year." I fall and fall and fall, and whumph!, land on the narrowest of bridges spanning the crevasse. As embar-rassed as I am to say it, I can only tell you that I landed like… a cat. Ten metres, on a

bridge that extended about a metre out on either side of me before the crevasse dropped off forever, I lay awaiting my doom.

Cold settled in quickly, with little dustings of spindrift covering me in sec-onds. I knew the boys had seen me disappear, and would soon come looking. The master simply couldn't last without his "chick magnet," but I thought I'd better scope out the scene in case they were too stupid to figure out a rescue. A long slot, widening quickly, with a couple of bridges like mine loomed in the bleak distance. One looked like a poodle, the other like a Milk Bone. I thought I'd try to jump to

the Milk Bone, because it might lead up and out of the hole, but when I got a paw on it, the thing collapsed into dust, and I just about went snout over tail into the abyss. I yelped and this seemed to waken the two above into action. It turned out later that the master had come to the edge, and not seeing me, had begun the funeral preparations a mite early. Shackleton, it seems, had moaned on about them being better off, because I was ruining the trip anyway…

When the master looked again after the yelp, he saw me this time and started in with that incredibly stupid baby-talk shit that humans try on the more dignified species. Like, I really want to have a conversation about "Whadda goo' boy" I am, when I'm on the edge of my eternal goddamn reward! Years of climbing training came in handy here as the master rapped into the hole and dumped about six tons of snow on top of me, burying me completely. He panicked because he thought I'd fallen off the ledge, and the last thing I wanted to do is shake the snow off and collapse my perch. He came all the way down to me though, and when I saw him step on the ledge, I realized it must be stronger than I thought if it could support his fat ass, so I stood up and he saw me just before he impaled me with his crampons.

After what seemed at least half an hour of them screwing up every system of rescue in the book, they finally figured out how to do a simple two-to-one pulley, and they smashed me back and forth up the sides of the crevasse. I finally flopped over the top…and then, they started yelling at me! Like I asked to be untied and exposed to my very own death! So when we started off again, and I had to endure nonsense from them like, "Jesus, we were lucky the dog found the slot — it could have been one of us!", and "Now he's all wet, he'll have to sleep outside…." I just smiled, and thought back to the day at the vet's when he told her to cut them off, and I thought to myself — one day when you're asleep, man, one day… CHOMP!

Peaks of the Exstew River range. Photo: John Clarke

Looking down from the summit of Mount Bute, Coast Mountains. Photo: Pat Morrow

1994 : FIFTH TIME LUCKY: BUTE MOUNTAIN

MICHAEL DOWN

M y long love affair with Bute Mountain began back in the mid-seventies when, fresh and tender out of high school, I was thrown into the hurly-burly of logging camps at the height of the green gold rush. At the time I had no qualms doing my part to liquidate the great Douglas fir forests of the lower coast; it was a quick fix to finance school and my newfound climbing habit. And besides, the remote camps were on the edge of a whole new and shining world of magic I was just discovering: the Coast Range.

My very first camp was tucked into the head of Bute Inlet, with the golden granite of Bute Mountain rising in full view above the flat, white rows of Atco trailers that made for home. It was here I shed my teenage skin. The heat and bugs and grinding hard work did their bit to whip me into manhood, but it was the uncouth culture of men, isolated in the bush and united by the sheer drudgery of their work, that had the biggest impact. The first few days I was in total shock from the unrelenting torrent of language so foul even the trees would cringe. But, being a natural with languages, in a few weeks I was talkin' loggin' with the best of them. A key element of my character was being formed.

Exhausted from labour and the bombardment of cultural stimulation, I'd take refuge every evening in the cookshack with triple desserts and sprawl out on the benches on the deck outside. Immobile and almost nauseous from overeating, I'd lay there in the fetid evening warmth, homesick as a puppy for my first great love, and gazing up at the flaming orange granite of Bute's West Wall. How many evenings did I recline there in a stupor, imagining myself on its massive flanks and kindling a passion to someday return and climb its great face?

I waited too long. In 1986, Greg Foweraker and Don Serl fired off one of the finest alpine rock climbs in all of Canada. Still, there remained a dramatic buttress framing the face to its left, and on this project I set my goal with a renewed desire. To this end I recruited Mike White, fittingly my only close friend to have endured from high school, and John Clarke, Grand Master of the Coast Range, who would provide us with instant credibility. Our plan was to fly to the base of the buttress by helicopter from Campbell River, climb the route, then exit via a two-day walk out Galleon Creek to the logging camp, which was ambitious given our staggering load of climbing gear.

With constant fog and drizzle, we didn't get much further than the landing pad. But we did get a suss on the soaring difficulties of the buttress, with the blank and compact upper headwall suggesting a bolt kit for future forays. After several days of John's tales of soiling summits, we packed up huge loads and wandered off into the mist.

John had previously thrashed out Galleon Creek many years before at the end of one of his trademark ski journeys, and had unequivocally declared it the most horrific bushwhack of his entire Coast Range career.

With its powerful themes of drive and persistence, Michael Down's piece from the 1994 Journal is a happy reminder of the continuing potential for significant personal achievement in our sport. Clearly, even in the age of helicopters and backroads and high-tech gear, the mountains still quietly await those with the right spirit.
– GP

Sometime before the war, the mid-valley had been felled and creamed, with many big trees left behind stacked up on the valley floor like pick-up-sticks. In the intervening half-century, a dense thicket of second growth had choked the valley with trees so tightly packed that one could barely wedge between them wearing a pack, and worse, matted out and filled the holes between old, fallen logs, making for trapdoors that could drop you fifteen feet with your pack following closely behind. If, with all his legendary time in the weeds, this was John's toughest bushthrash, it would certainly be so for Mike and I.

We planned to circumvent much of this nastiness by staying high, traversing slabs and boulderfields below the crest of the ridge arcing west out from the peak towards the inlet. Only a couple of hours on our way, I was carefully crab-walking down a pea-gravel-strewn slab, when my foot slipped on the ball bearings and my knee buckled backwards under the weight of my iron-laden load. A scream of pain shot through my knee as if jabbed with a red-hot firepoker, and in the time it took to roll over and pull up my pant leg, it had swollen up as fat and soft as an overripe grapefruit.

What to do? Two brutal days of bush ahead, and my knee could barely take body weight. After a couple of hours, the shooting pain dulled into a haze of 292s, and with a makeshift crutch I could hobble along. Now Mike came into his element. He became completely alive when called upon to fully engage his raw and immense physical power, with a frame as stout as a Douglas fir trunk, and just as durable. Mike's carefree demeanor carefully conceals a silent, almost brooding intensity that flushes with a cool and controlled desire when challenged by any ultimate endurance test. And here was an irrefutable opportunity. With barely a word of discussion, he seized my pack and lashed it on top of his.

With at least 120 pounds on his back, his neck bulging with pulsing purple veins, Mike never once complained, fighting through the bush and occasionally crashing headlong into the collapsing canopy of hidden tree wells. Mike's casual chuckle was working overtime; behind the grin you'd catch a quick but penetrating wince, revealing just how much pain he was pushing through—and how much he was relishing it. Never before or since have I witnessed such a feat of sheer endurance. Yet for Mike, a fireman by trade, it was just another act of the quiet and simple heroism that defines his character. This was his first trip into the Coast Range, and he hasn't been back. He's since chosen less arduous and more comfortable mountain projects like becoming the first Canadian to climb Jannu along with Rob Driscoll.

Within a few weeks my knee had cooled down, the weather had warmed up, and John and I were back with a revised strategy; we had in our pocket a top gun rope rocket by the name of Greg Foweraker to fire off the hard bits. Having already written his signature on the West Face years before, being first up the framing buttress would complete his ownership of one of the finest chunks of granite real estate in the Coast Range.

In the sweet coolness of an early dawn we quickly passed two easy pitches to the base of a steep, blank fin, and what turned out to be the technical crux of the entire route. Greg started up a narrow, diagonalling corner with delicate stemming and face moves until the corner dissolved into a thin facecrack, which continued to diagonal up the vertical wall of the fin. Several awkward A3 leeper stacks finished the pitch, and I jerked and dangled on aid through a roof, above spilling onto a fat ledge crowning the fin. We threw a rope down to John, who jumared straight up the wall of the fin while Greg dispatched tricky face climbing bordering another incipient and right-leaning facecrack.

Above, broken ground led to the base of a stiff offwidth and hand traverse, brutal to follow with a heavy pack. It was now early afternoon and, under a blazing sun, brains melting in helmets, we were slowing down. Greg and I waited for sometime, baking on an otherwise comfortable ledge. The jumar rope was tight, but our calls to John remained unanswered, so I rigged a rappel and headed down to check him out.

I found him with his jumars jammed under a roof, his face naive with a wide and innocent grin, chuckling to himself over his predicament, hanging in space and not being able to move up or down. You see, John had never jumared before and, true to his adventurous spirit, was learning this new skill on big granite, high in his beloved Coast Range. The arts and crafts of high-angle rock climbing he would learn on the peaks or not at all, for he had no taste for lowland life in places like seaside Squamish. With a little coaching and cursing, and a hearty, twisted laugh over the yawning exposure, John worked his wiry physique over the overhang, and then we sat down for a pow-wow.

It was obvious that, at the pace we were moving, we'd be on the route for a week, and John had lost enthusiasm for further big wall lessons upon perusing the headwall awaiting ahead. In his lighthearted and unassuming way, John was clear he would downclimb via a gully that intersected the ridge at our present point, one that funneled onto a steep, hanging glacier he could traverse back to base-camp, leaving Greg and I free to finish the buttress. We looked at each other with incredulity, Greg's eyebrows lifting high and his eyes popping wide as his chin lifted into a trademark leer of excited surprise. We were nobody to question John's plan, with his decades of safe soloing on just such terrain. He was so understated and matter-of-fact it would work, and it was what he wanted.

By evening Greg and I had fired several pitches to the base of the headwall, which immediately reared into a huge roof capping an initial corner. Bathed in softening hues of orange light, I watched him turn the roof aiding on solid Friends to the left, and break into a steep corner system that could carry us up most of the distance of the headwall. Jazzed about tomorrow's prospects, we settled in on a five-star ledge for an enchanted night hanging over the Coast Range.

Dawn came early, and with it a distant voice came wafting up on a breeze of first light. It was John's wake-up call; he had bivied where a 'schrund cut off the way down. So Greg and I began the rappels, leaving the route ahead with a shrug, and relieved to join him.

The summer of 1990 ended with a whimper, and one more, barely airborne, attempt. As we flew in, it became apparent a recent storm had dusted the higher peaks, and with the prospect of iced cracks, Greg and I had our pilot, Reto Glass, turn the helicopter back to Campbell River before Bute had even come into sight.

We were back next July, this time with Alan Fletcher. Alan was a long-time hiker and ski-tourer, fairly fresh to the technical alpine game, but eager for steep experience. With lungs like bellows and shoulders that straddle a doorway, he was the perfect support man for jugging up water and bivi gear while Greg and I shot ahead swapping leads. We made excellent time, gaining efficiency as the previous year's pitches were recalled and improved upon. Towards day's end, we were on new ground, working a steep dihedral, thinly plated onto the otherwise blank and bronzed headwall.

Exhilarating climbing! Wild exposure! I jammed my way up perfect finger-locks, cleanly shifting weight between my right shoe, tipped into the corner, and my left, pushing off of small knobs to wedge my butt into the corner for rests, and

dropping nuts into the crack. Aiding on a few baby angles pounded into a dirt-filled crack, and a full rope-length of purifying air on the blade of the buttress, the feature was done. Greg then made short work of a wide, low-angled corner above, finishing the 15th pitch of the day in fading light. Just as requested, a two-tiered ledge for three awaited us.

A dull grey infected the morning sky; rain threatened, but still seemed hours off. It was only some 60 m to the top of the buttress, but the gradient ran to overhanging on crackless rock where only a Hilti would have dared to travel. We pieced out a tentative traversing line from the bivi ledge, but with the brooding sky hanging heavy, we knew we would have to flash it fast. We asked Alan to wait on the ledge to lend us speed, and still playing the role of apprentice, he easily accepted.

Greg and I swung hard right on broken ledges, gaining height whenever flakes and corners offered upward movement. We were moving fast as the sky closed in, until I slowed down to negotiate some awkward and expanding aid, right off an intimidating ledge. One last gold-encrusted, razor-edged corner cut sharply to finish. His blood rising like a firebrand, Greg grabbed the wicked edge and grappled hand-over-hand, underclinging with powerful and flowing primate-like movements lightly clipped with an edge of impatience. I followed in his slip-stream as the first rain began to hit, exploding like tine bombs of pent-up anger. We dashed up the boulder-strewn terrace to a high point directly above Alan, and in two steep rappels, rejoined him on the bivi ledge.

We continued the rappels in lashing rain, picking up on anchors from our earlier attempt. The black lichen turned to grease, adding treachery to the misery of figure 8s squeezing freezing water out of ropes, and draining it directly into one's crotch. Then we heard a drone muffled in the folds of dismal, grey mist enveloping the buttress. Reto's helicopter emerged from the thick fog like a shadow, a day early for pickup, coming to check on our safety in the breaking storm. We madly waved bright colours and watched as his machine climbed the length of the buttress above, then spied us and plummeted straight down toward our stance like a raptor plunging after its prey. He hovered some 10 m off the buttress, and we could see his thick, black mustache underlined by a wild grin beaming out from the plastic bubble of the cockpit. The atmosphere was a cacophony of rotor blades and furious wind. We all laughed at the unreality of the moment, and in frenzied waving gestures, managed to communicate a game plan. Reto flew off, leaving us in ghost-like silence. He would park in basecamp, into which we would rappel in a couple of hours to fly off for some of his down-home hospitality.

We'd solved the crux lower buttress, but its cresting upper reaches remained inviolate, as did a second lower buttress splitting off in a Y-formation from the terraces, dropping off to the northwest. Lower-angled, and with a good dose of height gained by a glacier fanning up its flanks in an apron of ice, this lower northwest buttress could provide spicy climbing on perfect granite, as well as a direct connection to the upper buttress still waiting for completion.

Come September, it was a glorious Indian Summer. Newly a father, I could barely justify another attempt, but knew it would be my last chance to consummate a long-standing relationship with this mountain. Alan and I picked our weather, had Reto fly us to drop a cache at the base of the route, then continued on to the base of the north face of Mount Grenville standing in lonely vigil at the south end of the Homathko Icefield. We waved good-bye at noon, and by 4:00 were standing on the summit, after frontpointing up glassy-blue, autumn ice in a narrow gully hemmed in by rearing monolithic granite. The view was resplendent in the crystal September air, this remote sentinel at the centre of a circle whose radius takes in the full glory of the Waddington Range to the northwest, and sweeps around to take in Queen Bess, the Tchaikazan, Chilko Lake peaks through to Gilbert and Raleigh in the southeast, and on all the way down to Wahoo Tower and the edge of Whistler country. Accompanied by changing angles on one of the finest viewscapes the entire Coast Range has to offer, we spent the evening and all next day travelling back to Bute, following one of many tendrils of glacial ice radiating like fingers off a starfish from the southern end of the Homathko Icefield.

And now to the real task at hand. By first light, we'd cramponed up 300 m of ice apron and kissed cold, unblemished granite so clean there was barely a pebble on a ledge. The climbing was pure delight — pitch after pitch of 5.7 and 5.8 corners and cracks in ramps that zig-zagged upwards on the buttress crest to a final headwall, dressed with a vertical dihedral that went at 5.9 with stemming and handjams on rock imported from the Stovelegs of El Cap.

We quickly clambered up the terrace to get back on steep rock, moving quickly up the initial sections of the upper buttress. There was one last obstacle of consequence to decode — a flat-roofed overhand squatting on the buttress edge, jutting out like the chin of an Easter Island statue. I traversed under its cleft into a steep, shallow groove that started out with a seam in the crease of the corner. I got in a couple of dicey pins for protection, then started to stem the smooth rock, right foot and hand pushing inward on the left, slowly each short move with almost imperceptible weight shift. As I moved higher, the groove flattened out more and more, like a book opened on a table, until my cramping arms and legs were splayed behind my torso, elbows and knees locked in sharp angles like the limbs of a locust.

I became keenly aware of my fragility, my posture vulnerable to the slightest slip of friction being pressed out of the slight curves of wall to either side. I was in a serious position; the least bit of quivering would mean a dangerous fall. I thought of the warrior monks, like the Knights Templar, stern and disciplined, and soon I felt like one, my mind entering a place of cold and unforgiving vision. Then I saw it. A knife-blade hole in the moss-choked seam hinging the groove. I breathed out, staying still for a few seconds feeling for the stability in my stance. I breathed in security and on the next outbreath, freed my right hand as I pushed my limbs into maximum contact with the wall.

Without hesitation, my hand went to the rack and precisely picked the right piton, gently pushing it into the seam, and reached for my holstered hammer, taking excruciating care not to upset the delicate balance of body and rock. I let out a gasp from having held my breath too long, and took in a couple of deep drafts down to my belly in hopes of drawing some feeling back into my numbing feet and legs. With great delicacy, I managed some sharp, clean hammer blows, and with the knife blade singing tight, quickly clipped it and let my weight sag onto the tightened rope. I was flooded with courses of relief, like a riverbed washed clean with spring rain. Stepping onto the pin, I could reach a good edge, and the drama was over.

We finished up an offwidth just below the top in the last available light. There was no time to enjoy the summit. We scurried like frightened mice, searching for some shelter in the gathering darkness, and settled in with our backs against a dinner-table-sized boulder on the flat, wind-blasted summit. It was a very long night, all four feet stuffed in the daypack, with intermittent snow squalls for evening entertainment.

It was a strange intimacy, sharing an unplanned bivi, only layers of fleece and Goretex separating two cramped, sore, and sweaty male bodies, closely spooned together in an effort to find a moment of meager warmth. My nose was turned to the sky to avoid being muzzled into my partner's backside, trying to avoid breathing his smells, his body thick and heavy and hard and so unlike a woman's, body breathing with great heaves in fitful sleep, like some alien lover. I felt a distant gag in the gut, a faint disgust, like waking in the wrong woman's bed with no sense of pleasure or comfort, but only a near-panicked urge to get up and get out because being there feels so wrong. I caught a wave of that urge, that discreet repulsion, watching it rise from my guts with the witness of my mind. I smoothed it out, calmed it away, and snuggled in a little closer, homing in on spots of greater heat, searching for warmth, feeling like a hero for being in this forsaken place, before lapsing into a few minutes of shivering sleep. It was a long and cold night.

Bone-stiff and deeply chilled, we were slow to get moving in the morning. Our way up was our way down, rappelling the route, hammering in anchors, and sliding down the ropes well into the afternoon. Time was pressing in — Reto was soon due to pick us up, and beyond the raps, there was much ice to downclimb. Then, a good hour ahead of schedule, we heard the whomping of his rotor blades and watched the helicopter nose along the glacier into basecamp. A quick hover then, realizing nobody was home, Reto shot over to the buttress and followed it, zeroing in on our position on the last rappel. We all pointed to a huge platform on the lower ridge, where Reto put down and waited in the sunshine for us to scramble down the last of the rocks.

It was a fitting finish to decades of dreaming, years of trying, and many hours of helicopter time (too bad Highland Air doesn't offer frequent flyer points). And who needs interminable downclimbing on treacherously-angled ice to complete a long-standing adventure? Flying out, a rippling golden mirror stretched across the waters of Bute Inlet in the setting late September sun, we laughed off our guilt and helicopter-assisted debauchery of style, and I let myself bask in the sweet relief of putting behind me what had become an almost obsessive affair with this great, granite mountain. The time had finally come to let go and move on.

To a normal man, any high place is an invitation. Of course, not all men can become mountaineers. And though the calculating and practical man of the world has little use for the exploits of the mountaineer, the world owes little to its practical men, whereas great is its debt to its adventurers.
—G.K. *CAJ*, 1928

Middle Sister, the Three Sisters. Photo: Craig Richards

1994 : PEAK BAGPIPING IN THE CANADIAN ROCKIES

SCOTT DAVIDSON

W e'd come up with a plan; an idea that we were sure would guarantee us a footnote in the annals of the Canadian Rockies. Right up there with Conrad Kain and Charles Fay. A feat comparable to the first ascent of Mount Rundle — or at least Rundle Rock. It was August and we were ready. Plans were laid weeks in advance, then we sat around on the deck of the Sherwood House bar, sipping and waiting for good weather.

With a measure of luck and a lot of slogging, we pulled it off; a twist to two ascents that may alter the course of mountaineering in the Canadian Rockies. Well, maybe not really alter the course, but has anyone else ever heard the wail of the bagpipes on the summits of either Mounts Joffre or Assiniboine? It's been done now. Canmore sculptor and bagpiper Cam Douglas hauled his bagpipes to the summits of both peaks and enthralled all around with uplifting renditions of Amazing Grace and Scotland the Brave, demonstrating great lung power, puffing and blowing to keep the notes flowing mellifluously over 3350 m.

There was certainly nothing even mildly heroic in our ascents — no new routes, no record times, and thank God, no epics. I like reading about epics lying on my couch during those long winter months, but I've been climbing long enough to realize that reading and actually doing it are two different things. Doug Scott crawling down the Ogre with two broken legs may be tremendous reading, but the memory of biking out of Assiniboine with a full pack and rope after the climb is enough for me.

What the two climbers in this story did would have caused a sensation a century ago. Now ascents of Canada's tallest peaks are commonplace. The fact that Canadian mountains are far more accessible and crowded than ever before, however, has not diminished the challenge or the joy of climbing them. It only makes it more important to find a personal touch to apply to the style with which each peak is climbed.
— R W S

Before everyone's imagination runs off with visions of Cam struggling up the icy slopes with his bagpipes lashed to his back in the driving snow, I must point out that they do break down into a small six-pound bundle and there was no driving snow — the weather was near perfect on both ascents. He did make me carry the camera and he ate half of my supply of chocolate bars, but it was a noble feat nonetheless, sure to warm hearts from Edinburgh to Aberdeen.

The Joffre trip was an official A.C.C. Rocky Mountain Section outing, with nine participants, including a young woman from New York City who was an Outward Bound instructor at a high school in the Bronx. (And you thought climbing was inherently risky!) We went up to Aster Lake the first day, set up camp, then stood around in small groups brushing our teeth and pointing at the mountain. The consensus was that we would have to get up early the next morning and walk over a lot of broken rock to get to it.

At eight o'clock the next day we were under the face and we split into three rope teams, scoping out our chosen routes. Joffre is a good choice for rookie north face aspirants; there is only one rope length of forty-five degree ice, with panoramic views of the Royal Group and beyond, that are absolutely stunning.

Our rope team reached the summit first and the others were serenaded by the pipes as they came off the face and onto the final ridge. Adding to the inspirational setting, the two groups described the piping as both haunting and uplifting as they worked their way up those last few hundred metres to the summit. Everyone gathered happily on top, taking pictures and sharing granola bars and chocolate.

As we began to contemplate the descent, I cursed myself again for not investing a few measly thousand dollars in a parapente as the conditions would have allowed for a perfect take-off and an exhilarating six-minute ride back to camp with my knees thanking me all the way. But being parapenteless, we began the traditionally miserable descent and straggled back into camp in the mid-afternoon, laying around in various states of disrepair. When a ranger walked into camp and warned us that a grizzly bear had been spotted by the lake that morning, even that wasn't enough to rouse me from the prone position induced by the day's efforts.

We then turned our thoughts to Assiniboine.

There are few day-trips in the Canadian Rockies more fun than the mountain bike up Bryant Creek and over Assiniboine Pass, but being loaded down with thirty-pound packs because we were too cheap to have them flown in caused the fun factor to drop considerably. We consoled ourselves with the purity of our approach, although friend Dan, along for the ride, had generously offered to carry the rope on his bike. We accepted quickly, downgrading the style by only half a point. To make matters worse, it was a blistering hot day — blistering that is, by Rockies' standards. It must have been at least 25° C — an absolute scorcher.

We hoisted our bikes into a tree at the base of Assiniboine Pass and prayed to the Great Spirit that the porcupines wouldn't spot our delectable tires dangling temptingly from the branches; as if hanging the bikes up would deter the buck-toothed little buggers who spend half their lives sitting in trees. We climbed up and over the pass and stopped for lunch on the shore of Lake Magog — all the while staring up at Assiniboine. The grandeur and beautiful lines of this mountain never fail to overwhelm me. Dan, an artist by trade, voiced my very thoughts by stating that the Lake Magog setting with Assiniboine towering above it is surely one of the most beautiful places on earth. Dan bid farewell and headed for home, leaving us to scan for Gmoser's highway through the headwall. I'd been up to the

Hind hut once before, so we were spared the joys of routefinding, which made the trip pretty straightforward, though no less exhausting. It was seven hours from the Mount Shark parking lot to the hut.

As we made the final approach to the hut, we kept looking to our left at our towering host. I tried to take a photo from the hut, but couldn't get the whole thing in the frame. After a dinner of bread, cheese and chocolate, we lay about in the warm, evening air and contemplated the North Ridge. It didn't look as easy as everyone said it was, but we reassured each other that once on the mountain we'd figure it all out.

The next morning it was surprisingly warm, bringing smiles to our faces. I had envisioned gloves, toques and Gore-Tex, but instead we got by with a single pile jacket and the ubiquitous Co-op pants. We scrambled up the scree to the base of a gully just below the ridge. It was an abrupt transition from scree to mountain. From there to the base of the Red Band it was a meandering slog through small cliff bands and patches of snow and ice that grew in size the higher we got. They weren't supposed to be there. This was the August hot spell — you know, perfect conditions. Still, climbing through the Red Band was quite easy as we avoided the ice and climbed steadily to the base of the Grey Band where conditions finally justified crampons.

We shuffled sideways, still unroped, to an obvious weakness in the rock that would be our passage through to the top of the mountain. The entire thing was verglas. I started to have my doubts and voiced my concerns. Cam, short on experience but long on courage, immediately tied into the rope and climbed delicately upwards on front points to a waiting belay station above. There was no way I was going to let him down, so I tied into the rope and tiptoed up to the belay beside him.

From there to the summit was a matter of weaving upwards on the North Ridge with exposure down the East Face that was all the more incredible when one realized that it had been climbed.

The summit itself was windy and cold so we didn't stay long. Cam put the pipes together and managed a beautiful version of "Scotland the Brave" despite gasping for oxygen in the thin air. I photographed the event for posterity and sat looking out at Joffre and all the ice-capped peaks in between. I contemplated scrambling up to the very edge of the summit cornice to peek over the edge, but was convinced that it might not be such a great idea; breaking through the cornice to dangle on the end of a rope over the East Face of Assiniboine might have ruined what, up to then, had been a great day. We wandered back along the summit ridge and began a series of several rappels past the nasty icy sections. After rappelling the Red Band, we began the long, pounding walk down through the headwall to the Naiset cabins late in the afternoon.

In one of the cabins was a group of mountain bikers outfitted with the most dazzling collection of camping equipment and biking accessories I'd ever seen. More importantly, they had beer that they were willing to share. We told them about our day, and in exchange for another round, Cam put the pipes together and the meadows were filled with piping, laughter, and off-key singing.

Scottish rack for Mount Assiniboine, north face. Photo: Scott Davidson.

Lake Louise. Photo: Pat Morrow

1994: PASSION, PERFORMANCE, AND THAT PLASTIC KARMA

David Dornian

I'm gonna say important words here. And I don't want to have to put up with any more whole-wheat, beard-and-cycling-shorts, liberal apologia about "Games Climbers Play" or the "Partnership of the Rope" or "Life is at its Best When Risked" or any other of that trad-geezer-retro-runitoutontheslab drooling and puling I typically get from ski tourers(ists?), scree walkers, and Club members whose greatest outdoor achievement seems to have been the collection of the entire set of Mountain magazine back issues. The nineties have us by the throat, and all I hear is whining about the legitimacy of different personal experiences. I say it's time to scratch a line in the dirt. No more bowing and scraping and politely-mumbled excuses. I want to talk about athletics — real sports action — and what that term means in a climber's life.

Okay. What matters to me, and what should matter to you as a climber, is the naked human corpus excelling simply for the sake of doing more than it did yesterday. In other words, devotion to development of a mental and physical ideal. Here, the values inherent in the practice of sport climbing contrast sharply with conventional interpretations of mountaineering achievement. These latter are often best characterized, I want to claim, as charging your limit on the MasterLuck Card and hoping you can still make payment when the account comes due.

I think we should take a dim view of ego versus nature. In the grand scheme of things, anything that is said in support of vainglorious deeds is just shine, and, as always, no matter how glossy your finish, rubbing yourself is nothing more than rubbing yourself — best done in the dark and in private. If you're anything like me, you're tired to tears of the usual tales of big mountain masturbation, wooden with stubborn masochism in the face of random adversity. If you've ever read any of the literature, or ponied up a couple of bucks to a touring hardman when he drags his suite of Kodak carousels through your town, you know the tune. It's always sung with laboured breath, to a rhythm track of flapping ripstop. Feel free to hum along with me — "There we were, pinned down by the wind and the driving snow. Shivering and rubbing our feet into each other's stomachs to keep awake, with only the roar of the avalanches that split around the rib on which our tiny tent was perched to mark the abysmal hours 'til dawn." Okay, all together now, here comes the chorus — "Tomorrow would be our last chance for the summit."

Ick.

I want to argue that sport climbing — taken as single pitch, fair weather rock climbing on fixed protection, where a fall anywhere on the route offers little or no physical risk — embodies more of the ideas and values traditionally associated with climbing than does modern mountaineering or alpine rock work.

It seems unlikely that a more striking final piece to this volume could be found than Dave Dornian's rant from the 1994 Journal. This trundle on the heads of the traditional mountain philosophies takes us back to where the book began — evaluating what we do and why we do it. If the essay angers you, confuses you, or just makes you laugh, it has done its job; all good mountain writing reveals us to ourselves.

– GP

I'm going to take a few different tacks on this issue. To begin with, I want to contrast the perception — the received image — of mountain and multi-pitch climbing with some alternate interpretations of the experience, pointing out a couple of inconsistencies and, let's face it, downright idiocies in the views held by the gorp and GoreTex crowd. Then, I want to highlight some corresponding aspects of sport climbing that, while often held up to derision, actually demonstrate values that have been largely ignored in discussions of that activity. Finally, I'm going to ask, and answer, a couple of broad questions about the general worth of these two activities when they are placed in the wider context of human development and endeavour. There'll be oatmeal and powdered drink mix all over the topos before we finish. Ugly, but necessary. With luck, maybe someone will end up with one of those plastic six-pack rings wrapped around their necks or something.

THE "FREEDOM" OF THE HILLS...

An interesting cliché. Freedom doesn't really have much to do with a quality climbing experience. Freedom is what you get standing in the middle of a rural road in Nebraska at the end of a John Steinbeck novel, or what you have when your girlfriend tosses your collection of cassette tapes onto the front lawn at two in the morning. In such cases you have options — all the choices in the world. Freedom is what you have when you pause and say "Hmmmm, I wonder which one has the hazelnut centre?" Freedom is definitely not what you have when you're pinned down on the South Col, or tied off to some shaky pegs 1000 metres up on the North Face of North Twin. Freedom is about choice. Mountaineering is about commitment, and commitment, by definition, is about the limitation of choice. You've got an important mountaineering achievement when options are severely restricted by the situation and the heroes manage to survive and succeed despite the adversity. The feat might be impressive from the point of view of conventional human capability. It might even be interesting (in the same way that UFO cattle mutilations featured on the cover of Weekly World News are interesting; that is, curious) but it's not associated with freedom in any true sense.

On the other hand, with sport climbing, you have choice. When you're keeping it under 50 metres, with a body-length limit on runouts, you're not forced into a situation where you have to bivy under that cornice whether you want to or not; you can lower off and head to the mall for frozen yogurt at a moment's notice. You can step back on level ground and scope the difficulties of the next route on your tick list. You can pulley up, set the quickdraws so they open in the right direction, and then come back in the morning when the rock is cool and your guns are fresh and rested. That's freedom.

There's more. At the crags you can have a life. Sport climbers not only see their boy/girlfriends on a regular basis, they get to go climbing with them, too, even if said significant other doesn't climb him/herself. "Belay Billys/Bettys" are legion in the sport. Compare this domestic idyll with the life of the hardcore mountaineer — mountaineers often forget what their wives/husbands look like. Sometimes they forget whether or not they have children — and this can be just as well, as occasionally neither the spouse nor the children are there when he/she returns from the hills. And how about this? Anyone (just about) can pull your string at the crags, whereas on the big rigs, compatibility and competence in a partner are critical. While there are any number of willing accomplices already at a trendy crag when you arrive with a fist full of quickdraws, there are probably damn few perfect blends of Robin Williams and Mother Theresa anywhere on the continent with whom you would be willing to share a cramped tent on the ridge of K2 — and even fewer who would be willing to share that same tent with you and your much thumbed copy of Atlas Shrugged.

PSYCHOLOGY

This brings us to the broader concern of personality aberrations generally. What can be said about someone who volunteers repeatedly for confinement and conditions that put our most progressive prisons to shame? One thing is for sure — a robust approach to mental health has nothing to do with it. Where's Amnesty International when some third world customs officer starts screaming at you and confiscates all your gear? Where's your case worker when boredom on the second day of a whiteout causes you to eat half your first aid kit? I mean, what kind of perverse creature will accept and even favour freeze-dried farts and putrid polypro as preferred living conditions?

More briefly, what about physical health? Alpine climbing as a voluntary practice provides greater risk of illness, injury, and death than just about any other activity short of high school football.

And consider athleticism. If walking uphill with a heavy pack or breathing shallowly on some creaking hook placement are typical big mountain offerings of opportunities for physical expression, then apprenticing as a bricklayer's helper should be viewed as performing on a par with Olympic gymnasts.

The long climbs cost, too. They cost in terms of money, time, social ostracization, premature aging, physical debilitation, forced neglect of worthwhile alternatives, and opportunities lost. These are components of a satisfying, well-balanced existence? I think not.

They also cost your sense of humour. Life in the high places is too random for fun. The consequences are just too dire. Alpinists badly need to be able to laugh at the absurdity of summits. Most can barely manage a hysterical giggle as the pick breaks on their second tool fifteen metres out from their last screw. For instance, I'll bet that few committed crampon creepers will be able to read this article and take it in the spirit in which it is written.

SPORT CLIMBING — THREAT OR MENACE?

In sharp contrast to the above, sport climbers can laugh and dance in the sun. They have a life to live and a path to walk.

As an athlete, the sport climber trains and rehearses for performances that can compare favourably with the flow and expression of a figure skating routine, the energy demands of a powerlift, and the intuition, foresight, and mental acuity of a chess match. In opposition to the practice of mountaineering, success as a sport climber has little to do with simple doggedness and the seizure of windows of opportunity, and everything to do with insight and devotion to a physical and mental ideal — an ideal that sees the individual as able ultimately to deal gracefully and spontaneously with any specific climbing situation.

This is a good thing. The practice of sport climbing is a demanding but productive way through the world. It requires concentration and devotion, yet it need not detract from a well-rounded life. It isn't antipathetic to having a family, career, or secure old age. Neither does it require these things. It is physically healthy. It rewards a good diet, allows a proper sleep, and encourages personal hygiene and grooming habits (hey, gotta look good at the gym). If ambitions are high, training takes the long view. It is not enough to succeed on a single climb, no matter how major. This means that the development of a solid and enduring physical capability is all important. Power, endurance, composure, and flexibility are its grails. It is mentally healthy. Sport climbing is a social, friendly activity where participation and practice are open and easily shared with others. An individual's performance is accessible to all. There is often an audience when you climb, and, people being the way people are, gossip is rife. This penalizes indulgence in the vices of pride, laziness, lying, selfishness, and personal aggrandizement. A sport climber is a member of a community and, as such, suffers the community's responsibilities and reaps its rewards. Mountaineers tend to be closet misanthropes, excusing their reclusiveness by making the claim that aesthetic value in climbing demands isolation, when all it really does is echo their desire to avoid normal contact with other human beings.

Finally, and most telling to this case, sport climbing can demand a level of bravery unsurpassed by any other mountain activity. In competition — arguably the ultimate expression of any art — a sport climber must tighten his or her shoes one last time, find focus, and take the long walk out of the preparation area to their place under the lights in front of the crowd, turning to face the wall with wicked gravity raining all around.

Probably the first time the competitor has ever seen their belayer, at this moment there can be no "partnership of the rope" to serve as a crying towel for the timorous. When it comes to the "games climbers play," this is probably the only one where score is actually kept fairly. Avalanche hazard is low. The holds appear solid. The weather inside can only be described as good, and promises to hold stable for the duration of the competition, indeed for the next decade. Good visibility should last the few minutes until the route is either sent or sold, or until someone turns off the lights. It's a plain case of "life at its best when self image is risked." There are no excuses.

Very, very scary.

In the midst of the turmoil of living we may say "the mountains are still ours." They are ours because we have had direct, personal dealings with them. We know them in their many moods—in the warm sunshine when the very rocks seem friendly, in the misty half-light when the summits are lowering and remote, in the savagery of the howling storm, or in the heavenly pink of the alpenglow. We know them and may feel they are ours, but in reality they are ours only on loan.

—Frank Gaebelein, Sermon to the 54th Annual Camp,
at Bugaboos, July 26, 1959, *CAJ* 1960

The Catenary Ridge and the north side of Mount Logan, from the air. Photo: Whyte Museum Collection

Photographs

All the photographers have graciously donated their work to *Canadian Summits*.
Those listed below welcome requests for reprints.

Glen Boles
6 Riverside Place
Cochrane, Alberta T0L 0W3

Ray Kodama
9751 116th Street
Surrey, B.C. V3V 3Z8

Pat & Baiba Morrow
Box 2278
Canmore, Alberta T0L 0M0

Greg Horne
Box 2202
Jasper, Alberta T0E 1E0

Roger Laurilla
Box 864
Golden, B.C. V0A 1H0

Craig Richards
Box 2532
Banff, Alberta T0L 0C0

Pierre Lemire
Box 172
Field, B.C. V0A 1G0

Photographs from the Whyte Museum of the Canadian Rockies

Page 8, V653/NA80-1215; p. 11, V263/NA71-2262; p. 12, V14/AC00P-136b;
p. 17, V263/NA71-924; p. 22, V263/NA71-2294; p. 26, V653/NA80-1414;
p. 29, V48/NA65-375; p. 47, V14/AC 64P/1; p. 59, V14/AC 204P/9;
p. 75, V653/NG4-438; p. 102, V263/NA71-2267; p. 118, V469/2670;
p. 125, V751/A311; p. 187, V14/AC 0P-631

For information about ordering reprints, contact
Archives
Whyte Museum of the Canadian Rockies
Box 160
Banff, Alberta T0L 0C0